In the age of runaway global warming and widespread environmental destruction, it is vital that firms devote much more attention to green issues. This includes taking account of green issues across all the functional areas of management including HRM. This book consolidates and extends the most recent thinking on green HRM. It is an interesting, and above all, important volume, that deserves the attention of both the HR scholarly community and the world of practice.

Geoffrey Wood, *Dean of Essex Business School,*
Professor of International Business, University of Essex

Contemporary Developments in Green Human Resource Management Research

This book examines a new topic in Human Resource Management (HRM), Green – or environmental – HRM, analysing the role humans play in environmental management at work and environmental behaviours at workplaces around the world.

The book begins with a focus on negative workplace Green behaviours (e.g. toxic chemical leaks, air pollution, contaminated waste, etc.), and what such environmental problems mean for workers, managers and society as a whole.

The book outlines relevant underpinning academic theory and literature on how HRM is 'going Green', and details real-life organisational examples derived from original and secondary empirical research to illuminate the implications of adopting Green HRM practices for relevant stakeholders. In doing so, the book offers a new academic contribution to both the HRM and the environmental management literatures.

Douglas W.S. Renwick (Ph.D.) is Associate Professor of Sustainable Workforce Management at Nottingham Trent University, United Kingdom, and Visiting Professor at the Institute of Human Resource Management, Vienna University of Economics and Business, Vienna, Austria.

Routledge Research in Sustainability and Business

Contemporary Developments in Green Human Resource Management Research

Towards Sustainability in Action?

Edited by
Douglas W.S. Renwick

Routledge
Taylor & Francis Group

LONDON AND NEW YORK

First published 2018 by Routledge

2 Park Square, Milton Park, Abingdon, Oxfordshire OX14 4RN

52 Vanderbilt Avenue, New York, NY 10017

Routledge is an imprint of the Taylor & Francis Group, an informa business

First issued in paperback 2019

British Library Cataloguing in Publication Data
A catalogue record for this book is available from the British Library

Library of Congress Cataloging in Publication Data
Names: Renwick, Douglas W. S., editor.
Title: Contemporary developments in green human resource management research : towards sustainability in action? / edited by Douglas W.S. Renwick.
Description: Abingdon, Oxon ; New York, NY : Routledge, 2018. | Series: Routledge research in sustainability and business | Includes bibliographical references and index.
Identifiers: LCCN 2017032312| ISBN 9781315768953 (hardback) | ISBN 9781317667995 (adobe reader) | ISBN 9781317667988 (epub) | ISBN 9781317667971 (mobipocket)
Subjects: LCSH: Personnel management–Environmental aspects. | Management–Environmental aspects.
Classification: LCC HF5549 .C72195 2018 | DDC 658.3/01–dc23
LC record available at https://lccn.loc.gov/2017032312

ISBN: 978-1-138-78285-3 (hbk)
ISBN: 978-0-367-37687-1 (pbk)

Typeset in Bembo
by Wearset Ltd, Boldon, Tyne and Wear

This research-based book is dedicated to the memory of the late, great Professor Tom Redman, Chair in HRM at Durham University, United Kingdom, and his family. My thanks go to the publisher and chapter authors for the opportunity to compile this research volume. Any faults, errors and omissions arising are mine alone.

Dr. Douglas W.S. Renwick,
Bournemouth, England,
United Kingdom.

Contents

Figures

Tables

Contributors

Ina Aust (was Ehnert) is Professor of Human Resource Management with a specialization in CSR/sustainability at Louvain School of Management/ILSM, Université Catholique de Louvain in Belgium.

Susanne Blazejewski is Chair for Sustainable Organization and Work Design at Alanus University of Arts and Social Sciences in Germany.

Anke Buhl works at Alanus University of Arts and Social Sciences in Germany.

Luca Carollo is a Post-Doctoral Researcher at the Department of Social and Political Sciences, Università degli Studi in Milan, Italy.

Franziska Dittmer is based at Alanus University of Arts and Social Sciences in Germany.

Ante Glavas is Assistant Professor of Corporate Social Responsibility at the University of Vermont, USA.

Paul J. Gollan is Professor of Management and Director and Head, Australian Institute of Business and Economics, at the University of Queensland, Australia.

Anja Gräf is based at Nuertingen-Geislingen University, Germany.

Marco Guerci is Assistant Professor of Human Resource Management and Organization Studies, at the Department of Social and Political Sciences, Università degli Studi in Milan, Italy.

Julie Haddock-Millar is an Associate Professor (Practice) in Learning and Development at Middlesex University Business School and a Visiting Professor in Organisational Behaviour at the International University of Monaco.

Christopher Hill is Director Environmental Sustainability at Mater Misericordiae Limited in South Brisbane, Australia.

Brian Matthews is a PhD Candidate at the Institute for Human Resource Management, Vienna University of Economics and Business, in Vienna, Austria.

Michael Müller-Camen is Full Professor at the Institute for Human Resource Management, Vienna University of Economics and Business, in Vienna, Austria.

Lisa Obereder is a Research and Teaching Associate at the Institute for Human Resource Management, Vienna University of Economics and Business, in Vienna, Austria.

Douglas W.S. Renwick is Associate Professor of Sustainable Workforce Management at Nottingham Trent University, UK, and Visiting Professor at the Institute of Human Resource Management, Vienna University of Economics and Business, Vienna, Austria.

Sally V. Russell is Associate Professor of Business, Organisations, and Sustainability at the University of Leeds, UK.

Chandana Sanyal is a Senior Lecturer (Practice) in Human Resource Management and Development at Middlesex University Business School, UK.

Amy Tian is a Senior Lecturer in Human Resource Management in the School of Management at Curtin Business School, Curtin University, Australia.

Kerrie L. Unsworth is Professor of Organisational Behaviour and Director of the Workplace Behaviour Research Centre at Leeds University Business School, University of Leeds, UK.

Adrian Wilkinson is Professor of Employment Relations and Director of the Centre for Work, Organisation and Wellbeing at Griffith Business School, Australia.

Cathy Xu is Lecturer in the Department of Marketing and Management at Macquire University, Sydney, Australia.

Foreword

The importance of addressing the detrimental effects that industrializa-
tion and economic development have had on our environment is now
recognized by nearly everyone. Despite the unfortunate foot dragging
of a few politicians, private and public organizations around the world
are beginning to address concerns about environmental sustainability as
they plan their futures. Pressure to change how organizations behave is
coming from many directions. National and local governments are
imposing regulations to reduce environmental damage and some also
are offering incentives to reward organizations that promote environmental preservation, conservation, and repair. Many consumers are
shifting their buying behaviour to align with their pro-environment
values. Increasingly, employees are taking into account the environmental records of organizations as they choose where to work. After
many decades of grass-roots environmental activism, finally the world is
paying attention! For human resource scholars and managers alike, there
has never been a greater need for our expertise; by understanding how
people's knowledge, attitudes, values, and emotions shape their behaviours, Human Resource Management (HRM) experts can improve the
effectiveness of organizational efforts to address environmental threats
and leverage new opportunities to improve the health of our planet and
the well-being of the people who inhabit it.

In this edited volume, the best Green HRM (GHRM) scholars from
several countries bring a variety of perspectives to illuminate how the
emerging field of GHRM can promote environmental sustainability.
Taking a broad view of what GHRM encompasses, the chapters in this
volume consider the role of GHRM practices in shaping both employee
behaviours and the spill-over effects that can influence how employees
behave in other settings, such as at home and in their communities.
Thus, GHRM is shown to be relevant for informing actions that affect
a wide variety of different stakeholders. Furthermore, whereas some

authors adopt the perspective of strategic HRM and thus emphasize the linkage between GHRM and a firm's financial performance, others adopt humanistic or political perspectives. Regardless of the particular perspectives taken, however, each chapter is theoretically grounded and rigorous in its analysis.

In compiling this collection of cutting-edge GHRM scholarship, the editor has created a book that should be of interest to readers interested in advancing academic knowledge, practitioners seeking new ideas for managing greener organizations effectively, and those who create and/ or seek to enforce environmental policies. Contributions are organized to reflect a multi-level framework that will be familiar to many readers, with chapters progressing from those that address primarily "micro" phenomena such as employee motivation and engagement to those that address primarily "meso" or middle-level phenomena such as organizational HRM policies and initiatives to those that consider how more "macro" or contextual dynamics influence the direction and effectiveness of GHRM initiatives.

In Chapter 1, Renwick introduces readers to the relatively young field of GHRM by explaining the meaning of the term "Green HRM," providing a brief historical synopsis of the field's origins, and summarizing several of the major themes addressed in contemporary research. Subsequent chapters are organized into two parts that focus first on phenomena within organizations (Part I) and second on contextual conditions that impinge on intra-organizational phenomena (Part II).

The dynamic interplay between the motives and attitudes of individual employees and the goals and management structures adopted by organizations is clearly illustrated throughout the chapters that comprise Part I. In Chapter 2, Unsworth and Tian discuss how HRM practices can be used to motivate employees to engage in environmentally friendly behaviours. In addition to summarizing how HRM practices can be used to promote the achievement of environmental goals established by the organization, Chapter 2 also addresses the motivational challenges faced by employees whose personal pro-environmental values are in conflict with the achievement of work goals that ignore the negative environmental effects (such as increased carbon emissions) of one's work. In Chapter 3, Sanyal and Haddock-Millar describe an interesting case study that illustrates how two subsidiaries of McDonald's, the fast food company, employed GHRM initiatives to involve and engage employees in improving the company's environmental performance. Using a combination of volunteerism, training, teamwork, effective leadership, and performance measurement, McDonald's succeeded in engaging employees in the company's routine pro-environment activities to achieve results such as reducing litter and increasing the cardboard recycling in the company's UK and Swedish subsidiaries. In Chapter 4, Russell and Hill present another case study that illustrates effective GHRM practices. Located in eastern Australia, Mater is a health care provider comprising hospitals and health centres, a medical research institute, and pathology and pharmacy businesses. After reviewing evidence from HRM research, Mater implemented initiatives to improve sustainability-focused communications, change employees' green behaviours, and assess employees' environmental knowledge. In addition to describing the many specific actions undertaken by Mater, this chapter illustrates the importance of bringing together experts from many different parts of an organization when attempting to improve environmental performance. Thus, the Director of Sustainability worked with the marketing department to design and implement the communications strategy, information technology experts were involved in creating an intranet tool central repository for relevant information such as energy usage, administrators and supervisors made face-to-face presentations to staff in departments with limited access to electronic communication tools, training took place during orientation and dedicated education sessions, and HR staff provided expertise in conducting, analysing and interpreting employee surveys. Thus, through a variety of initiatives that required many different types of expertise, Mater gradually embedded environmental sustainability into its business practices.

The final two chapters in Part I highlight the importance of recognizing that the workforce of most organizations includes diverse employees who bring to their work a variety of differing attitudes, values, identities, and mind-sets. Thus, in Chapter 5, Blazejewski, Gräf, Buhl and Dittmer focus on a specific and growing sector of the workforce – namely green activists and agents who are intrinsically motivated to engage in green behaviour at work – and argue different support structures and unique approaches to GHRM should be used with such employees. For readers who have wondered whether green activists can or should be managed differently from peers who are less personally committed to or concerned about ecological issues, this study of employees in large and mid-sized German firms will be of particular interest.

Part II shifts our attention to the external context of organizations and shines new light on the powerful ways in which political, ethical, and community concerns can shape how organizations and management scholars alike frame environmental challenges and potential solutions. Specifically, in Chapter 6, Carollo and Guerci argue that GHRM practice and scholarship could become more useful and relevant by attending more closely to the social, ethical, and political contexts within which GHRM is embedded. This chapter prods readers to consider questions such as: To what extent are GHRM systems just another form of management control versus a potential means for supporting employee self-direction and self-determination? To what extent are corporations misappropriating concerns about environmental sustainability as a means to gain legitimacy for corporate activities aimed primarily at achieving economic goals and/or minimizing the regulatory and consumer pressures they might otherwise experience? And, under what conditions does the pursuit of environmental sustainability create ethical dilemmas such as choosing between actions that bring immediate benefits to an organization's current employees versus actions that are costly in the short term in hopes of bringing benefits to future generations? In Chapter 7, Matthews, Obereder, Aust and Müller-Camen present an expansive discussion of how the urgent need to address environmental as well as social sustainability should, as perhaps it already has, cause a re-imagining of how to evaluate an organization's HRM system, shifting from an emphasis on economic outcomes as the defining characteristic of effective HRM to a perspective that evaluates HR professionals based on how well they "critically reassess and redesign their role as mere administrators and managers of human capital towards authentic, trustful, convincing leaders and nurturers of real holistic organizational change" (p. 128, Chapter 7). In Chapter 8, Xu, Gollan, and Wilkinson continue the discussion of how the changing external context and increasing concerns about sustainability are changing our views of the goals to be achieved by effective HRM. For organizations at the beginning of their journey toward sustainability, the authors offer a framework that can be used as a diagnostic tool to identify the ways in which HRM can be used to most effectively address a specific organization's sustainability concerns. For organizations that are further along the journey to sustainability, the authors argue that achieving sustainable HRM requires attending to several core principles that should be followed in efforts to effect change within the context of complex social systems.

Part II's discussion of contextual influences is brought to a close with Chapter 9 by Glavas, who asks readers to envision how a radical shift in the perspective one takes when managing human resources might result in new and quite different solutions to the problem of sustainability. Viewing our mental model of HRM as a contextual condition that shapes our approach to GHRM, Glavas asks readers to ponder what HRM would look like if we started by assuming that HRM's role is to satisfy the needs of individuals rather than the needs of an organization. That is, "how can HRM inspire individuals, organizations, and society/

planet to thrive?" In such a world, HRM would stand for "humans really matter," and the goal of achieving environmental sustainability would be viewed as a stimulus for adopting HRM practices that enable employees to achieve meaningfulness and purpose while simultaneously pursuing organizational goals. Drawing from a wide range of literature, Glavas alerts us to the danger of merely hoping that HRM systems designed to improve environmental performance will also address human concerns and instead argues that a better way forward is to use environmental management to prod the redesign of organizations and thereby create the conditions in which human beings will thrive as individuals who experience a sense of meaningfulness and purpose.

Bringing this stimulating edited volume to a close with Chapter 10, Renwick considers the future of GHRM. What's next for this emerging field of scholarship? Given that GHRM is still in its infancy, the opportunities for research that contributes to our current understanding seem nearly limitless. For readers seeking guidance in choosing how to proceed, Renwick endorses diverse theoretical and methodological approaches and provides specific suggestions concerning research questions worthy of attention. Among the topics Renwick covers are green leadership, individual attributes associated with green workplace behaviours, organizational barriers, institutional pressures, cross-national comparisons, ethical issues, green jobs, and including the GHRM research agenda under the broad umbrella of "Sustainable Workforces in Management Studies." As this volume makes clear, together the early GHRM pioneers represented in this volume have built a strong foundation upon which others can build. Ideally, this volume will inform and inspire readers from around the world to apply their own unique resources and talent to rapidly improving the environmental conditions that currently threaten our planet and our humanity.

Susan E. Jackson
Distinguished Professor of Human Resource Management
School of Labor and Management Relations
Rutgers University, USA

Abbreviations

ACSI	American Customer Satisfaction Index
AMA	American Management Association
AMO	Ability–Motivation–Opportunity
AMOS	Analysis of a Moment Structures
CAS	Complex Adaptive System
CIPD	Chartered Institute of Personnel and Development
CPA	Corporate Political Activity
CSR	Corporate Social Responsibility
ECG	Economy for the Common Good
EGB	Employee Green Behaviour
EM	Environmental Management
EMS	Environmental Management Systems
ES	Environmental Sustainability
GHRM	Green Human Resource Management
HPWS	High Performance Work Systems
HR	Human Resources
HRD	Human Resource Development
HRM	Human Resource Management
MNE	Multi-National Enterprise
OB	Organisational Behaviour
OCB	Organisational Citizenship Behaviour
OCBE	Organisational Citizenship Behaviours to the Environment
PM	Personnel Management
RBV	Resource-Based View
SDG	Sustainable Development Goal
SEM	Structural Equation Modelling
SHRM	Strategic HRM
SWiM	Sustainable Workforces in Management Studies
WEFB	Workplace Environmentally Friendly Behaviour

1 Towards an understanding of Green Human Resource Management

Douglas W.S. Renwick

Recently, some scholars argue that protecting the natural world and its resources for the next generation(s) has emerged as an urgent priority for society, policy-makers and managers (Pinzone *et al.*, 2016, p. 201). Green Human Resource Management (GHRM), defined as 'HRM activities which enhance positive environmental outcomes' (Kramar, 2014, p. 1075 in Shen *et al.*, 2016, p. 2), is developing as one way to help tackle this ecological priority (Jackson *et al.*, 2011). As such, the purposes of GHRM workplace-based practices (Renwick *et al.*, 2013) and organizational staff enacting Voluntary Workplace Green Behaviours (Kim *et al.*, 2017) are to help organizations reduce factory and office emissions and increase recycling, so organizations can help mitigate the effects of global climate change through reduced workplace-driven pollution and waste and better energy use (Saifulina and Carballo-Penela, 2016, p. 3). In terms of take-up, one Society of Human Resource Management (2011) survey revealed that nearly two thirds of organizations sampled engaged in environmental sustainability initiatives, and over 85 per cent of Fortune 500 companies reported environmental sustainability efforts (Wiernik *et al.*, 2016, p. 1). Such initiatives mean GHRM practices can help to 'improve organizational green performance' (Shen *et al.*, 2016, p. 7).

Although some researchers see Corporate Social Responsibility (CSR) studies as a field where 'the environmental dimension seems to be the most examined social dimension' (Wang *et al.*, 2016, p. 537), others note GHRM as an emerging concept which has received inadequate empirical research attention (Shen *et al.*, 2016, p. 20). Such findings may appear puzzling, as recent research has also demonstrated that employee behaviour makes 'significant contributions to organizational environmental performance' (Norton *et al.*, 2017, p. 1), and others argue that workplace pro-environmental behaviour research potentially has important implications for environmental protection as 'human activity within organizations is a major cause of ecological degradation' (Inoue and Alfaro-Barrantes, 2015, p. 138). Of course, one barrier argu-ably restricting GHRM research is promotion by fossil fuel industries and their supporters of a 'neoliberal, free market ideology as a solution for large-scale environmental issues' (Teeter and Sandberg, 2016, p. 3). This is because it may reduce the desire for government-funded GHRM research, which has been seen in the context for research scoping and funding under the Donald Trump administration in the USA.[1] Nonetheless, benefits for organizations from enacting GHRM-researched initiatives include helping save firms money through reduced use of raw materials and energy (see Wehrmeyer, 1996, for examples), and a positive impact on external company image (Shen *et al.*, 2016, p. 7). Such results lead some organizational practitioners concerned about Green issues to 'accept that "being green" makes good business sense' (Norton *et al.*, 2017, p. 1).

So, what is the rationale for this research volume? The original idea for it arose from my experiences as a UK A-level student being intro-duced to the great books in sociology and political science by respected tutors such as Dave Rawlinson, Chris Carter and Tony Ward in the 1980s. Then, as now, I have always been persuaded by memorable tomes that others remember, and my own desire to do 'a book', however small, or in whatever form. My academic interest in environ-mental management, HRM and sustainability was sparked by having the pleasure of reading Dr Walter Wehrmeyer's (1996) book, *Greening People: Human Resources and Environmental Management*, and the joy of reading *Managing Human Resources for Environmental Sustainability* by Professor Susan Jackson and colleagues (2012). I would recommend both books very highly to any interested scholars wondering where to begin reading on the GHRM-related field.

What appears in this book are a series of research papers on GHRM written (in my opinion) by some of the most respected and relevant researchers working globally on it today. As Jackson stated in the *Foreword* to this volume, the chapters following this one are show-cased using the micro–meso–macro frame familiar to many manage-ment researchers (e.g. George *et al.*, 2016, pp. 1890, 1892), beginning with micro-level internal organizational initiatives and meso-level external ones (in Part I), before then detailing more macro-level con-textual issues (in Part II).

The purpose of this work is to respond to calls from the *Academy of Management Journal's* 20th editorial team for research which explores global problems including climate change (George *et al.*, 2016, p. 1880). Here, tackling climate change is seen as a United Nations Sustainable

Development Goal (SDG), because the global average sea level has risen by 7 inches (178 mm) over the past 100 years. This problematic circumstance is due to the 'scale, scope and time horizon over which mitigation efforts must take place, without central authority', and because of water scarcity, famine and food waste, as 'the number of forcibly displaced people worldwide at the end of 2014 is about 60 million, the highest level since World War II (UNHCR, 2015)' (in George *et al.*, 2016, pp. 1883, 1886, 1893).

My own interest in GHRM stems from four personal experiences, which I now detail. First, as a young boy in the late 1970s, I wondered when passing through the old Esso (now Exxon Mobil) refinery at Fawley[2] (UK), why so many fumes were being allowed to drift into people's residential homes nearby. Second, while attending University in Newcastle (UK), I saw a fellow student gathering polluted water from the River Tyne in the late 1980s and was puzzled how local rivers could get so polluted, and why this was not being stopped. Third, after the Chernobyl disaster, and visiting Kiev in the Ukraine on a research visit in 1991, I remember coughing on acrid air fumes there, and asking local people what was being done to reduce pollution in the air and waterways. Fourth, and more positively, when visiting my older brother working in Brazil in the early 2000s, I saw some cars running on sugar cane fuel (not gas/petrol), and wondered if I would ever see more such 'Green cars' globally. These four personal experiences shaped my understanding of the downsides and upsides of environmental and ecological management. Indeed, later reading the life story of a European-based work colleague who showed Green leadership by building their own house in a pro-Green way in the early 2010s made me re-examine the size of my own carbon footprint. Of course, and like others, external events and news also helped form my Green knowledge, as I remember reports of the incidents and accidents at nuclear power plants at Three Mile Island (Pennsylvania, USA) and Chernobyl (Ukraine),[3] and chemical leaks at Union Carbide in Bhopal (India) and at BP in the Texas Gulf (USA) making headline news (see Renwick *et al.*, 2013). Such events appear to partly involve some kind of human error as drivers of them and to have produced much environmental damage too.

Most recently, the possible need for humans to physically adapt to climate change events and the potential and actual development of people's resilience to do so fascinates me. Here, television documentaries charting the lives of people in desert areas such as Jordan in the Middle East (Channel 4, 2017), and in and around the Arctic Circle in Alaska (USA) such as *Life Below Zero* (on the UK Travel Channel), and their love of such lands, are, for me, essential viewing. This is because such programmes surface real insight into the many ways humans innovate to cope with changing weather events to live in extreme physical environments. In doing so, such documentaries may provide lessons for many people to learn if any of our next generation(s) globally (eventually) ever have to move into, become prone to, or cope with, such harsh climatic conditions. Although perhaps somewhat ethnocentric, other environmental television programmes shown in the UK, USA and Canada may provide accessible, much needed learning for any English-language speakers curious to know more about changes to local and global ecologies. Such are the origins of my own academic and personal interests in the natural environment.

The aim for my own chapters is not to develop new theory, but instead to highlight current yet lesser known theory and practice in the GHRM literature and to provide interesting new research avenues in GHRM. My intention for this book is that it helps moves forward research efforts aimed at highlighting HRM scholarship on the environmental roles of corporations and individual and organizational actions that may work to increase it (Wang *et al.*, 2016, p. 534). In doing so, I send huge thanks and congratulations to all of the authors appearing in this research collection for their excellent chapter contributions. I think all their works move GHRM research forward in varying, subtle and important ways. I hope that readers of this research volume enjoy it as much as I have in putting it together.

To combat known limitations emerging from the methodology-as-technique genre (Bell *et al.*, 2016. p. 1), I use a combination of orthodox (review)[4] and non-orthodox (current press/media analysis) in my own contributions to challenge views that climate change is not happening, or is somewhat alien. While my use of secondary analysis and mainstream media may be a controversial use of current contemporaneous evidence, my hope is that reporting such different sources also offers an immediate, basic triangulation of event accuracy (see Hampton, 2015, p. 7). I am aware of, and accept that my own pro-Green attitudes, values, and professional involvement in environmental management education may introduce bias and prejudice into this work, and that 'objectivity' seems difficult to achieve when such personal pro-Green sympathies are involved. Nonetheless (see Hampton, 2015, p. 7), I hope my own transparency and critical analysis of interpretations on GHRM provides a less partisan account overall. In doing so, I also accept that tackling 'grand challenges'[5] such as climate change involves the idea of CSR, and of 'businesses bearing a responsibility to society and a broader set of stakeholders beyond its shareholders', and is thus relevant, as 'over 8,000 companies from more than 150 countries are signatories to the United Nations Global Compact covering issues [including the] environment' (Wang *et al.*, 2016, p. 534).

To me, any effort towards introducing and understanding GHRM requires us to briefly note (1) what is happening to our external, ecological environment, and then to more extensively detail (2) what GHRM theory and practice could potentially indirectly contribute to help tackle climate change. I begin below by briefly charting what I feel are some key external environmental changes in our weather and climate. Here, I use the micro–meso–macro analytical frame already detailed internationally, i.e. to examine such changes from my locality, the UK, and then up to more regional, comparative and global perspectives.

The external ecological environment

In 2016, the UK saw several changing atmospheric events occur such as strange humming sounds in Bristol giving rise to Britain being labelled the perfect 'tornado alley', and winds on the English east coast sweeping an oil rig inland. A very rare heatwave was reported in Glasgow (Scotland) in June, which contrasted with hailstones and snow in Rochdale and heavy flooding in London where 40 mm of rain fell in one hour. These events reveal recent UK weather patterns as both changeable and unpredictable (BBC, 2017a). Climate change and global warming seem to impact Britain via the basic physics of the UK generally being warmer overall, and increased rainfall and flooding in particular. Here, figures for Britain reveal the coldest UK winter (2008), the coldest winter in Scotland (2009), and the coldest UK December in 100 years (2010). Whatever the exact drivers of such changes to UK weather, seasoned observers note seeing a definite future pattern for the UK of prolonged, extreme weather occurring[6] (BBC, 2014).

In the USA, 'fracking' for energy may produce an increased risk of small earthquakes and water contamination emerging, while one of the most extreme weather events in Hurricane Sandy in 2012 left at least 70 people dead, and a clean-up bill of over $50 billion. West Texas has seen record rainfall in 2016 and then record droughts and dust storms in 2017, while the increased population in Las Vegas has produced rising energy use there, which in turn is draining the lake of the Hoover dam (BBC Four, 2017; Channel 4, 2017). Further north, the Arctic appears to be warming twice as fast as the rest of the world, with 2007 recording reduced Arctic sea ice and 2012 seeing record lows of Arctic ice, and with such ice being thinner too. Further afield, the Aral Sea in Kazakhstan/Uzbekistan has shrunk by 90 per cent from the 1960s, a development which has come as a shock to some observers (BBC, 2014), the bleaching of the Great Barrier Reef in Australia still continues (George *et al.*, 2016, p. 1890), glaciers at the summit of Mount Kilimanjaro on Africa's highest peak are reducing (Channel 4, 2017), and ground-level hurricanes are anticipated in Dubai and the Persian Gulf (BBC Four, 2017).

In the East, China has emerged as a (reforming) powerhouse of carbon emissions, and yet also a victim of world waste, as unwanted parts from Western mobile phones, personal computers and tablets are buried in Chinese-based landfill sites, producing solid waste pollution. China currently burns 60,000 tons of coal in 90 minutes, with visibility in cities like Shijiazhuang down to less than two metres along a 2,000-mile-long cloud stretch of toxic smog. There, some locals state: 'you can taste coal in the air'; 'we don't go outside', and 'the whole of China is polluted' (Shudworth, 2017). Beijing in particular suffers from polluting smog produced by coal power stations (BBC, 2014), which are linked to one million premature deaths in China per year due to lung cancer, and many children there developing asthma (Shudworth, 2017).

Globally, 34 square kilometres of land turn to desert every 90 minutes, and one-fifth of the world's trees have disappeared. Planet Earth's temperature has changed (upwards) by 1° Celsius, which has a big impact, as global humidity has increased by 4° due to more water being dumped. Overall, global temperatures are rising, with dry regions getting drier and wet locales getting wetter (BBC Four, 2017). Moreover, the world population also continues to rise. Estimates are that 23,000 children are born every 90 minutes, and that the global population will equal around nine billion people or so by 2050, up two billion from the roughly seven billion humans living now (BBC, 2014). Overall, the world population has doubled in size since 1945 (Channel 4, 2017), which means that, if continued, more people may produce more carbon emissions, and thus increases in climate change. Such developments could impact heavily on low income and developing countries, because most of the increase in world population occurs in the continents of Africa and Asia. Further, in countries such as Malaysia, urbanization also places a great challenge on government agencies in terms of environmental waste disposal (Ju *et al.*, 2015, p. 1). Additionally, the Intergovernmental Panel on Climate Change reports detail a consensual understanding that our climate system is significantly warming, is likely to carry on doing so, that human activities are a major cause of it, and that, if this continues, possibly 'serious impacts' are likely to both humans and Planet Earth (Hampton, 2015, p. 1).

Building on the points above, it is clear that *something* is happening 'out there' to Planet Earth from changes to local, regional and global weather and climate patterns, which seem to impact negatively on humans, animals and the natural environment, and are arguably not good global developments. Here, the pro-green activist Arnold Schwarzenegger estimates that 'every day, 19,000 people die due to pollution from fossil fuels' (in Werber, 2015, p. 1), and at least 30,704 human deaths have been associated with heatwaves globally (Milman, 2017, p. 1). These seem staggering and depressing statistics, as such phenomena appear avoidable. I now consider what GHRM is, and then what GHRM research could possibly do to indirectly mitigate climate change impacts.

What is GHRM?

GHRM currently exists as a series of environmental HRM processes (from staff originally entering to finally exiting work organizations) (Renwick *et al.*, 2013, 2016), underpinned by Ability–Motivation–Opportunity (AMO) theory (Appelbaum *et al.*, 2000), as Pinzone *et al.* (2016), Rayner and Morgan (2017), Renwick *et al.* (2013), and Russell and Hill (in this volume) all use AMO theory as a theoretical lens to view and explain relevant stakeholder behaviour in GHRM. The upside of using AMO theory in GHRM research is that it has a practical relevance in guiding organizations, managers and practitioners forward on what workplace GHRM interventions they might possibly consider implementing to help combat climate change. For example, GHRM is focused on using *indirect* links between organizations adopting pro-GHRM practices to change staff behaviour towards taking enhanced care when using energy resources, and employees undertaking more recycling and conducting better waste management. Such staff-based, pro-Green actions may help the planet over time, as factory smoke emissions are reduced, local water supplies become less polluted from factory outputs and organizations present lower energy demands and needs. As such, keywords for GHRM impact regarding the environment may perhaps be: indirect, long-term and variable.

However, using AMO theory in GHRM also has constraints, as AMO theory can seem somewhat instrumental, pro-managerial and arguably Orwellian at first sight too, because it looks to change staff behaviour towards increasing concern for the external environment. Yet on closer inspection, GHRM may appear to have an authoritarian tendency or undercurrent for good reason(s). This is because, if society at large wants work organizations to shape staff behaviours to become greener to help deliver reductions in external environmental degradation, doing so could seem to be both a noble cause and a social outcome. In essence, some may see GHRM workplace interventions as a means to justify the end goal of helping society to indirectly reduce climate change overall.

Moreover, the term and concept GHRM itself may also be 'contested terrain' (see Edwards, 1979), as it does not appear as union-focused as other areas of HRM scholarship. To tackle such limitations, Hampton's (2015) work provides an alternative viewpoint, and route, on how union and non-managerial stakeholders may help tackle global warming. In it, he uses 'critical realism' to critique positivist, constructivist and post-modern conceptualizations of climate change and establish an alternative philosophical framework for humans 'to take transformative action', where structure and agency[7] 'magnify the potential of workers and their organisations as "strategic climate actors"' (Hampton, 2015, p. 4).

Building on such a wider understanding of GHRM, while the financial crisis of the late 2000s may have been a key opportunity for work organizations to move away from primarily chasing profits, and instead, to pursue wider goals such as 'the three Ps' (of people, planet and profit) to meet social needs for a more sustainable biosphere (Hampton, 2015, pp. 4–5), the financial aspects of GHRM may still dominate. This is because a key driver for some case study examples of GHRM organizational best practices (especially in USA-based or US-origin organizations) lies in the financial, monetary-based value of 'going Green', i.e. the desire not to spend resources twice, to save resources, or to recycle resources[8] (see Wehrmeyer, 1996, for examples). As such, from the points above, GHRM has some limitations, which need acknowledging. I now build upon prior literature reviews (see Jackson et al., 2011; Renwick et al., 2013, 2016) to detail some new trends emerging in GHRM research.

Contemporary research trends in GHRM

Relevant theory in GHRM

While some scholars argue that strong theoretical and analytical frameworks for GHRM 'have yet to emerge', a wide range of theoretical lenses currently influence GHRM themes which draw on institutional theory, systems theory, process theory, stakeholder theory, resource-based theory and AMO theory (Arulrajah and Opatha, 2016, p. 153). Additionally, the theoretical perspective of organisational citizenship behaviours to the environment (OCBEs),[9] in which collective OCBEs are aggregations of individual OCBEs, has now 'gained significant consensus' (Pinzone *et al.*, 2016, pp. 201–202).

Some recent studies of top management tangible competencies among UK and New Zealand chief executive officers and managing directors detail the micro-foundations of environmental sustainability based on the resource-based view theory, and relationship-based business networks entrenched in social network theory (Anonymous, 2017, p. 1). Indeed, other new works draw on social cognitive theory to theorize on the imitation of sustainability behavioural modelling by leaders placing supervisors as role models for employees (Saifulina and Carballo-Penela, 2016, pp. 3–4). Here, servant leadership theory has been highlighted as especially useful for predicting sustainability actions in theorizing that an environmentally specific servant leadership style can affect targeted Green outcomes (Robertson and Barling, 2017, p. 30), and in investigations of employee attitudinal and behavioural responses to perceived GHRM to understand employee reactions to perceived CSR (Shen *et al.*, 2016, p. 4).

In environmental psychology, a major review reveals three major pro-environmental workplace behaviour theoretical frameworks being used: the theory of reasoned action, the theory of planned behaviour and value-belief-norm theory (Inoue and Alfaro-Barrantes, 2015, pp. 140–141). Complementary but less frequently used theories include expectancy-value theory, cognitive action and stress theory, eco-feminist theory, social dilemma frameworks, broaden-and-build/positive emotions theory and transformational leadership theory (Inoue and Alfaro-Barrantes, 2015, p. 152). Other theories utilized in environmental sustainability include natural resource-based views of the firm (Alt and Spitzeck, 2016, p. 49), open systems theory and the 'line of sight' concept (Buller and McEvoy, 2016, p. 1).

Organizational Citizenship Behaviours to the Environment, pro-environmental workplace behaviour, Employee Green Behaviours, and Green psychological climate

Recent findings on OCBEs from a study of the English NHS[10] reveal GHRM practices as conducive to collective voluntary behaviours towards the environment. Staff willingness to support firm-level ecological initiatives partially mediate this relationship, as 'Green competence building, performance management and employee involvement practices' all positively influence collective OCBEs (Pinzone *et al.*, 2016, pp. 201, 207). As such, sharing a vision with staff is positively associated with organizations adopting proactive environmental practices (Alt and Spitzeck, 2016, pp. 48–49), as both eco- and organization-centric rationales at individual and organizational levels relate to employee OCBEs, and interactive effects such as staff perceptions of company rationales are key determinants of such OCBEs (Tosti-Kharas *et al.*, 2016, p. 1).

Researchers have found three types of workplace pro-environmental behaviour in the environmental psychology literature, namely: environmental activism, non-activist behaviour in the public sphere[11] and private sphere environmentalism. Determinants of pro-environmental behaviour and attitudinal variables[12] are 'significant predictors' of pro-environmental behaviour, female staff 'scored higher in environmental activism' than males and individual pro-environmental behaviours are influenced by various situational and external factors[13] (Inoue and Alfaro-Barrantes, 2015, pp. 139, 149, 150). Additionally, in the Spanish public sector, 'harmonious environmental passion of employees' and 'organizational environmental support, gender and perceived incomes' all influence employee workplace environmentally friendly behaviour (WEFB)[14] (Saifulina and Carballo-Penela, 2016, pp. 1–2).

For Employee Green Behaviours (EBGs), recent studies find GHRM both directly and indirectly influencing in-role green behaviour, and only indirectly influencing extra-role green behaviour through the mediator of psychological climate. Individual green values moderate the impact of psychological green climate on extra-role green behaviour, but not the effect of GHRM or psychological green climate on in-role green behaviour (Dumont *et al.*, 2016, pp. 1–3). One related study of 11 countries reveals that 'contrary to popular stereotypes, age showed small positive relationships with pro-environmental behaviours' (Wiernik *et al.*, 2016, p. 1), while another reveals culture as unlikely to be a 'major moderator of age-employee green behaviour relations' (Wiernik *et al.*, 2016, p. 11).

Current works find Green psychological climate[15] positively related to corporate environmental strategy and, in turn, moderating the relationship between 'green behavioural intentions and next-day employee green behaviour'[16] when 'employees perceive a positive green psychological climate' (Norton *et al.*, 2017, p. 1). Contextual factors also impact on 'general green behaviour', as 'within-person relationship' between green behavioural intentions may occur on one day and EGB the next, and roughly 'one third of variance in daily employee green behaviour resides at the within-person level' (Norton *et al.*, 2017, pp. 1, 4, 13, 14).

Leadership

Some studies of Green leadership find links between leadership, organizational and individual-level environmental performance (Andersson *et al.*, 2013) and that participants exposed to environmentally specific transformational leadership not only rate their leader's environmental values and priorities more highly, but also seem engaged in higher levels of pro-environmental behaviours (Robertson and Barling, 2017, p. 2). Additionally, perceived GHRM is positively related to employee task performance and organizational citizenship behaviour (OCB) and negatively related to employee intention to quit, with organizational identification and perceived organization support moderating such relationships (Shen *et al.*, 2016, p. 20). Moreover, related work in Nigeria reveals that:

> After controlling for age, education and gender, environmentally specific transformational leadership had a significant positive relationship with environmental concern, which in turn predicted green behaviour at work in a positive direction ... [while] environmental concern mediated the relationship between environmentally specific transformational leadership and green behaviour at work.
>
> (Kura, 2016, p. 1)

Additional studies

Other separate, individual studies on GHRM also provide new and interesting findings. One study of social exchanges among Mexican employees found organizations and supervisors not linked to eco-initiatives, yet peer relationship quality mediating the influence of organizations and supervisors, meaning that 'social exchange with peers' seems crucial to developing such eco-initiatives (Raineri *et al.*, 2016, pp. 47, 55). A related study on CSR and pro-environmental behaviour showed that perceived CSR has both direct and indirect influences via organizational identification on pro-environmental behaviour (Gkorezis and Petridou, 2017, p. 1). Moreover, case-study work among senior managers in Saudi Arabia found that HRM practices can promote and support Green workplace behaviour, but 'are not used effectively', and that senior managers can 'only marginally' facilitate pro-environmental behaviour in such organizations as 'other management-related issues may be more important than environmental sustainability' (Abdulghaffar, 2017, p. 25). One survey of HR professionals in Malaysian manufacturing and service companies found only strategic positioner and change champion roles being significantly related to GHRM practices (Yong and Mohd-Yusoff, 2016,

p. 416), while in-depth interview study of procurement experts in three Brazilian public universities revealed alignment between sustainable procurement levels and environmental training adoption, but a lack of training and support from senior management as barriers to implementing environmental procurement practices (Aragao and Jabbour, 2017, p. 48). Further, findings from one study of GHRM systems[17] in Malaysia highlight their significant role in promoting the implementation of cleaner organizational sustainability strategies (Gholami *et al.*, 2016, p. 159).

Workers, trade unions and the regulatory context

Critical Marxist-inspired work by Hampton (2015) has researched worker and trade union roles in building 'climate solidarity', and views the 'ecological[18] context' and social agents 'most able and willing to tackle' climate change as ones occurring 'in the realm of work' (Hampton, 2015, pp. 4–7). This is because he argues that the contemporary labour process 'modifies the climate', as:

> Workers as climate agents organised in trade unions can offer what might be called 'climate solidarity': distinctive framings of climate questions, together with specific forms of representation and mobilisation on climate matters.[19] Unions offer a potential pole around which a revived climate movement might coalesce.[20]
>
> (Hampton, 2015, pp. 6–8)

Hampton's work draws upon an extensive review of files produced by UK trade unions on climate change and his own data on the UK Vestas occupation as a case study (Hampton, 2015, pp. 9–10). His work has been complemented by other recent studies which have empirically researched the environmentally active role of UK trade unions. Findings from one survey of 22 UK unions' environmental activism suggests that:

> Although an environmental agenda appears popular with members and encounters little resistance from employers, few unions currently evidence serious or regular engagement, and environmental work is largely confined to large and/or public-sector workplaces where the union is already well established. This limited adoption may be attributable to a combination of the absence of supportive legislation and public funding, the agenda's inability to generate an attractive 'product' for members, and already-crowded local

agendas. However, most unions surveyed anticipate that their environmental agenda will expand in the future.

(Farnhill, 2016, p. 257)

A study on the regulatory context surrounding organizational environmental initiatives has recently been undertaken in Australia. In it, scholars revealed that Australia's brief carbon pricing scheme has seen policy uncertainty[21] forcing organizations there 'to focus their responses on short-term investments', which preclude 'the development of green capabilities and preventing flexible environmental regulations from achieving their intended policy results' (Teeter and Sandberg, 2016, pp. 1, 14).

Sustainability

Some new studies seek to connect environmental management, HRM and sustainability together. In them, researchers analysing sustainability reports in the Forbes Top 250 global companies find that the higher perceived visibility of environmental issues among consumer opinion in the developed world does not mean that 'the world's largest corporations do not report less on "labour and decent work" than on "environmental" indicators'. Indeed, nor do they 'support the notion that organisations focus their attention in sustainability activities on "green matters" while neglecting "people matters"' (Ehnert *et al.*, 2016, p. 100). As such, organizational support for sustainability:

> Can influence how employees respond to sustainability messages … [and] further, that the intensity of emotions change agents display, and how appropriate [they] are within organizational contexts will influence how employees perceive those individuals and the success of their efforts to influence green outcomes.
>
> (Blomfield *et al.*, 2016, pp. 1–2)

Finally, qualitative data collected as part of a Finnish (European) HR Barometer inquiry reveals that, contrary to expectations in the prior GHRM literature, 'ecological responsibility was largely ignored' as a dimension of Sustainable HRM by top managers (Jarlstrom *et al.*, 2016, p. 1).

From all the studies detailed above, one thing seems clear. If the *indirect* role that GHRM theory and practice(s) could play in helping to tackle climate change through re-configuring organizational greening initiatives is accepted, doing so could suggest that GHRM might *matter* for humans, our planet and the ecology. Indeed, doing so may mean the wider impact of GHRM theorizing and empirical research is wholly surfaced. The next chapters build upon, extend and enhance such an understanding.

Notes

1 Private correspondence from a US-based researcher (2017).

2   The Esso refinery at Fawley, near Southampton, is the largest in the UK and one of the most complex in Europe, with a mile-long marine terminal that handles around 270,000 barrels of crude oil a day and provides 20 per cent of UK refinery capacity.
(Source: www.exxonmobil.co.uk/UK-English/about_what_refining_fawley.aspx Accessed 6 March 2017)

3   On 26th April 1986, the Chernobyl nuclear reactor leak in the Ukraine exposed on-site workers and fire-fighters trying to fix it to high levels of radiation which burnt human skin, broke down DNA and led to cancers. The World Health Organization estimates that 2,200 such 'liquidator' clean-up staff died, or will die, from the radiation received at Chernobyl. If the current 'fix' sarcophagus Chernobyl shell collapses, it may break into particles site workers could inhale, and stay in their bodies causing further new cancers.
(BBC, 2017b)

4 I follow the methods used in prior works to review the relevant GHRM literature (see Renwick *et al.*, 2013, p. 2; 2016, p. 115).

5 'At a historic summit in September 2015, 193 member states of the UN adopted goals to protect the planet, for example in "affordable and clean energy" (SDG 7)' (George *et al.*, 2016, p. 1881).

6 The coldest UK winter was recorded in 1683–1684, where sunspots disappeared for 50 years and ice courses reveal the sun had a strange rhythm of low ultra-violet light for decades, but is an exception. Global warming in Britain means an increased chance of record-breaking maximums of cold and heat appearing, which gives rise to the notion of the UK's 'weird weather' (BBC Four, 2017).

7 'Structure includes context and refers to the setting within which social, political and economic events occur and acquire meaning, while agency refers to action, specifically political conduct' (Hay, 2002, pp. 91–94, in Hampton, 2015, pp. 3–4).

8 As 'management theory and practice departmentalizes and abstracts the natural environment into an economic framework … [which] has created a lack of empathy for nonhumans and the inanimate world' (Whiteman and Cooper, 2000, p. 1267).

9 'OCBEs are defined as individual and discretionary social behaviours not explicitly recognized by the formal reward system, and the contextual factors that enable the manifestation of OCBEs at the unit level' (Alt and Spitzeck, 2016, p. 48).

10   The NHS in England accounts for 25 per cent of public sector emissions in the UK, and is the largest public sector contributor to climate change in England. It has committed to reducing its carbon footprint by 28 per cent in 2020, and has a dedicated unit, the Sustainable Development Unit (SDU), [to help] organisations change their attitudes and behaviours in regard to the environment.
(Pinzone *et al.*, 2016, pp. 204–205)

11 'which can be further decomposed into environmental citizenship and policy support' (Inoue and Alfaro-Barrantes, 2015, p. 140).
12 'Such as: personal beliefs, personal norms, satisfaction, motivation, citizenship, and attitudes related to given pro-environmental behaviour' (Inoue and Alfaro-Barrantes, 2015, p. 149).
13 'Including social norms, incentive, support from supervisors, information and constraints' (Inoue and Alfaro-Barrantes, 2015, p. 150).
14 'WEFB is an umbrella concept describing all types of voluntary or prescribed activity and can be conceptualized as organizational citizenship behaviour (OCB), for instance, switching off lights, recycling garbage and the use of environmentally friendly sprays' (Saifulina and Carballo-Penela, 2016, pp. 2–3).
15 'Defined as employees' perceptions and interpretations of their organization's policies, procedures, and practices regarding environmental sustainability' (Norton *et al.*, 2017, p. 5).
16 'A workplace-specific form of green behaviour ... [where] the workplace represents a context in which factors beyond the control of employees can, to varying degrees, create variation in daily behaviour' (see Norton *et al.*, 2017, pp. 3–4). 'EGBs can be required or discretionary, [as] organizations are seeking to understand which personal characteristics lead to good and poor environmental performance at the individual level' (Wiernik *et al.*, 2016, p. 2).
17 GHRM systems are of emerging interest in countries such as Brazil too (see Jabbour *et al.*, 2017).

18   Ecologism argues that care for the environment ... presupposes radical changes in our relationship with it, and thus in our mode of belief that [environmental problems] can be solved without fundamental changes in present values or patterns of production and consumption (Dobson, 1990, p. 13).
(In Hampton, 2015, p. 12)

19   By 2010, a significant breakthrough had been made in the number of UK union representatives who saw themselves as carrying out an environmental role, whatever formal position they held ... they proved capable of instigating, directing and supporting significant reductions in workplace carbon emissions ... [with such] climate representation initiated by individual unions and supported by the UK Trades Union Congress (TUC).
(Hampton, 2015, p. 151)

20 'Trade unions in Britain still constitute the largest voluntary organisation in the country, representing seven million workers, and negotiating on behalf of one-third of all employees' (Hampton, 2015, p. 7).
21 Plus 'seesawing carbon policies in Australia, Canada, China, the EU, India, Japan, New Zealand and the US' (Teeter and Sandberg, 2016, p. 1).

References

Abdulghaffar, N. (2017) 'Green workplace behaviour in Saudi Arabia: The case of EnviroCo', *Journal of Management and Sustainability*, vol. 7, no. 1, pp. 19–28.
Alt, E. and Spitzeck, H. (2016) 'Improving environmental performance through unit-level organizational citizenship behaviours for the environment: A capability perspective', *Journal of Environmental Management*, vol. 182, pp. 48–58.

Andersson, L., Jackson, S.E. and Russell, S.V. (2013) 'Greening organizational behaviour: An introduction to the special issue', *Journal of Organizational Behavior*, vol. 34, pp. 151–155.

Anonymous (2017) 'Essential micro-foundations for contemporary business operations: Top management tangible competencies, relationship-based business networks and environmental sustainability', *British Journal of Management*, forthcoming, pp. 1–36.

Appelbaum, E., Bailey, T., Berg, P. and Kalleberg, A. (2000) *Manufacturing Advantage: Why High-Performance Work Systems Pay Off*. Ithaca, NY: Cornell University Press.

Aragao, C.G. and Jabbour, C.J.C. (2017) 'Green training for sustainable procurement? Insights from the Brazilian public sector', *Industrial and Commercial Training*, vol. 49, no. 1, pp. 48–54.

Arulrajah, A.A. and Opatha, H.H.D.N.P. (2016) 'Analytical and theoretical perspectives on Green Human Resource Management: A simplified understanding', *International Business Research*, vol. 9, no. 12, pp. 153–164.

Bell, E., Kothiyal, N. and Willmott, H. (2016) 'Methodology-as-technique and the meaning of rigor in globalized management research', *British Journal of Management*, forthcoming, pp. 1–17, DOI: 10.1111/1467-8551.12205.

Blomfield, J.M., Troth, A.C. and Jordan, P.J. (2016) 'Emotional thresholds and change agent success in corporate sustainability'. In Askkanasy, N., Hartel, C.E.J. and Zerbe, W.J. (Eds) *Emotions and Organizational Governance (Research on Emotion in Organizations, Volume 12)*. Bingley, UK: Emerald Group Publishing Limited, pp. 191–216.

British Broadcasting Corporation (BBC) (2014) 'What is wrong with our weather?' *Horizon*, 17 April 2014.

British Broadcasting Corporation (BBC) (2017a) 'Britain's wildest weather 2016', *BBC Two*, 8 January 2017.

British Broadcasting Corporation (BBC) (2017b) 'Inside Chernobyl's mega tomb', *BBC One*, 14 January 2017.

British Broadcasting Corporation (BBC Four) (2017) 'Horizon: Global weirding', *BBC Four*, 9 April 2017.

Buller, P.F. and McEvoy, G.M. (2016) 'A model for implementing a sustainability strategy through HRM practices', *Business and Society Review*, vol. 121, no. 4, (Winter), pp. 465–495. DOI: 10.1111/basr.12099.

Channel 4 (2017) 'Man made planet: Earth from Space', *Channel 4*, 22 April 2017.

Dobson, A. (1990) *Green Political Thought*. London: Unwin Hyman.

Dumont, J., Shen, J. and Deng, X. (2016) 'Effects of Green HRM practices on employee workplace green behavior: The role of psychological climate and employee green values', *Human Resource Management*, pp. 1–15. DOI: 10.1002/hrm.21792.

Edwards, R. (1979) *Contested Terrain: The Transformation of the Workplace in the Twentieth Century*. London: Heinemann.

Ehnert, I., Parsa, E., Roper, I., Wagner, M. and Müller-Camen, M. (2016) 'Reporting on sustainability and HRM: A comparative study of sustainability reporting practices by the world's largest companies', *The International Journal of Human Resource Management*, vol. 27, no. 1, pp. 88–108.

Farnhill, T. (2016) 'Characteristics of environmentally active trade unions in the United Kingdom', *Global Labour Journal*, vol. 7, no. 3, pp. 257–278.

George, G., Howard-Grenville, J.H., Joshi, A. and Tihanyi, L. (2016) 'Understanding and tackling societal grand challenges through management research', *Academy of Management Journal*, vol. 59, no. 6, pp. 1880–1895.

Gholami, H., Saman, M.Z.M. and Rezaei, G. (2016) 'State-of-the-art Green HRM system: Sustainability in the sports centre in Malaysia using a multimethods approach and opportunities for future research', *Journal of Cleaner Production*, vol. 124, March, pp. 142–163.

Gkorezis, P. and Petridou, E. (2017) 'Corporate social responsibility and pro-environmental behaviour: Organisational identification as a mediator', *European Journal of International Management*, vol. 11, no. 1, pp. 1–20.

Hampton, P. (2015) *Workers and Trade Unions for Climate Solidarity: Tackling Climate Change in a Neoliberal World*. Abingdon, Oxon: Routledge.

Hay, C. (2002) *Political Analysis*. Basingstoke, UK: Palgrave.

Inoue, Y. and Alfaro-Barrantes, P. (2015) 'Pro-environmental behavior in the workplace: A review of empirical studies and directions for future research', *Business and Society Review*, vol. 120, no. 1, pp. 137–160.

Jackson, S.E., Ones, D.S. and Dilchert, S. (eds.) (2012) *Managing Human Resources for Environmental Sustainability*. San Francisco, CA: Jossey-Bass.

Jackson, S.E., Renwick, D.W.S., Jabbour, C.J.C. and Müller-Camen, M. (2011) 'State-of-the-art and future directions for Green Human Resource Management', *Zeitschrift für Personalforschung (German Journal of HR Research)*, vol. 25, no. 2, pp. 99–116. ISSN 0179–6437/1862–0000.

Jabbour, C.J.C., Vazquez-Brust, D., Ubeda, J.A.P. and Jabbour, A.B. (2017) 'Stakeholders, green human resource and environmental proactivity in Brazil', *Unpublished working paper*, pp. 1–32.

Jarlstrom, M., Saru, E. and Vanhala, S.J. (2016) 'Sustainable human resource management with salience of stakeholders: A top management perspective', *Journal of Business Ethics*, pp. 1–22. DOI: 10.1007/s10551-0160-3310-8.

Ju, S.Y., Azlinna, A. and Thurasamy, R. (2015) 'Environmental leadership and employees' organizational citizenship behavior towards the environment (OCBE): Psychological distance as a moderating variable'. In *Advances in Global Business Research: Proceedings of the 12th Annual World Congress of the Academy for Global Business Advancement (AGBA)*, 16–19 November 2015, Faculty of Industrial Management, University of Malaysia Pahang, Kuantan, Pahang, vol. 12, no. 1, pp. 949–953.

Kim, A., Kim, Y., Han, K., Jackson, S.E. and Ployhart, R. (2017) 'Multilevel influences on voluntary workplace green behavior: Individual differences, leader behavior, and coworker advocacy', *Journal of Management*, vol. 43, issue 5 (May), pp. 1335–1358.

Kramar, R. (2014) 'Beyond strategic human resource management: Is sustainable human resource management the next approach?' *International Journal of Human Resource Management*, vol. 25, no. 8, pp. 1069–1089.

Kura, K.M. (2016) 'Linking environmentally specific transformational leadership and environmental concern to green behavior at work', *Global Business Review*, pp. 1–20. DOI: 10.1007/s10551-016-3228-1.

Milman, O. (2017) 'A third of the world now faces deadly heatwaves as result of climate change', *Guardian*, pp. 1–5. www.theguardian.com/environment/2017/jun/19/a-third-of-the-world-now-faces-deadly-heatwaves-as-result-of-climate-change. Accessed 19 June 2017.

Norton, T.A., Zacher, H., Parker, S.L. and Ashkanasy, N.M. (2017) 'Bridging the gap between green behavioural intentions and employee green behaviour: The role of green psychological climate', *Journal of Organizational Behavior*, pp. 1–20, DOI: 10.1002/job.2178.

Pinzone, M., Guerci, M., Lettieri, E. and Redman, T. (2016) 'Progressing in the change journey towards sustainability in healthcare: The role of "Green" HRM', *Journal of Cleaner Production*, vol. 122, pp. 201–211.

Raineri, N., Mejia-Morelos, J.H. and Francoeur, V. (2016) 'Employee eco-initiatives and the workplace social exchange network', *European Management Journal* (February), vol. 34, pp. 47–58.

Rayner, J. and Morgan, D. (2017) 'An empirical study of "green" workplace behaviours: Ability, motivation and opportunity', *Asia Pacific Journal of Human Resources*, Early View, pp. 1–23, DOI: 10.1111/1744-7941.12151. Accessed 4 May 2017.

Renwick, D.W.S., Jabbour, C.J.C., Müller-Camen, M., Redman, T. and Wilkinson, A. (2016) 'Introduction: Contemporary developments in Green (environmental) HRM scholarship', *The International Journal of Human Resource Management*, vol. 27, no. 2, pp. 1–16.

Renwick, D.W.S., Redman, T. and Maguire, S. (2013) 'Green HRM: A review and research agenda', *International Journal of Management Reviews*, vol. 15, no. 1, pp. 1–14.

Robertson, J.L. and Barling, J. (2017) 'Contrasting the nature and effects of environmentally specific and general transformational leadership', *Leadership & Organization Development Journal*, vol. 38, no. 1, pp. 1–46.

Saifulina, N. and Carballo-Penela, A. (2016) 'Promoting sustainable development at an organizational level: An analysis of the drivers of workplace environmentally friendly behaviour of employees', *Sustainable Development*, pp. 1–14. DOI: 10.1002/sd.1654.

Shen, J., Dumont, J. and Deng, X. (2016) 'Employees' perceptions of Green HRM and non-Green employee work outcomes: The social identity and stakeholder perspectives', *Group & Organization Management*, pp. 1–29. DOI: 10.1177/1059601116664610.

Shudworth, J. (2017) 'China report on Shijiazhuang', *BBC News*. Accessed 6 January 2017.

Teeter, P. and Sandberg, J. (2016) 'Constraining or enabling Green capability development? How policy uncertainty affects organizational responses to flexible environmental regulations', *British Journal of Management*, forthcoming, pp. 1–17. DOI: 10.1111/1467-8551.12188.

Tosti-Kharas, J., Lamm, E. and Thomas, T.E. (2016) 'Organization *or* environment? Disentangling employees' rationales behind organizational citizenship behavior for the environment', *Organization & Environment*, 2016 (1), pp. 1–20.

Wang, H., Tong, L., Takeuchi, R. and George, G. (2016) 'From the editors. Thematic issue on Corporate Social Responsibility. Corporate Social Responsibility: An overview and new research directions', *Academy of Management Journal*, vol. 59, no. 2, pp. 534–544.

Wehrmeyer, W. (Ed.) (1996) *Greening People: Human Resources and Environmental Management*. Sheffield, UK: Greenleaf Publishing.

Werber, C. (2015) 'From the future: Arnold Schwarzenegger believes in climate change and doesn't "give a damn" if you don't'. Accessed on 6 January 2017 at: https://qz.com/568412.

Whiteman, G. and Cooper, W.H. (2000) 'Ecological embeddedness', *Academy of Management Journal*, vol. 43, no. 6, pp. 1265–1282.

Wiernik, B.M., Dilchert, S. and Ones, D.S. (2016) 'Age and employee green behaviors: A meta-analysis', *Frontiers In Psychology*, (April), pp. 1–15. DOI: 10.3389/fpsyg.2016.00194.

Yong, J.Y. and Mohd-Yusoff, Y. (2016) 'Studying the influence of strategic human resource competencies on the adoption of green human resource management practices', *Industrial and Commercial Training*, vol. 48, no. 8, pp. 416–422.

Part I

Internal and external organisational GHRM initiatives

2 Motivation and GHRM

Overcoming the paradox

Kerrie L. Unsworth and Amy Tian

Introduction

Pro-environmental behaviours are simultaneously crucial and tangential. They are crucial for the state of the planet and for mitigating further climate change; yet they are tangential for most employees who will be focused on their own work goals and performance. Given this paradox, what can Human Resource Management (HRM) do to help motivate employees to engage in pro-environmental behaviours? In this chapter, we will explore the role of motivation in human resource (HR) practices, identify how 'green motivation' is different to traditional work performance motivation, highlight how conventional HR practices will affect green motivation and suggest some ways forward.

Motivation and traditional HRM

Motivation is defined as the initiation, direction and persistence of behaviour (Campbell and Pritchard, 1976; Klein, 1989). Over the years, many views on how motivation is engendered and maintained have been theorised with varying levels of support for each. Some of the most well-supported theories that are relevant for the workplace include: goal-setting theory, which states that people are more motivated by specific challenging goals on which they get feedback than on vague or general do-your-best goals (Locke and Latham, 1990, 2002); theory of planned behaviour, which states that motivation (intention to act) is greater when people have a positive attitude towards the action, feel that other people have positive attitudes towards the action and have control over performing that action (Ajzen, 1985, 1991); self-determination theory, which states that people are motivated by activities that are enjoyable or personally meaningful and are dis-motivated by activities they feel they have to do or are doing because of a reward

(Deci, 1975; Deci and Ryan, 1985; Gagne and Deci, 2005); social exchange theory (Blau, 1964), which is based on reciprocity of support with motivation and performance; and the job characteristics model, which states that people are motivated when performing a task that is autonomous, significant, varied, complete and provides feedback (Hackman and Oldham, 1976, 1980).

Based on these and other theories, HR practices have been developed to foster employee motivation. Strategic HRM research has long suggested that the use of HR practices can increase employees' motivation and organisational performance (e.g. Combs *et al.*, 2006; Jiang *et al.*, 2012; Paauwe and Boselie, 2005). To begin, many of the current HR practices are underpinned by social exchange theory (Blau, 1964). According to this approach, employees interpret HR practices as indicative of organisational trust and support for them. Thus they are motivated to reciprocate that support in some way, such as through increased motivation to performance (O'Boyle Jr *et al.*, 2012; Rhoades and Eisenberger, 2002).

An alternative approach to motivating employees in HRM is through direct motivational practices. This bundle of practices can be seen as the 'M' in the AMO (ability–motivation–opportunity) framework of HRM (Gardner *et al.*, 2011; Jiang *et al.*, 2012; Kehoe and Wright, 2013; Lepak *et al.*, 2006; Subramony, 2009). More broadly, the AMO framework of HRM proposes that HRM systems comprise three sub-systems (bundles of HRM practices) that focus on enhancing employees' (a) ability/skill (e.g. training and development), (b) motivation (e.g. rewards), and (c) opportunity to perform (e.g. teamwork design) (Jiang *et al.*, 2012; Lepak *et al.*, 2006; Subramony, 2009). The motivation-enhancing HRM practices, in particular, aim to motivate discretionary employee effort and behaviour and are based predominantly on goal setting (Locke and Latham, 1990, 2002) and operant conditioning (Skinner, 1953) theories. Specific practices include individual and group incentives, promotion opportunities, benefits, job security and performance appraisal. As would be expected, Jiang *et al.* (2012) found that motivation-enhancing HR practices are related to extrinsic motivation because of the link to specific goal-driven and reinforcement mechanisms (either rewards seeking or punishment avoidance).

Finally, the 'O' in the AMO framework represents opportunity-enhancing HRM practices. These are designed to provide employee opportunities and motivation to contribute to organisational objectives, and include practices such as teamwork, flexible job design, participation in decision-making and information-sharing (Gardner *et al.*, 2011;

Jiang *et al.*, 2012; Kehoe and Wright, 2013; Lepak *et al.*, 2006; Subra-mony, 2009). Opportunity-enhancing HR practices are rooted in job design (e.g. Hackman and Oldham, 1976, 1980) and intrinsic motiva-tion (Deci, 1975; Deci and Ryan, 1985; Gagne and Deci, 2005) the-ories and, as such, focus upon motivating employees through heightened feelings of autonomy, sense of achievement and fulfilment from work (Jiang *et al.*, 2012; Shin *et al.*, 2016).

As noted above, to date these HR practices have worked well to foster employee motivation towards traditional work behaviours. But pro-environmental behaviour in the workplace is not a traditional work behaviour because it is outside traditional work goals and performance. A pertinent question, therefore, is to what extent these traditional HR practices are relevant for 'green motivation' and do we need any different practices to complement them? To address this question, we first outline the peculiarities associated with green motivation before discussing how green motivation might be affected by HR practices.

Green motivation

Although we tend to conduct research on single goals and focused motivation, life is more complex and generally involves dealing with multiple goals and multiple motivations (see Unsworth *et al.*, 2014). This is even more pertinent at work, where people are juggling both work and life goals. Employees are contracted to work on the core business of the organisation and, for most people, their core goal while at work is based around this; in addition to this, many employees will have other goals at work based on their needs, such as getting on with colleagues, getting a promotion or maintaining work/ life balance. On top of all of these diverse goals, we are now con-sidering pro-environmental goals.

Pro-environmental goals are usually tangential to the core business of the organisation and to the core needs of the employee and thus are usually of a much lower priority to employees. For example, a secretary will probably be highly motivated to keep clear, documented records of discussions and decisions made but probably much less motivated to do so in an environmentally friendly way. He may not be against acting in a pro-environmental fashion, but he may be less proactive and less per-sistent when facing barriers to do so.

Because of the tangential nature of pro-environmental behaviour to most core businesses and the core needs of most employees, we must consider the role of HR in green motivation separately. To date, tradi-tional HR practices have generally focused on the traditional work goals based on the core business of the organisation and have begun to deal with other employee needs-based goals such as work/life balance. Given the difference between these and pro-environmental goals, though, we cannot assume that traditional HR practices will address all aspects of green motivation. We believe there are two ways we can consider this: (1) change the focus to having a primary pro-environmental goal; and (2) deal with the fact that the pro-environmental goal will be secondary. We will now outline theories from the pro-environmental literature which will inform each of these considerations.

Encouraging a primary pro-environmental goal

The first consideration is to see whether we need to, and can, make the pro-environmental goal a primary focus for employees. Indeed, most theorists and researchers examining pro-environmental behaviour have assumed a green value- or attitudinal-based motivation; in other words, they have assumed that pro-environmental goals are primary. This was driven most strongly by Stern and colleagues in their delineation of the Values–Beliefs–Norms model (e.g. Stern, 2000; see Stern and Dietz, 1994; Stern *et al.*, 1995, 1999). From the perspective of this model, motivation comes predominantly from biospheric values (valuing the environment and ecology for its own right), but is also generated when a person with altruistic values sees that environmental damage is harming society or other people and/or when a person with egoistic values see that environmental damage could be harmful to him or her personally.

Research into attitudinal-based motivation comes from the application of the Theory of Planned Behaviour (e.g. Chan and Bishop, 2013; Fielding *et al.*, 2008; Lam, 2006). In this theory, motivation to act in a pro-environmental manner comes from a positive attitude towards pro-environmental behaviour and from believing that others think that acting pro-environmentally is a good thing to do. These attitudinal and normative factors are, however, complemented by the ability to control behaviour.

Finally, Pelletier and colleagues (Pelletier, 2002; Pelletier and Sharp, 2007; Pelletier *et al.*, 1998) applied the self-determination theory constructs of intrinsic, identified, introjected, extrinsic and amotivation to the realm of pro-environmental behaviour. These five types of self-regulation lead to different motivations: (1) intrinsic motivation comes from the pleasure and fun of engaging in pro-environmental behaviours; (2) identified motivation comes from believing in the importance of engaging in the behaviour; (3) introjected motivation comes from a feeling of guilt if one did not engage in the behaviour; (4) extrinsic motivation comes from 'having to' engage in the behaviour because of external constraints; and (5) amotivation is a lack of motivation to engage in pro-environmental behaviour (e.g., Deci and Ryan, 1985; Deci *et al.*, 1994; Gagne and Deci, 2005; Pelletier *et al.*, 1998). Intrinsic and identified motivation are both classified as 'autonomous' motivations, indicating that a person is engaging in the behaviour by their own volition (Deci and Ryan, 1985; Pelletier *et al.*, 1998). On the other hand, introjected and extrinsic motivations are classified as 'controlled' motivations because a person lacks a sense of volitional control over their engagement (Deci and Ryan, 1985; Pelletier *et al.*, 1998). Pelletier and colleagues find that autonomous motivation for the environment leads to engagement in pro-environmental behaviours; controlled motivation is unrelated and amotivation is negatively related to engagement in pro-environmental behaviours (Lavergne *et al.*, 2010; Pelletier and Sharp, 2007; Pelletier *et al.*, 1998).

From this very quick overview we can identify three main issues. First, from this approach, employees' values and attitudes towards the environment will play an important role. Second, the ability to control one's pro-environmental behaviour will enable motivation. Finally, we must keep in mind that, for those whose primary motivation is driven by environmental concerns, intrinsic motivation is positive but extrinsic motivation may be irrelevant or potentially harmful for motivation to engage in pro-environmental behaviour at work.

So, when environmental concerns are the primary goal for the employee, how can HR practices improve motivation towards pro-environmental behaviour? According to the AMO framework, ability/skill-enhancing HR practices (e.g., comprehensive recruitment, rigorous selection, and extensive training) can directly influence the types and levels of employees' abilities and skills, and the types of employees to recruit and retain. For example, training programmes were indicated as the most effective HRM practices in promoting pro-environmental behaviour (i.e., green behaviour) in a recent study by Zibarras and Coan (2015). Although it is focused on skills and not directly related to motivation, training can increase employees' green motivation by increasing employees' awareness of environmental concerns (e.g., climate change) on the organisation's activities and beyond and by helping to equip employees with the necessary knowledge, skills and abilities to engage effectively in pro-environmental behaviours (Shen *et al.*, 2016).

In addition to training, organisations can also attract and select job candidates whose green values are congruent with those of the organisations (Dumont *et al.*, 2016). For example, Renwick and colleagues suggest that green HRM can be seen as 'a form of "employer branding" in order to improve their selection attractiveness for an increasingly environmentally aware younger generation' (Renwick *et al.*, 2013, p. 4). While selecting for pro-environmental values in the absence of other characteristics is unlikely, selecting for value fit with the organisation is common practice (see e.g., Cable and Judge, 1997).

Finally, the opportunity aspects of AMO may also be relevant when employees have green values. For example, high involvement of employees in the decision-making process, when that process involved pro-environmental criteria, would heighten their sense of psychological ownership of organisational green objectives. This would then increase the employees' overall green motivation. However, for this practice, as with the previous practices, the organisation must already hold pro-environmental objectives.

In sum, we anticipate that ability/skill-enhancing and opportunity-enhancing HR practices in the green HRM field promote employees' green motivation through three main mechanisms: first, by increasing the employees' knowledge and ability to control their engagement in pro-environmental behaviours; second, by creating and shaping employees' pro-environmental values and norms and their commitment to those values; and third, by changing the profile of the employees to include more who hold pro-environmental values as primary goals.

What is notable about this approach is that they all focus on a conscious pro-environmental goal that must be held by both employees and the organisation (Unsworth, 2015). However, this is not the only approach we could adopt when increasing green motivation at work. We now discuss theories which consider factors that may help green motivation when the pro-environmental goal is secondary to, or conflicting with, the primary work goals.

Dealing with a secondary/conflicting pro-environmental goal

As noted earlier, at work, most employees are focused on work goals. Thus, there is a large potential for personal goal conflict between the green motivation and other work-based motivation (Unsworth *et al.*, 2013). This can be seen most clearly when pro-environmental behaviours are not aligned with work goals and/or are a low priority for an organisation. For example, a mechanic in a mining organisation in a growth period will be focused on fixing machinery as quickly as possible because his work goal is to enable more minerals to be mined; if the mechanic is in a situation where he has to choose between doing a quick fix that gets the truck moving again or doing a longer-term solution that might reduce carbon emissions, he is much more likely choose the former, regardless of his own personal pro-environmental values. When a person has multiple goals that are in conflict, that person will be less likely to achieve either goal (e.g., Soman and Min, 2011), will experience stress (e.g., Dickson and Moberly, 2010) and will be driven to resolve the conflict (e.g., Stroebe *et al.*, 2008), usually by prioritising the more important or salient goal and literally forgetting the other goal (e.g., Louro *et al.*, 2007; Shah *et al.*, 2002; Unsworth *et al.*, 2014). Pro-environmental goals are likely to be less important and less salient in a workplace than conflicting productivity or performance goals (Unsworth *et al.*, 2013), thus are likely to be the one that is forgotten.

However, there are ways that environmental goals that are secondary to or conflicting with work goals can be included. The first, and most obvious, approach is to ensure alignment at the level of the individual employee. Unsworth and colleagues (2014) examined various literatures surrounding goal conflict and suggested that goal alignment can be an alternative to goal prioritisation – that is, if a person is able to align their goals then they do not necessarily have to choose one over the other. In their review of the literature, Unsworth and colleagues (2014) find that alignment can be achieved through focusing on shared features or identification of a higher-order composite goal; in the realm of green HRM, this might include, for example, identifying 'keeping the organisation financially viable' as a higher-order personal goal that can align work efficiency and pro-environmental efficiency goals. Similarly, for a HR employee focused on attracting and selecting 'bright young things', using pro-environmental behaviours as a means of improving organisational branding for younger generations (see Renwick *et al.*, 2013) is also a way in which goal alignment can emerge. In this instance, the person has reduced conflict between her selection goals and her pro-environmental goals and green motivation will ensue.

Reducing goal conflict can also be achieved by aligning organisational goals with the employee's personal goals. Researchers such as Dumont *et al.* (2016) and Shen *et al.* (2016) suggested that, if employees' pro-environmental values (i.e., green value) are congruent with those demonstrated and supplied by the organisation, this will have a positive effect on employee pro-environmental motivation and behaviours (i.e., green motivation and behaviours). In doing so, employees are likely to be more motivated and emotionally involved in environmental issues as a result of their enhanced green awareness, KSAs, cognition and values (Dumont *et al.*, 2016; Renwick *et al.*, 2013, 2016; Shen *et al.*, 2016).

If goal alignment is not possible, then goal prioritising must occur (see Unsworth et al., 2014). To do this in a structured and systematic way, we suggest that HR first needs to be aware of instances where goal conflict might be arising. To our knowledge, there is little work that has addressed this in the pro-environmental or the GHRM literature. However, given the personal stress that goal conflict can create and the likelihood that pro-environmental goals will be forgotten, it may be an interesting way forward. In this instance, HR would first need to conduct new job analyses and outline which desirable pro-environmental behaviours need to be included in job descriptions. A detailed analysis would then be undertaken to pinpoint any areas of conflict. For example, academics often have a goal to disseminate and discuss their work with colleagues from around the world. The implementation of this goal often requires a great deal of airborne travel – which conflicts with a goal of reducing one's carbon footprint. Requiring people to work every day in an office building outside a city centre is likely to conflict with a goal of reducing one's commuting in a car. Conducting an audit of potential goal conflicts will allow HR managers to determine which goal should be prioritised in which situation and to subsequently change the job or the context to minimise these conflicts.

Finally, a different approach to green motivation has more recently been taken forward. This approach contrasts with the traditional approaches by diluting the focus on pro-environmental values and attitudes (see Unsworth, 2015). Instead, it proposes increasing motivation to engage in green behaviours through a 'selfish', indirect route (Unsworth and McNeill, 2016). This indirect route uses self-concordance as the motivating mechanism; self-concordance is the degree to which a behaviour is related to enduring values, identities and goals (Adriasola et al., 2012; Sheldon and Elliot, 1999; Sheldon and Kasser, 1995; Unsworth et al., 2011). For example, one employee may be highly motivated to respond to emails if she believes that doing so will help her get promoted (and getting promoted is important to her), another may be highly motivated to enact leadership behaviours because he values developing and caring for others. Research has generally shown that self-concordance is more likely to be related to engagement and persistence (i.e., motivation) across a range of work and home behaviours (Adriasola et al., 2011; Bono and Judge, 2003; Chatzisarantis et al., 2008, 2010; Greguras and Diefendorff, 2010; Judge et al., 2005; Koestner et al., 2002; Sheldon and Houser-Marko, 2001).

With regards to green motivation, it has been theorised that self-concordance will affect the degree to which workplace interventions are successful in changing behaviour – if the behaviour or the goals being addressed in the intervention are not self-concordant then it is likely that the intervention will fail or, at best, result in only short-term change (Unsworth *et al.*, 2013). Unsworth and McNeill (2017) conducted three studies with employees to show that self-concordance for pro-environmental behaviours could be changed and that it was indeed related to behaviours and intentions to behave in a more green way. One of their experiments involved participants who were told to imagine that their organisation was removing the car park but would subsidise public transport; the participants needed to decide how they would react. One third of the participants were asked to think about how catching public transport could help them with achieving goals that were important to them (e.g., if leisure was an important goal, then using public transport could enable them to read a book or relax); this was the self-concordance condition. Another third of the participants were asked to think about how catching public transport helped to mitigate against climate change, while the final third were simply asked to describe what catching public transport would be like for them. These last two conditions were designed as comparisons to see whether the self-concordance intervention worked better than nothing at all, and whether it worked better than a traditional pro-environment attitudinal intervention. As you might expect, the self-concordance condition did result in more people being willing to use public transport, indicating support for linking pro-environmental behaviours to 'selfish' reasons for increasing green motivation.

The most obvious way in which HR has attempted to address a form of pro-environmental self-concordance is through motivation-enhancing HRM practices (e.g. performance-based compensation, incentives and benefits, promotion opportunities). For example, Dumont *et al.* (2016) suggested that 'organizations should properly appraise employee green behaviour, and link this behaviour to promotional opportunities, pay, and compensation, for employees to be encouraged and motivated to participate in green activities, and to contribute to green management objectives' (p. 11). For example, using longitudinal data from 469 US firms operating in high-polluting industries, Berrone and Gomez-Mejia (2009) study revealed that firms' environmental performance was significantly better when it was related to chief executive officer total pay. A recent survey of 214 UK organisations found rewards as one of the top ten prevalent HR practices encouraging employees to become more pro-environmental (Zibarras and Coan, 2015, p. 2133).

Non-monetary rewards such as recognition programmes are another popular form of reward practices which have been demonstrated to be effective in motivating employees to engage in green activities (Renwick *et al.*, 2016; Zibarras and Coan, 2015). In fact, Handgraaf *et al.* (2013) found that recognition (e.g. positive comments) were more effective than monetary rewards in reducing energy use in a Dutch organisation. We posit that these effects are derived from self-concordance motivation that works for those who value either the reward or the recognition offered.

Performance-based compensation/incentives can be seen as a strong extrinsic motivation based HRM practice, and there is a tendency for these rewards to undermine intrinsic motivation (Deci *et al.*, 1999). However, such HRM practices can also boost intrinsic motivation. This is because they can satisfy employees' needs for competence and relatedness (Gardner *et al.*, 2011). For example, in cases where an employee demonstrates a high level of pro-environmental behaviour and is compensated accordingly, this signifies excellent performance and the use of performance-based compensation/incentives affirm competence, thus offsetting the potential detrimental effects of tight control (Deci *et al.*, 1999). Furthermore, social exchange theory suggests that the availability of various official appraisal, recognition and rewards in relation to green behaviour, is often seen as reflective of the value of the organisation. Thus, engagement in green activities followed by rewards also conveys feelings of belonging and relatedness to the organisation as a whole. As such, it is important to note that motivation-enhancing HRM practices need to be well designed and relevant to exert maximal positive effort, and offset potential detrimental effects on employees' intrinsic motivation to engage in green activities (Renwick *et al.*, 2013, 2016; Zibarras and Coan, 2015).

On the other hand, for those who do not value monetary rewards or recognition, self-concordance will not be gained by reward-based practices and crowding out effects can occur (Frey, 1997; Unsworth *et al.*, 2013). As such, we suggest that HR needs to consider alternative means of increasing self-concordance for some employees. This might include a link to learning goals, social justice goals, leisure goals and so forth. In each instance, HR would enable employees to see how engaging in the pro-environmental behaviour helps them to achieve these other goals. For example, in an organisation where employees value social justice, HR could arrange for the money that was saved from energy efficiency behaviours to be donated to a local charity. As was found in Unsworth and McNeill (2016), pro-environmental behaviours do not need to be linked to the environment for them to produce green motivation.

Enabling green motivation

So far, we have considered factors that create green motivation and have only briefly mentioned the role of control. However, regardless of whether the pro-environmental is primary or secondary, the employee must be able to act upon their green motivation for it to be maintained. As noted earlier, the theory of planned behaviour labels this 'perceived behavioural control'. From an HR perspective, perceived behavioural control is most often associated with opportunity-enhancing practices. Thus, increasing the amount of autonomy and flexibility in job design (Gardner *et al.*, 2011; Jiang *et al.*, 2012; Kehoe and Wright, 2013; Lepak *et al.*, 2006; Subramony, 2009) should allow employees to act on their green motivation and to engage in pro-environmental behaviour.

Practical implications and conclusion

We have outlined a number of pro-environmental theories and discussed how they might relate to both traditional and new HR practices. In summary, we believe there are many ways in which HR can promote green motivation. Some of these fall within traditional practices already considered within the AMO framework, such as training, attraction and selection, and rewards. However, some new HR practices must also be considered, which involve conducting detailed job analyses and considering alternative goals beyond financial reward and recognition.

The practices we have identified include:

- training that makes the pro-environmental goal primary;
- training that increases the skills of the employee to enable them to engage in pro-environmental behaviour;
- attraction and selection of staff that hold pro-environmental values;
- involvement in decision-making that includes pro-environmental decision criteria;
- aligning employees' personal goals so that pro-environmental goals do not conflict with work goals;
- aligning the employees' pro-environmental goal with the organisation's goals to reduce conflict;
- conducting audits of job roles to identify where pro-environmental and work goals conflict;
- linking pro-environmental goals to rewards and recognition programmes; and
- linking pro-environmental goals to other employee goals such as social justice.

In conclusion, we believe that traditional HR practices can help with increasing green motivation. However, the paradox of pro-environmental behaviours is such that goal conflict may interfere with these practices. We suggest therefore that additional practices are needed which explicitly deal with the fact that pro-environmental behaviours, in an organisational setting, are both crucial and tangential.

References

Adriasola, E., Steele, A., Day, D. V., and Unsworth, K. L. (2011) 'Leader identity: Using goal hierarchy self-concordance to understand leader emergence', *26th Annual SIOP Conference*. Chicago.

Adriasola, E., Unsworth, K. L. and Day, D. V. (2012) 'Goal self-concordance: Understanding its effects through a new conceptualisation and task differentiation', *Academy of Management Conference*. Boston, USA.

Ajzen, I. (1985) 'From intentions to actions: A theory of planned behavior'. In Kuhl, J. and Beckmann, J. (Eds) *Action Control: From Cognition to Behavior*. Berlin: Springer Verlag, pp. 11–39.

Ajzen, I. (1991) 'The theory of planned behavior', *Organizational Behavior and Human Decision Processes*, vol. 50, no. 2, pp. 179–211.

Berrone, P. and Gomez-Mejia, L. R. (2009) 'Environmental performance and executive compensation: An integrated agency–institutional perspective', *Academy of Management Journal*, vol. 52, no. 1, pp. 103–126.

Blau, P. M. (1964) *Exchange and Power in Social Life*. New York: John Wiley & Sons.

Bono, J. E. and Judge, T. A. (2003) 'Self-concordance at work: Toward understanding the motivational effects of transformational leaders', *Academy of Management Journal*, vol. 46, no. 5, pp. 554–571.

Cable, D. M. and Judge, T. A. (1997) 'Interviewers' perceptions of person–organization fit and organizational selection decisions', *Journal of Applied Psychology*, vol. 82, no. 4, pp. 546.

Campbell, J. and Pritchard, R. (1976) 'Motivation theory in individual and organizational psychology'. In: *Handbook of Industrial and Organizational Psychology*. Chicago: Rand McNally.

Chan, L. and Bishop, B. (2013) 'A moral basis for recycling: Extending the theory of planned behaviour', *Journal of Environmental Psychology*, vol. 36, pp. 96–102.

Chatzisarantis, N. L. D., Hagger, M. S. and Thogersen-Ntoumani, C. (2008) 'The effects of self-disconcordance, self-concordance and implementation intentions on health behavior', *Journal of Applied Biobehavioral Research*, vol. 13, no. 4, pp. 198–214.

Chatzisarantis, N. L. D., Hagger, M. S. and Wang, J. C. K. (2010) 'Evaluating the effects of implementation intention and self-concordance on behaviour', *British Journal of Psychology*, vol. 101, pp. 705–718.

Combs, J., Liu, Y., Hall, A. and Ketchen, D. (2006) 'How much do high-performance work practices matter? A meta-analysis of their effects on organizational performance', *Personnel Psychology*, vol. 59, no. 3, pp. 501–528.

Deci, E. L. (1975) *Intrinsic Motivation.* New York: Plenum Press.

Deci, E. L. and Ryan, R. M. (1985) *Intrinsic Motivation and Self-Determination in Human Behavior.* New York: Plenum.

Deci, E. L., Eghrari, H., Patrick, B. C. and Leone, D. R. (1994) 'Facilitating internalization: The self-determination theory perspective', *Journal of Personality*, vol. 62, pp. 119–142.

Deci, E. L., Koestner, R. and Ryan, R. M. (1999) 'A meta-analytic review of experiments examining the effects of extrinsic rewards on intrinsic motivation', *Psychological Bulletin*, vol. 125, no. 6, pp. 627–668.

Dickson, J. M. and Moberly, N. J. (2010) 'Depression, anxiety and reduced facilitation in adolescents' personal goal systems', *Cognitive Therapy and Research*, vol. 34, no. 6, pp. 576–581.

Dumont, J., Shen, J. and Deng, X. (2016) 'Effects of green HRM practices on employee workplace green behavior: The role of psychological green climate and employee green values', *Human Resource Management*, pp. 1–15. DOI: 10.1002/hrm.21792.

Fielding, K. S., McDonald, R. and Louis, W. R. (2008) 'Theory of planned behaviour, identity and intentions to engage in environmental activism', *Journal of Environmental Psychology*, vol. 28, pp. 318–326.

Frey, B. (1997) *Not Just For the Money: An Economic Theory of Personal Motivation.* Cheltenham, UK: Edward Elgar.

Gagne, M. and Deci, E. L. (2005) 'Self-determination theory and work motivation', *Journal of Organizational Behavior*, vol. 26, pp. 331–362.

Gardner, T. M., Wright, P. M. and Moynihan, L. M. (2011) 'The impact of motivation, empowerment, and skill-enhancing practices on aggregate voluntary turnover: The mediating effect of collective affective commitment', *Personnel Psychology*, vol. 64, no. 2, pp. 315–350.

Greguras, G. J. and Diefendorff, J. M. (2010) 'Why does proactive personality predict employee life satisfaction and work behaviors? A field investigation of the mediating role of the self-concordance model', *Personnel Psychology*, vol. 63, no. 3, pp. 539–560.

Hackman, J. R. and Oldham, G. R. (1976) 'Motivation through the design of work: Test of a theory', *Organizational Behavior and Human Performance*, vol. 16, no. 2, pp. 250–279.

Hackman, J. R. and Oldham, G. R. (1980) *Work Redesign.* Reading, MA: Addison-Wesley Publishing Company.

Handgraaf, M. J., de Jeude, M. A. V. L. and Appelt, K. C. (2013) 'Public praise vs. private pay: Effects of rewards on energy conservation in the workplace', *Ecological Economics*, vol. 86, pp. 86–92.

Jiang, K., Lepak, D. P., Hu, J. and Baer, J. C. (2012) 'How does human resource management influence organizational outcomes? A meta-analytic investigation of mediating mechanisms', *Academy of Management Journal*, vol. 55, no. 6, pp. 1264–1294.

Judge, T. A., Bono, J. E., Erez, A. and Locke, E. A. (2005) 'Core self-evaluations and job and life satisfaction: The role of self-concordance and goal attainment', *Journal of Applied Psychology*, vol. 90, no. 2, pp. 257–268.

Kehoe, R. R. and Wright, P. M. (2013) 'The impact of high-performance human resource practices on employees' attitudes and behaviors', *Journal of Management*, vol. 39, no. 2, pp. 366–391.

Klein, H. J. (1989) 'An integrated control theory model of work motivation', *Academy of Management Review*, vol. 14, no. 2, pp. 150–172.

Koestner, R., Lekes, N., Powers, T. A. and Chicoine, E. (2002) 'Attaining personal goals: Self-concordance plus implementation intentions equals success', *Journal of Personality and Social Psychology*, vol. 83, no. 1, pp. 231–224.

Lam, S. P. (2006) 'Predicting intention to save water: Theory of planned behavior, response efficacy, vulnerability and perceived efficiency of alternative solutions', *Journal of Applied Social Psychology*, vol. 36, no. 11, pp. 2803–2824.

Lavergne, K. J., Sharp, E. C., Pelletier, L. G. and Holtby, A. (2010) 'The role of perceived government style in the facilitation of self-determined and non self-determined motivation for pro-environmental behavior', *Journal of Environmental Psychology*, vol. 30, no. 2, pp. 169–177.

Lepak, D. P., Liao, H., Chung, Y. and Harden, E. E. (2006) 'A conceptual review of human resource management systems in strategic human resource management research'. In Martocchio, J. J. (Ed.), *Research in Personnel and Human Resources Management*, Vol. 25, Greenwich, CT: JAI, pp. 217–271.

Locke, E. A. and Latham, G. P. (1990) *A Theory of Goal Setting and Task Performance*. Englewood Cliffs, NJ: Prentice Hall.

Locke, E. A. and Latham, G. P. (2002) 'Building a practically useful theory of goal-setting and task motivation: A 35 year odyssey', *American Psychologist*, vol. 57, no. 9, pp. 705–717.

Louro, M. J., Pieters, R. and Zeelenberg, M. (2007) 'Dynamics of multiple-goal pursuit', *Journal of Personality and Social Psychology*, vol. 93, no. 2, pp. 174–193.

O'Boyle Jr, E. H., Forsyth, D. R., Banks, G. C. and McDaniel, M. A. (2012) 'A meta-analysis of the dark triad and work behavior: A social exchange perspective', *Journal of Applied Psychology*, vol. 97, no. 3, pp. 557–579.

Paauwe, J. and Boselie, P. (2005) 'HRM and performance: What next?', *Human Resource Management Journal*, vol. 15, no. 4, pp. 68–83.

Pelletier, L. G. (2002) '10: A motivational analysis of self-determination for pro-environmental behaviors', *Handbook of Self-Determination Research*, no. 205.

Pelletier, L. G. and Sharp, E. C. (2007) 'From the promotion of pro-environmental behaviors to the development of an eco-citizen: The self-determination theory perspective', *The Annual Conference of the Canadian Psychological Association*. Ottawa, Ontario.

Pelletier, L. G., Tuson, K. M., Green-Demers, I., Noels, K. and Beaton, A. M. (1998) 'Why are you doing things for the environment? The motivation toward the environment scale (mtes) 1', *Journal of Applied Social Psychology*, vol. 28, no. 5, pp. 437–468.

Renwick, D. W., Jabbour, C. J., Müller-Camen, M., Redman, T. and Wilkinson, A. (2016) 'Contemporary developments in Green (environmental) HRM scholarship', *The International Journal of Human Resource Management*, vol. 27, no. 2, pp. 114–128.

Renwick, D. W., Redman, T. and Maguire, S. (2013) 'Green human resource management: A review and research agenda', *International Journal of Management Reviews*, vol. 15, no. 1, pp. 1–14.

Rhoades, L. and Eisenberger, R. (2002) 'Perceived organizational support: A review of the literature', *Journal of Applied Psychology*, vol. 87, no. 4, pp. 698–714.

Shah, J. Y., Friedman, R. and Kruglanski, A. W. (2002) 'Forgetting all else: On the antecedents and consequences of goal shielding', *Journal of Personality and Social Psychology*, vol. 83, no. 6, pp. 1261–1280.

Sheldon, K. M. and Elliot, A. J. (1999) 'Goal striving, need satisfaction, and longitudinal well-being: The self-concordance model', *Journal of Personality and Social Psychology*, vol. 76, no. 3, pp. 482–497.

Sheldon, K. M. and Houser-Marko, L. (2001) 'Self-concordance, goal attainment and the pursuit of happiness: Can there be an upward spiral?', *Journal of Personality and Social Psychology*, vol. 80, no. 1, p. 152.

Sheldon, K. M. and Kasser, T. (1995) 'Coherence and congruence: Two aspects of personality integration', *Journal of Personality and Social Psychology*, vol. 68, pp. 531–543.

Shen, J., Dumont, J. and Deng, X. (2016) 'Employees' perceptions of green HRM and non-green employee work outcomes the social identity and stakeholder perspectives', *Group & Organization Management*, doi:10.1177/1059601116664610.

Shin, S. J., Jeong, I. and Bae, J. (2016) 'Do high-involvement HRM practices matter for worker creativity? A cross-level approach', *The International Journal of Human Resource Management*, Doi: 10.1080/09585192.2015.1137612.

Skinner, B. F. (1953) *Science and Human Behavior*. New York: Free Press.

Soman, D. and Min, Z. (2011) 'The fewer the better: Number of goals and saving behavior', *Journal of Marketing Research*, vol. 48, no. 6, pp. 944–960.

Stern, P. C. (2000) 'Toward a coherent theory of environmentally significant behavior', *Journal of Social Issues*, vol. 56, no. 3, pp. 407–424.

Stern, P. C. and Dietz, T. (1994) 'The value basis of environmental concern', *Journal of Social Issues*, vol. 50, no. 3, pp. 65–84.

Stern, P. C., Dietz, T., Abel, T., Guagnano, G. A. and Kalof, L. (1999) 'A value-belief-norm theory of support for social movements: The case of environmental concern', *Human Ecology Review*, vol. 6, no. 2, pp. 81–97.

Stern, P. C., Dietz, T. and Guagnano, G. A. (1995) 'The new ecological paradigm in social psychological perspective', *Environment and Behavior*, vol. 27, pp. 723–745.

Stroebe, W., Mensink, W., Aarts, H., Schut, H. and Kruglanski, A. W. (2008) 'Why dieters fail: Testing the goal conflict model of eating', *Journal of Experimental Social Psychology*, vol. 44, no. 1, pp. 26–36.

Subramony, M. (2009) 'A meta-analytic investigation of the relationship between HRM bundles and firm performance', *Human Resource Management*, vol. 48, no. 5, pp. 745–768.

Unsworth, K. L. (2015) 'Green me up Scotty: Psychological interventions to increase pro-environmental behaviours'. In Barling, J. and Robertson, J. (Eds) *The Psychology of Green Organizations*. New York: Oxford University Press.

Unsworth, K. L. and McNeill, I. (2017) 'Increasing pro-environmental behaviors by increasing self-concordance: Testing an intervention', *Journal of Applied Psychology*, vol. 102, no. 1. pp. 88–103.

Unsworth, K. L., Adriasola, E., Johnston-Billings, A., Dmitrieva, A. and Hodkiewicz, M. R. (2011) 'Goal hierarchy: Improving asset data quality by improving motivation', *Reliability Engineering and System Safety*, vol. 96, pp. 1474–1481.

Unsworth, K. L., Dmitrieva, A. and Adriasola, E. (2013) 'Changing behaviour: Increasing the effectiveness of workplace interventions in creating pro-environmental behaviour change', *Journal of Organizational Behavior*, vol. 34, no. 2, pp. 211–229.

Unsworth, K. L., Yeo, G. and Beck, J. W. (2014) 'Multiple goals: A review and derivation of general principles', *Journal of Organizational Behavior*, vol. 35, no. 8, pp. 1064–1078.

Zibarras, L. D. and Coan, P. (2015) HRM practices used to promote pro-environmental behavior: A UK survey' *The International Journal of Human Resource Management*, vol. 26, no. 16, pp. 2121–2142.

3 Employee engagement in managing environmental performance

A case study of the Planet Champion initiative, McDonalds UK and Sweden

Chandana Sanyal and Julie Haddock-Millar

Introduction

This chapter examines an employee involvement initiative in two McDonald's subsidiaries in the United Kingdom (UK) and Sweden, and the relationship with human resource development (HRD) factors such as employee engagement and leadership with environmental performance. The case study explores: (1) a specific green initiative used to involve and engage employees; and (2) employee perceptions of the key levers necessary to achieve positive environmental impact. The case study organisation was chosen because of its existing commitment to environmental responsibility and strategic aim to improve environmental sustainability, in addition to the recent development of initiatives which seek to involve, empower and engage staff. The organisation's global environmental vision is to maximise positive environmental impact through key stakeholder groups: suppliers, employees and customers. The central initiative focuses primarily on the relationship between the organisation, employees and related human resource development outcomes in the context of environmental sustainability.

The relationship between employee involvement and environmental management is well researched and grounded in theory (Renwick *et al.*, 2013) and why organisations choose to engage the workforce in environmental management is well documented too (Aragon-Correa *et al.*, 2013; Boiral, 2009; Brio *et al.*, 2007). Hiring new employees who are willing to engage in positive environment activities, alongside working with current employees to develop green training and involvement initiatives, are growing trends (Guerci *et al.*, 2016; Haddock-Millar *et al.*, 2016; Ramus and Steger, 2000). Recognising that green training has the ability to develop an employee's awareness and understanding of green issues, it is no surprise that 'green training is also shown to be the most adopted practice in HRM practices' (Guerci *et al.*, 2016, p. 267). Of significant importance is the relationship between the proactive adoption of green practices and firm performance (O'Donohue and Torugsa, 2016). The concept of performance has broad connotations, incorporating revenue flows and reduced costs (O'Donohue and Torugsa, 2016; Torugsa *et al.*, 2012, 2013). A recent empirical study in two Australian-based organisations highlighted that participation in environmental initiatives was directly associated with higher levels of employee engagement within the organisation and its green performance, reducing staff intentions to leave the organisation (Benn *et al.*, 2015). More recently, O'Donohue and Torugsa's (2016) quantitative study of 1,278 small firms in the Australian machinery and equipment-manufacturing sector reported a positive association between proactive environmental management, Green Human Resource Management (GHRM) and financial performance. Furthermore, a shared understanding of the organisation's strategic and operational goals, employee involvement in relevant business processes and the opportunity to contribute are all regarded as essential to secure the benefits of investing in GHRM. The following section explores specific aspects of GHRM activities theory connected to the case study.

Theoretical background

Green employee engagement and environmental management

The meaning of employee engagement is ambiguous among both academic researchers and practitioners. Research shows that the term is used at different times to refer to psychological states, behavioural engagement and trait engagement (Macey and Schneider, 2008). Employee involvement can be described as cultivating employee interest and dedication for greater employee participation in the workplace (Cotton, 1993). Kahn (1990) argues that employee engagement is different from other employee role constructs such as job involvement. Similarly, Hallberg and Schaufeli (2006) highlight that work engagement, job involvement and organisational commitments are empirically distinct constructs and, thus, reflect different aspects of work attachment. However, in the context of GHRM, the terms employee involvement and employee engagement appear to be used interchangeably.

There is wide recognition that employees are one of the, if not the, most important source of knowledge, expertise and innovation in the area of GHRM (Brio *et al.*, 2007; Perron *et al.*, 2006; Renwick *et al.*, 2013). The literature identifies several key levers to involve and engage the workforce in environmental management. In the context of this research study, the authors focused on the practice of involving employees in GHRM policies and processes, which led to, or was aimed at, maximising employee engagement. A recent development is the emphasis on the 'green work–life balance' of the employee which proposes that organisations should consider employees in their two-fold role – for the organisation and their family. The green work–life balance concept is suggested to facilitate environmentally friendly behaviour in both life domains: eco-friendly behaviour as an employee and as a consumer (Muster and Schrader, 2011). This in turn can increase staff motivation, commitment and job retention (Frank *et al.*, 2004; Jackson *et al.*, 2011). Organisations will, therefore, need to consider both the 'what' (outcomes) and 'how' (processes) to achieve effective employee engagement (Muster and Schrader, 2011; Yusoff *et al.*, 2015).

Team formation

Involving employees in environmental management has been proven to positively correlate with environmental outcome measures (Brio *et al.*, 2007). Empirical studies have identified the development of team formation (Hanna *et al.*, 2000; Robertson and Barling, 2013) and employee training (Alberti *et al.*, 2000; Teixeira *et al.*, 2012) as key initiatives for increasing employee involvement in green activities. Many commentators recommend the use of green teams to involve the workforce in green management practices (Jabbour, 2011; Jabbour *et al.*, 2013), which can be defined as a team of people who work together to solve environmental problems that can be used to generate ideas, resolve environmental management conflicts and foster environmental learning. Green teams have been classified into different categories. On the one hand, green teams can be either functional or cross-functional, distinguished by membership from the same or different organisational units (Daily *et al.*, 2009). On the other hand, green teams can comprise top management, focusing on environmental policy formation; be action-orientated, analysing opportunities and improving environmental performance; or be responsible for specific processes to bring about improvement (Anderson Strachan, 1996). However, whatever the shape or orientation of the green teams, they can play a key role in engaging wider employees and support the process of environmental management.

Employee training

Employee education and training is a core element of most, if not all, environmental management systems (Perron *et al.*, 2006). Industry standards such as BS7750 and ISO14001 incorporate training at all levels of the organisation, for the purpose of understanding the goals of the environmental management system. Here, the goal is to train employees to develop environmental organisational citizen behaviours and green competences (Boiral, 2009; Subramanian *et al.*, 2016) and environmental action (Daily and Huang, 2001; Govindarajulu and Daily, 2004). In addition, key outcomes of education and training are, first, to raise employee alertness and commitments towards going green and, second, to equip employees with the knowledge and skills to make a positive contribution to the long-term performance of the business. Relevant employee environmental training and increasing awareness, together with a heightened level of motivation, make it possible for companies to improve their environmental performance (Alberti *et al.*, 2000). Green training and development educate employees about the value of environmental management, train them in working methods that conserve energy, reduce waste, diffuse environmental consciousness inside the organisation and offer an opportunity to engage employees in environmental problem-solving (Pande, 2016). Training programmes tailored to addressing environmental concerns should involve a three-stage planning process, beginning with establishing the need and rationale for the training, defining the training programme objectives and developing content which aligns with the corporate objectives (Fernandez *et al.*, 2003). Likewise, Teixeira, Jabbour, de Sousa Jabbour, Latan and de Oliveira (2016) suggest that, when focusing on 'green training', organisations should invest in systematic analysis of training gaps and needs, the content of training and opportunities for employers to apply green knowledge. Jackson and Seo (2010) identify three GHRM training perspectives, from the basic premise of compliance, enabling conformance in the areas of regulations and technicality, to raising employee awareness in relation to the corporate agenda and, finally, creating a shift in organisational culture. More recently, Jabbour *et al.*'s (2013) empirical study links environmental training positively and significantly to the level of maturity in environmental management in companies. Similarly, Teixeira *et al.*'s (2016) recent study has shown that alignment of green training, organisational learning and green human resource practices are crucial to the greening of firms.

Green leadership and management

The development of green leadership and commitment from top management is seen by many as a pre-requisite for employee engagement (Egri and Herman, 2000; Govindarajulu and Daily, 2004; Robertson and Barling, 2013). Organisational structural changes, such as the creation of a specialist management role/department, are being increasingly implemented by companies to raise the importance of environmental issues. Renwick *et al.* (2013) classify a number of different roles that HR managers may take up in environmental management. These range from 'light green' to 'dark green', based on environmental competencies and business experience. This variation in the green capabilities of managers could also have an impact on the level of staff's green engagement. Research suggests that employees are more willing to undertake environmental initiatives when their supervisors embrace a democratic and open style of communication in regard to environmental ideas (Ramus, 2001; Ramus and Steger, 2000), and when managers and supervisors actively involve employees at all levels towards improving environmental goals (Govindarajulu and Daily, 2004). Aragon-Correa and Rubio-Lopez (2007) suggest that a lack of expertise will probably lead to wasted time and inefficiencies, tending to limit any major financial returns from environmental progress. A 'passive approach' from managers to environment sustainability has led to managerial reluctance to champion sustainability initiatives (Harris and Tregidga, 2012). Here, position, status and power are important levers within the context of management and leadership roles (Robertson and Barling, 2013). To win the hearts and minds of employees, and keep them motivated and engaged in environmental initiatives, the role of the manager is crucial. Therefore, encouraging employees to make suggestions and engage in activities that improve the environment is imperative for employee engagement (Renwick *et al.*, 2013).

Integration of green performance measures

Another lever for engaging employees in environmental practices is the integration of corporate GHRM strategy into the performance management system (Länsiluoto and Jarvenpää, 2010). Incorporating green management into the everyday language and fabric of the organisation is a growing phenomenon. The 'greening' of the Balanced Score Card has received growing attention, focusing on the relationship between environmental management, financial performance and stakeholder interests (Marcus and Fremeth, 2009; Sharma, 2000). Performance evaluation and regular review of goals and accountabilities can instil a sense of shared responsibility for environmental outcomes amongst key stakeholders, including employees (Ones and Dilchert, 2013; Ramus, 2001). More recently, an empirical study has highlighted that there is strong relationship between the internal workplace practices of GHRM within organisational systems – in which environmental performance is correlated to employee involvement and empowerment; culture and supportive climate is related to pay and reward systems; and recruitment, training, development and union role is correlated to employee involvement and environmental management (Gholami *et al.*, 2016). Here, leaders and managers have a responsibility to apply strategic and operational tools to engage employees and encourage participation in environmental management.

Overall, the human factor is a key success factor in organisational environmental activities (Brio *et al.*, 2007) and is now almost a first step when organisations introduce new environmental initiatives to involve the wider workforce (Renwick *et al.*, 2013). Although employee engagement is a well-researched area, what appears to be lacking is the rich insight and narrative accounts of the individual employee experience in the field of GHRM when developing and implementing new environmental initiatives, to which we now turn.

McDonald's business model

McDonald's is the leading global brand in the 'informal eating out' market, with a presence in over 100 countries and 35,000 restaurants. McDonald's global system comprises both company-owned and franchised restaurants, owned or operated via conventional franchise, developmental licence or affiliate. Over 80 per cent of McDonald's restaurants globally are currently franchised and over 90 per cent in the USA; the goal is to shift to 95 per cent franchisee in the longer term. Franchise restaurants are owned and operated by approximately 5,000 independent, small- and mid-sized businesses. Their business relationship is supported by an agreement that requires adherence to standards and policies regarded as essential to protect the McDonald's brand. Company-owned restaurants allow McDonald's to improve the operations and success of all restaurants. Innovations from franchisees can be tested and, when viable, implemented across the globe where appropriate. Furthermore, company-owned restaurants provide a location for training experience of restaurant operations. Company-owned restaurants employ more than 420,000 people.

McDonald's four pillars of strategic focus are: food, sourcing, people and planet. The next section focuses on the strategic pillar of *planet*.

McDonald's and the environment

McDonald's aspiration is to develop and operate the most environmentally efficient restaurants, delivering value to the business and the communities in which their restaurants operate. The regulatory environment worldwide causes complex compliance risks that can affect McDonald's operations. New, potential or changing regulations constantly influence business plans, which need to be responsive to the legal and regulatory environment. Furthermore, the increased public focus, including by governmental and nongovernmental organisations on environmental sustainability matters (e.g., packaging and waste, animal health and welfare, deforestation and land use) and the increased pressure to make commitments, set targets or establish additional goals and take actions to meet them, adds an ever-growing layer of complexity. McDonald's 'Good Planet' aspirational goals for 2020 include:

*   achieve 20 per cent increase in energy efficiency of company-owned restaurants;
*   increase energy efficiency through restaurant standards; and
*   increase amount of in-restaurant recycling to 50 per cent and minimise waste.

Moving towards 2020 and beyond, McDonald's will continue to focus on energy management, waste minimisation and recycling, and water efficiency. The environmental management strategic focus and organisational culture in previous years meant doing less harm; today McDonald's focuses on opportunities and innovations to do good. Success depends on a number of factors, including the independent franchisees' willingness and ability to implement major initiatives and the leadership and management needed to drive innovation and progress, in addition to the need to involve and engage the workforce. The Planet Champion initiative is one example of the way in which McDonald's is attempting to engage and leverage the commitment of the workforce.

Planet Champions

Planet Champions is a voluntary McDonald's programme, which began in the UK and is aimed at leveraging the environmental enthusiasm of restaurant teams. Helen McFarlane, Environmental Consultant, McDonald's UK explained:

> McDonald's UK asks staff members to be the environmental voice in the restaurant, to help business managers with existing environmental

initiatives and to generate new ideas. The volunteers receive a day of training on broad environmental issues, the company's activities and how they can contribute. They have a year-long calendar of activities focusing on the key issues of litter, recycling and energy. A regular newsletter keeps them up-to-date, informs them about competitions and gives them a forum to share ideas.

So far, approximately 1,100 restaurant staff in the UK have volunteered to be Planet Champions in over 650 restaurants. As a network group, Planet Champions have increased cardboard recycling and realised energy savings. This initiative has also helped to increase awareness of environmental initiatives among non-champion crew in pilot restaurants. The Planet Champions programme won the Green Apple Award for employee engagement. The Green Apple Award was launched in 1994 by The Green Organisation. The Green Apple Awards take place annually to recognise, reward and promote environmental best practice around the world. The initiative and was shortlisted for the PEER Awards, recognising commitment to community, customers and people. In 2011, the programme was extended to Ireland, Norway and Sweden.

Research approach

The case study research was conducted in the UK and Swedish subsidiaries of McDonald's. In this chapter, we refer to them as UK Ltd and Sweden Ltd. The authors adopted an interview-based multi-case study approach (Eisenhardt, 1989; Eisenhardt and Graebner, 2007). Multiple cases provide the opportunity to gain a fuller picture of the subject of study by having different contexts to compare and contrast and to identify patterns and underlying relationships through the close examination of themes and evidence (Bryman and Bell, 2015; Miles and Huberman, 1994; Yin, 2013). The study involved ten one-to-one semi-structured interviews with a sample of employees from different levels in the organisational hierarchy (Drever, 1995), including directors and managers, and five focus groups which involved a total of 23 managers and frontline workers (see Table 3.1).

The hierarchical structure varied across the two countries and the table shows this by identifying the role as not applicable where this position is not within the structure (N/A). When the authors were not able to interview a role representative, this is acknowledged by a dash (–). As convenience dictated the sample size, the composition of the sample has a degree of homogeneity in the sense that all participants had been involved in a green initiative, had experience of green initiatives

Table 3.1 Interview respondents

Job role	UK	Sweden
Category: Head Office staff		
HR Director	1	1
Head of Environment Department	1	N/A
Environment Manager/Consultant	1	1
Operations Manager/Consultant	1	1
Category: Restaurant Managers		
Restaurant Business Manager/Franchisee	3	3
Restaurant Assistant/Shift Manager	11	–
Category: Frontline Staff		
Restaurant Trainer	1	–
Restaurant Frontline Staff	–	8
Total Participants	**19**	**14**

at head office or restaurant level, or had a general awareness of the organisation's current approach to environmental sustainability. The participants were drawn from both company-owned and franchised restaurants. The overarching interview questions were drawn from a review of the recent literature on green employee involvement and engagement.

Data analysis

There were three inter-related phases in the data analysis. The first phase involved within-case study analysis, building individual write-ups of each national location (Byrne and Ragin, 2009; Eisenhardt, 1989). Collecting data from secondary and primary sources and drawing on different methods, including one-to-one interviews and focus groups, facilitated a degree of methodological triangulation, insofar as it enabled the authors to develop a more detailed picture of the UK and Swedish subsidiaries. Next, the authors read through the transcripts independently, following a descriptive coding process. Once the descriptive codes were agreed, the next stage involved interpretative coding, which identified a smaller number of codes. The authors followed a manual coding and thematic process. This process allowed for preliminary themes to be developed and embedded in the green employee involvement and engagement literature. Following this, the authors conducted cross-case analysis to identify consistent themes across the subsidiaries

(Ryan and Bernard, 2003), reviewing the transcripts again for recurrent themes and comparisons to understand the degree of convergence across different national, regional and local contexts.

Planet Champions and employee engagement

At the time of our interviews, the key initiative in UK Ltd and Sweden Ltd was the launch of 'Planet Champions'. In UK Ltd, the Planet Champion pilot was tested in a small number of restaurants from July to September 2010 before the decision was made to roll it out nationally. The UK initiative was rolled out in January 2011 on a voluntary basis, and over 279 members of staff attended training workshops in eight regional locations throughout the country. Building on this pilot, the training gave Planet Champions the opportunity to understand the role requirements and expectations, participate in a range of practical activities to encourage engagement and enhance knowledge, and form a community of practice within their local region, creating a reflective structure to encourage and foster a learning and innovative culture (Brown and Duguid, 1991). By 2013, 1,100 staff members had volunteered to be Planet Champions in 674 restaurants. In October 2012, Sweden Ltd launched their Planet Champion initiative, based on the UK model. At the initial stage, 15 volunteers attended the first Sweden Ltd training session, which was regarded as a pilot, in order to test the training materials. In 2013, four further training sessions were held with 50 Planet Champions. The Planet Champions were a combination of managers and frontline restaurant staff.

The implementation of Planet Champions in UK Ltd and Sweden Ltd is a strong indicator of the commitment to employee engagement to environmental sustainability in these McDonald's subsidiaries. The literature highlights the use of green teams to address environmental issues, generate new ideas and foster environmental learning (Hartman and Stafford, 1997; Jabbour, 2011). UK Ltd and Sweden Ltd have implemented Planet Champions.

The purpose of the Planet Champion was to:

> … raise awareness of environment initiatives within restaurants feeding new ideas and insights back to head office and – hopefully – improve our (environmental) performance against some key measures.
>
> (Head Office respondent, UK Ltd)

The overall aim was to raise the profile of the environment within restaurants and encourage staff to think – and act – in a way which is better for the restaurant and the planet. This initiative was perceived by the leadership of the team as a key lever to enhance the level of staff commitment and engagement and to reinforce the behaviours that drive environmental performance.

Both UK Ltd and Sweden Ltd pitched the Planet Champion position as a voluntary role and recruited individuals with drive and passion to maximise employee engagement. However, the hierarchical level varied across the two subsidiaries; in UK Ltd, the role was undertaken primarily by shift managers, who had responsibility for staff training. In Sweden Ltd, the roles were more filled in a way that was inclusive of frontline workers, with less focus on hierarchical position. All respondents felt that Planet Champions should demonstrate a bias for action through their behaviour and positive attitude, and have sound operational knowledge of the business. Time served in the organisation was less important. Specific comments included: 'Need people with energy, passion, persistence, the right attitude. Knowledge can be learned, anyone can pick up a book.'

In Sweden Ltd, where the implementation of the Planet Champion initiative was at the developmental stage, there was concern about ownership and accountability. The research team was able to obtain staff views concerning the appropriateness of the initiative in relation to the tackling of environmental concerns. Consistency and uniformity is present across many aspects of the business; however, in respect of environmental routines and practices this is not the case. Three participants in the focus group discussed the importance of accountability and ownership in relation to routines and operational practices. One participant claimed that there was a 'lack of ownership in restaurants – no dedicated person, therefore no one accountable and responsible'. This theme was reinforced by the response from a restaurant manager in Sweden Ltd that:

> You can have a Planet Champion within the restaurant when you have the routines in place. When you have made sure that this is the way we are doing it, this is how we train people, this is how we follow up, this is how the management team is responsible, then you have a Champion. Otherwise, Champion is just a title.
>
> (Restaurant manager, Sweden Ltd)

> To take the first step we need to have that awareness not only at the restaurant level but also at the operational level.
>
> (Head Office respondent, Sweden Ltd)

Another theme which emerged was the need to embed the green initiatives and practices in the operations function and restaurant routines. All restaurant managers and a senior head office management participant identified the importance of embedding environmental practices into the operations function and restaurants routines. Connections were made between practice and behaviours: 'Environment is about people and people behaviour, so it needs to be grounded in operations, otherwise it will not happen; hamburgers are made by people not machines, operations are about people'.

The commitment to invest in staff development and training at all levels of the hierarchical structure is consistent across both subsidiaries. Respondents also highlighted the role of managers as a key factor in staff engagement with environmental initiatives. Frontline respondents in UK Ltd and Sweden Ltd highlighted the importance of having the 'right leader' to face the current challenges and provide clear direction in the future. Leadership was seen by the respondents as a key lever for achieving positive environmental impact. In UK Ltd, senior manager commitment was clearly evidenced, as green initiatives were championed at all levels of the hierarchy. Role modelling was identified as a way of demonstrating the 'right thing to do'. Focus group respondents referred to the 'shadow of the leader – people will do what I do not what I say' and confirmed that this message is communicated in their basic shift management training.

Addressing environmental concerns through employee engagement and behavioural change was discussed with respondents from both countries. In UK Ltd, over half of the respondents felt that engaging and embedding environmental practices were the greatest HRM challenges, with employees facing ever increasing targets and heightened expectations around the core fundamentals, such as service and quality. As yet, environmental performance indicators are not perceived by the majority of respondents as a core requirement. In both countries, the performance indicators consist of four quadrants, focusing on the customer experience, staff, finance and leadership. In the majority of respondents' views, these indicators drive the key priorities and performance outcomes and are therefore perceived as levers to achieve both involvement and engagement. The majority of respondents also acknowledge that the challenge is to raise the importance of environmental impact reduction. This might be achieved through the alignment of the organisation's strategic aim to improve environmental sustainability, operationalised in environmental practices and translated into key performance indicators. Respondents from both locations understand the need to measure performance in a results-orientated business: 'If we can't measure it doesn't exist … we are competitive; if we can't measure it is not important ... performance is mainly about bottom lines, targets and goals' (Business manager, Sweden Ltd). This strength of feeling was reflected in the UK Ltd and Sweden Ltd by the majority of respondents. Other than financial key performance indicators, such as waste reduction and recycling, respondents did not recognise the integration of environmental indicators into the performance measures at restaurant level. The importance of transparency and visibility in relation to restaurant environmental performance was cited by respondents across both countries.

Discussion and concluding remarks

This study confirms the need for active involvement and engagement of employees in green management as highlighted in the literature (Brio *et al.*, 2007; Jackson *et al.*, 2011; Renwick *et al.*, 2013). People development strategies such as the Planet Champion initiative and team formation are examples of employee involvement which may lead to greater impact and improvement in the organisation's environmental performance, thereby making a noticeable difference in the business (Ones and Dilchert, 2013). The commitment to invest in staff development and training at all levels of the hierarchical structure is an essential lever in raising awareness of environmental initiatives and encouraging individuals and teams to think – and act – in a way which is better for the restaurant and the planet. Consistent with the literature, training employees can lead to the development of environmental organisational citizen behaviours and green competencies (Boiral, 2009; Subramanian *et al.*, 2016). Furthermore, employee environmental training has been shown to increase awareness and heighten levels of motivation and proactive behaviour. This, in turn, leads to improved environmental performance (Alberti *et al.*, 2000; Daily and Huang, 2001).

Developing management and leadership behaviours to establish ownership and create accountability and commitment to environmental practices are essential HRD strategies. The role of the Planet Champion in this case study is intended to create accountability and ownership at all levels of the hierarchy, many of which are at middle-management level. Clearly, there is some degree of convergence with the literature, as a number of studies have underscored the importance of managers and leaders actively involving employees at all levels towards improving environmental goals (Ergi and Herman, 2000; Govindarajulu and Daily, 2004). There is widespread recognition that role modelling can be effective in engaging and garnering support for proactive environmental behaviours, as also demonstrated in this case study.

Integration of environmental performance indictors within individual and organisational performance management processes will strengthen and influence employee engagement in environmental practices. In this case study, there was widespread recognition that performance indicators drive priorities and outcomes and therefore are perceived to be a key lever in the development of positive environmental practices. Notwithstanding this, the degree to which relevant performance indicators are embedded within the performance framework needs further consideration by organisations committed to environmental sustainability. As highlighted in the literature, the 'greening' of the overall business performance matrix is an area in which interest is growing, largely because of the potential for this to have a positive impact on financial and non-financial performance (Marcus and Fremeth, 2009; Sharma, 2000).

The literature has clearly highlighted the need for active engagement of employees in green management (Aragon-Correa *et al.*, 2013; Boiral, 2009; Ramus and Steger, 2000; Renwick *et al.*, 2013). This study highlights that, even with organisational commitment, staff engagement can vary across subsidiaries. Overall, it appears that engaging the workforce and embedding pro-environmental behaviours should be considered as the first steps to enhanced environmental management. The success of initiatives such as the Planet Champions requires the involvement and engagement of all stakeholders within the organisation, supportive HR people strategies and practices such as developing strong environmental leadership, effective environmental performance management and green learning and development opportunities for employees.

A key implication for management practice from this empirical study is that embedding routines within operational systems is essential to the successful implementation of any environmental initiative within a global foodservice company. Whether it is the green teams or restaurant managers, their aim should be to embed green activities within the day-to-day routines and practices of the restaurants to embed employee engagement. Our results show that some practices, such as litter patrol and cardboard recycling, are part of everyday McDonald's practice. Here, environmental training can be planned and designed to develop such behavioural competencies. However, to achieve proactive environmental management (Jabbour *et al.*, 2013, Teixeira *et al.*, 2012), the focus has to be on organisational behaviours that support environmental engagement, as, in a people-orientated business, employee engagement is fundamental to the organisation's success. At a societal level, this study highlights the need for ownership and accountability of people and community to support and replicate such behaviours.

There are a number of limitations in this empirical study, some of which provide consideration for further research. First, this study incorporates both company-owned and franchised restaurants. Second, the research was restricted to Europe, and therefore does not include the perspective of the parent organisation, and the extent to which the parent strategy influences the development of subsidiary strategies and practices, including the alignment of the HR and environment functions and the ways in which subsidiaries are able to engage their workforce in sustainability practices. Third, although the study identifies the introduction of the Planet Champions role as a key employee engagement strategy in UK Ltd and later in Sweden Ltd, the extent to which this role is effective in demonstrating positive organisational employee outcomes is yet unclear and therefore an area for further research.

References

Alberti, M., Marzluff, J.M., Shulenberger, E., Bradley, G., Ryan, C. and Zumbrunnen, C. (2000) 'Integrating humans into ecology: Opportunities and challenges for studying urban ecosystems', *Bioscience*, vol. 53, pp. 1169–1179.

Anderson Strachan, P. (1996) 'Achieving environmental excellence through effective teamwork', *Team Performance Management: An International Journal*, vol. 2, no. 1, pp. 25–29.

Aragón-Correa, J.A. and Rubio-Lopez, E.A. (2007) 'Proactive corporate environmental strategies: Myths and misunderstandings', *Long Range Planning*, vol. 40, no. 3, pp. 357–381.

Aragón-Correa, J.A., Martin-Tapia, I. and Hurtado-Torres, N.E. (2013) 'Proactive environmental strategies and employee inclusion: The positive effects on information sharing and promoting collaboration and the influence of uncertainty', *Organization and Environment*, pp. 1–23.

Benn, S., Teo, S.T. and Martin, A. (2015) 'Employee participation and engagement in working for the environment', *Personnel Review*, vol. 44, no. 4, pp. 492–510.

Boiral, O. (2009) 'Greening the corporation through organisational citizenship behaviours', *Journal of Business Ethics*, vol. 87, pp. 221–223.

Brio, J.A., Fernandez, E. and Junquera, B. (2007) 'Management and employee involvement in achieving an environmental action-based competitive advantage: An empirical study', *The International Journal of Human Resource Management*, vol. 18, no. 4, pp. 491–522.

Brown, J.S. and Duguid, P. (1991) 'Organizational learning and communities-of-practice: Toward a unified view of working, learning, and innovation', *Organization Science*, vol. 2, no. 1, pp. 40–57.

Bryman, A. and Bell, E. (2015). *Business research methods*. Oxford University Press.

Byrne, D. and Ragin, C.C. (2009) *The Sage handbook of case-based methods*. SAGE Publications.

Cotton, J.L. (1993) *Employee involvement: Methods for improving performance and work attitudes*. Sage Publications, Inc.

Daily, B.F. and Hung, S. (2001) 'Achieving sustainability through attention to human resource factors in environmental management', *International Journal of Operations and Production Management*, vol. 21, pp. 1539–1552.

Daily, B.F., Bishop, J.W. and Govindarajulu, N. (2009) 'A conceptual model for organizational citizenship behaviour directed toward the environment', *Business and Society*, vol. 48, pp. 243–256.

Drever, E. (1995) *Using semi-structured interviews in small-scale research. A teacher's guide*. Scottish Council for Research in Education.

Eisenhardt, K.M. (1989) 'Building theories from case study research', *The Academy of Management Review*, vol. 14, no. 4, pp. 532–550.

Eisenhardt, K.M. and Graebner, M.E. (2007) 'Theory building from cases: Opportunities and challenges', *Academy of Management Journal*, vol. 50, no. 1, pp. 25–32.

Egri, C.P. and Herman, S. (2000) 'Leadership in the North American environmental sector: Values, leadership styles, and contexts of environmental factors and their organizations', *Academy of Management Journal*, vol. 43, pp. 571–604.

Fernandez, E., Junquera, B. and Ordiz, M. (2003) 'Organizational culture and human resources in the environmental issue', *International Journal of Human Resource Management*, vol. 14, pp. 634–656.

Frank, F.D., Finnegan, R.P. and Taylor, C.R. (2004) 'The race for talent: Retaining and engaging workers in the 21st century', *Human Resource Planning*, vol. 27, no. 3, pp. 12–25.

Gholami, H., Rezaei, G., Saman, M.Z.M., Sharif, S. and Zakuan, N. (2016) 'State-of-the-art Green HRM System: Sustainability in the sports center in Malaysia using a multi-methods approach and opportunities for future research', *Journal of Cleaner Production*, vol. 124, pp. 142–163.

Govindarajulu, N. and Daily, B.F. (2004) 'Motivating employees for environmental improvement', *Industrial Management and Data Systems*, vol. 104, no. 4, pp. 364–372.

Guerci, M., Longoni, A. and Luzzini, D. (2016) 'Translating stakeholder pressures into environmental performance – the mediating role of green HRM practices', *The International Journal of Human Resource Management*, vol. 27, no. 2, pp. 262–289.

Haddock-Millar, J., Sanyal, C. and Müller-Camen, M. (2016) 'Green human resource management: A comparative qualitative case study of a United States multinational corporation', *The International Journal of Human Resource Management*, vol. 27, no. 2, pp. 192–211.

Hallberg, U.E. and Schaufeli, W.B. (2006) ' "Same same" but different? Can work engagement be discriminated from job involvement and organizational commitment?' *European Psychologist*, vol. 11, no. 2, pp. 119–127.

Hanna, M.D., Rocky Newman, W. and Johnson, P. (2000) 'Linking operational and environmental improvement through employee involvement', *International Journal of Operations & Production Management*, vol. 20, no. 2, pp. 148–165.

Harris, C. and Tregidga, H. (2012) 'HR managers and environmental sustainability: Strategic leaders or passive observers?', *International Journal of Human Resource Management*, vol. 23, no. 2, pp. 236–254.

Hartman, C.L. and Stafford, E.R. (1997) 'Green alliances: Building new business with environmental groups', *Long Range Planning*, vol. 30, no. 2, pp. 184–149.

Jabbour, C.J.C. (2011) 'How green are HRM practices, organisational culture, learning and teamwork?' *Industrial and Commercial Training*, vol. 43, no. 2, pp. 98–105.

Jabbour, C.J.C., Santos, F.C.A., Fonseca, S.A. and Negano, M.S. (2013) 'Green teams: Understanding their roles in the environmental management of companies located in Brazil', *Journal of Cleaner Production*, vol. 46, pp. 58–66.

Jackson, S.E. and Seo, J. (2010) 'The greening of strategic HRM', *Organisation Management Journal*, vol. 7, pp. 278–290.

Jackson, S. E., Renwick, D.W., Jabbour, C.J. and Müller-Camen, M. (2011) 'State-of-the-art and future directions for green human resource management: Introduction to the special issue', *German Journal of Human Resource Management: Zeitschrift für Personalforschung*, vol. 25, no. 2, pp. 99–116.

Kahn, W.A. (1990) 'Psychological conditions of personal engagement and disengagement at work', *Academy of Management Journal*, vol. 22, no. 4, pp. 692–724.

Länsiluoto, A. and Jarvenpää, M. (2010) 'Greening the balanced scorecard', *Business Horizons*, vol. 53, pp. 385–395.

Macey, W.H. and Schneider, B. (2008) 'The meaning of employee engagement', *Industrial and Organizational Psychology*, vol. 1, no. 1, pp. 3–30.

Marcus, A.A. and Fremeth, A.R. (2009) 'Green management matters regardless', *Academy of Management Perspectives*, vol. 8, pp. 17–26.

Miles, M.B. and Huberman, A.M. (1994) *Qualitative data analysis: An expanded sourcebook*. Sage.

Muster, V. and Schrader, U. (2011) 'Green work–life balance: A new perspective for green HRM', *German Journal of Human Resource Management: Zeitschrift für Personalforschung*, vol. 25, no. 2, pp. 140–156.

O'Donohue, W. and Torugsa, N. (2016) 'The moderating effect of "Green" HRM on the association between proactive environmental management and financial performance in small firms', *The International Journal of Human Resource Management*, vol. 27, no. 2, pp. 239–261.

Ones, D.S. and Dilchert, S. (2013) 'Measuring, understanding, and influencing employee green behaviors'. In: Huffman, A.H. and Klein, S.R. (Eds), *Green organizations: Driving change with IO psychology*, Routledge, pp. 115–148.

Pande, B.H. (2016). 'A study on work behaviour on HR personnel towards environment to endorse Green HRM practice in workplace', *Journal of Advances in Business Management*, vol. 2, no. 2, pp. 88–89, DOI: 10.14260/jadbm/2016/22.

Perron, G.M., Côté, R.P. and Duffy, J.F. (2006) 'Improving environmental awareness training in business', *Journal of Cleaner Production*, vol. 14, no. 6, pp. 551–562.

Ramus, C.A. (2001) 'Organisational support for employees: Encouraging creative ideas for environmental sustainability', *California Management Review*, vol. 43, no. 3, pp. 105–121.

Ramus, C.A. and Steger, U. (2000) 'The roles of supervisory support behaviours and environmental policy in employee eco-initiatives at leading-edge European companies', *Academy of Management Journal*, vol. 41, no. 4, pp. 605–626.

Renwick, D., Redman, T. and Maguire, S. (2013) 'Green Human Resource Management: A review and research agenda', *International Journal of Management Reviews*, vol. 15, pp. 1–14.

Robertson, J.L. and Barling, J. (2013) 'Greening organizations through leaders' influence on employees' pro-environmental behaviors', *Journal of Organizational Behavior*, vol. 34, no. 2, pp. 176–194.

Ryan, G.W. and Bernard, H.R. (2003) 'Techniques to identify themes', *Field Methods*, vol. 15, no. 1, pp. 85–109.

Sharma, S. (2000) 'Managerial interpretations and organizational context as predictors of corporate choice of environmental strategy', *Academy of Management Journal*, vol. 43, no. 4, pp. 681–697.

Subramanian, N., Abdulrahman, M.D., Wu, L. and Nath, P. (2016) 'Green competence framework: Evidence from China', *The International Journal of Human Resource Management*, vol. 27, no. 2, pp. 151–172.

Teixeira, A.A., Jabbour, C.J.C and Jabbour, A.B.L. (2012) 'Relationship between green management and environmental training in companies located in Brazil: A theoretical framework and case studies', *International Journal Production Economics*, vol. 40, pp. 318–329.

Teixeira, A.A., Jabbour, C.J.C., de Sousa Jabbour, A.B.L., Latan, H. and de Oliveira, J. H.C. (2016) 'Green training and green supply chain management: Evidence from Brazilian firms', *Journal of Cleaner Production*, vol. 116, pp. 170–176.

Torugsa, N.A., O'Donohue, W. and Hecker, R. (2012) 'Capabilities, proactive CSR and financial performance in SMEs: Empirical evidence from an Australian manufacturing industry sector', *Journal of Business Ethics*, vol. 109, no. 4, pp. 483–500.

Torugsa, N.A., O'Donohue, W. and Hecker, R. (2013) 'Proactive CSR: An empirical analysis of the role of its economic, social and environmental dimensions on the association between capabilities and performance', *Journal of Business Ethics*, vol. 115, no. 2, pp. 383–402.

Yin, R.K. (2013) *Case study research: Design and methods*. Sage publications.

Yusoff, Y.M., Othman, N.Z., Fernando, Y., Amran, A., Surienty, L. and Ramayah, T. (2015) 'Conceptualization of Green Human Resource Management: An exploratory study from Malaysian-based multinational companies', *International Journal of Business Management & Economic Research*, vol. 6, no. 3, pp. 1–15.

4 A case study of Mater Misericordiae Limited

Sally V. Russell and Christopher Hill

Introduction

In this chapter, we present a case study of Mater Misericordiae Limited (Mater) to demonstrate how green human resource management (GHRM) practices can be effectively integrated into organisational practice. We draw on the work of Renwick, Redman, and Maguire (2013) and frame the case using the Ability–Motivation–Opportunity (AMO) theory (Applebaum *et al.*, 2000, p. 1324). In the first section of the chapter, we describe the organisation, its history and underlying ethos, and the origins of the organisation's sustainability journey. We then go on to identify each of the key dimensions of the AMO theory (Renwick *et al.*, 2013) and demonstrate how Mater has effectively embedded these dimensions into their day-to-day practice.

The case study information presented in this chapter is based on data collected through an action research approach led by the two chapter authors. The approach, which could also be termed co-creation (Chen *et al.*, 2012), involves a group of people working together to co-create positive outcomes for both parties (McNiff and Whitehead, 2001; Thompson and Perry, 2004). Businesses and researchers are increasingly using action research (McNiff and Whitehead, 2001) and co-creation (Chen *et al.*, 2012) to bring together knowledge from researchers and practitioners in order to have a positive influence on organisational practice as well as ensuring scientific scholarship.

Data collected to inform this case study have included interviews with senior management, focus groups with staff, intervention studies, as well as documentary data collection. Where part of the research has been published with the organisation's permission, this is noted in the text.

In the following section, we introduce the organisation and its background and describe the beginnings of the sustainability journey. We then present the GHRM initiatives that the organisation has undertaken within each of the components of ability, motivation, and opportunity (Renwick *et al.*, 2013). By organising the case study in this way, our aim is to demonstrate to practitioners and scholars how a collaborative approach and the co-creation of sustainability knowledge can have a positive effect on GHRM in practice.

Background and organisational context

Mater is a large healthcare provider in Eastern Australia and comprises several hospitals, health centres, a medical research institute, and pathology and pharmacy businesses. The overarching aim of the organisation is to provide exceptional care. The Sisters of Mercy established the organisation in 1906 and the organisation currently employs 6,500 staff and volunteers and provides care to hundreds of thousands of people each year. The five core values of the organisation reflect the spirit of the Sisters of Mercy:

- mercy: the spirit of responding to one another
- dignity: the spirit of humanity, respecting the worth of each person
- care: the spirit of compassion
- commitment: the spirit of integrity
- quality: the spirit of professionalism.

Mater is involved in education and research and hosts several research institutes and centres, including the Nursing Research Centre, the Queensland Centre for Evidence-Based Nursing and Midwifery, the Mater Medical Research Institute, and the Queensland Injury Surveillance Unit. Mater is governed by a Board of Directors (10 Members) and the Executive team (14 roles, including Group Chief Executive Officer, Chief Financial Officer, Chief Information Officer, Chief Marketing Officer, and a number of Group Directors and CEOs for Education, Foundation, and Research). Mater is a ministry of Mercy Partners, a Catholic Church entity established in 2008.

The beginning of a sustainability journey

The journey towards a more sustainable Mater began in 2007, when legislation for the Australian National Greenhouse and Energy Reporting Act 2007 was introduced, along with reporting requirements for the National Pollutant Inventory. Following these developments, the Mater Board identified areas to be addressed in Mater's strategic plan, which stated:

Mater will increase its activities to ensure we optimise our position as responsible corporate citizens. Initially we will work to reduce our water usage before increasing the scope of our activities to other areas such as energy, recycling and the effective use of products.

In the same year, the Board of Directors committed to a set of environmental sustainability principles and agreed to ensure that the organisation will "seek to minimise our impact on the environment in the delivery of our services". Within the strategic plan for the organisation, a set of key actions was identified in order to progress environmental sustainability.

In 2008, further work was commenced with the creation of a multidisciplinary sustainability committee, comprising executive directors and senior directors from across Mater. Research collaborations between university researchers and Mater began in 2009 and continue to date. In 2010, a full-time dedicated position was created by Mater to coordinate the initiatives, identify new opportunities, monitor results, and collaborate on research opportunities.

In 2009, Mater began an annual carbon footprint process in order to accurately identify environmental issues and annual improvements. Environmental reporting was also included in the organisation's Annual Review from 2010, with an overview of the progress of the *Sustainability at Mater* program and consumption data sets included from 2014.

Ability, motivation, opportunity

The AMO model was initially proposed by Bailey (1993, as cited in Kaifeng *et al.*, 2012) and developed further by Appelbaum *et al.* (2000). AMO theory suggests that employee performance is a function of the three essential components of ability, motivation, and opportunity. This theory has become an effective framework to explain how HR policies can influence performance. AMO theory proposes that HR practices contribute to improved employee performance by developing employees' abilities (A) and skills to do their job, improving an employee's motivation (M) for discretionary effort, and providing employees with the opportunity (O) to make full use of their skills and be motivated. Renwick *et al.* (2013) applied this theory to a sustainability context and suggested that it is a useful tool by which to examine how HRM practices can influence and facilitate a 'green' or sustainability agenda. In the following sections, we examine each of the components of the AMO theory and demonstrate how Mater has integrated each dimension effectively into their GHRM practices.

Ability

According to AMO theory (Applebaum *et al.*, 2000), ability can be influenced in recruitment and selection as well as through training, learning, and development. The key focus of the ability component of the AMO model is to ensure employees have adequate skills and abilities to perform necessary functions. In applying this to a green context, Renwick *et al.* (2013) identify the key needs for ability in GHRM as: (1) recruitment and selection; (2) employee training; and (3) leadership. In the case of Mater, the focus has been very much on training and leadership, with little emphasis on initiatives to improve recruitment and selection. The focus of this section, therefore, is on employee training and leadership, with each addressed in turn.

Employee training

Training is considered a key GHRM intervention and is of utmost importance in ensuring employees have the skills and abilities necessary to perform effectively (Renwick *et al.*, 2013). Training may involve increasing staff awareness of the environmental impact of their organisation's activities (Bansal and Roth, 2000), improving skills such as environmentally relevant data collection (May and Flannery, 1995), and increasing the level of 'eco-literacy' and environmental expertise in the firm (Roy and Therin, 2008).

Within Mater, the link into established HR processes has built up during the sustainability journey and it is now well supported through a variety of methods. Commencing with the *Mater Behavioural Standards* booklet that is given to all new staff and linking from the core value of Care, Mater sets the agenda by "exercising care towards our environment and the use of resources" as a responsibility for all staff. Similarly, the *Code of Conduct* has four key principles, with stewardship encouraging all staff to "be a steward for the sustainability of Mater, both financial and non-financial and acknowledging our impact upon the environment, appropriate selection and use of resources, as well as their disposal". The *Code of Conduct* also references the *Mater Environmental Sustainability Policy* as a supporting document along with the delegation's manual in setting the accountabilities for stewardship.

Education is a key component in ensuring staff awareness and engagement with dedicated campaigns and in challenging current business practices. Environmental Sustainability (ES) presentations and content are now included in the following formal education packages coordinated through the Mater Education Centre:

- Diploma of Nursing
- Mater Managers Programme
- clinical orientation – waste segregation
- clinical in-services – simulation-based waste segregation education to all clinical areas.

ES education has also been previously delivered within the:

- Diploma of Management
- Certificate 4 in Frontline Management
- Certificate 3 in Nutrition and Dietetic Assistance.

Furthermore, dedicated education and awareness programmes are delivered in:

- monthly orientation to all new staff;
- department presentations;
- online education packages that can be accessed by staff through the education centre; and
- short face-to-face seminars and feedback sessions that are delivered to clinical in-services, clinical, and non-clinical areas.

It has been noted that there can be issues in staff training and development as they relate to ES (Renwick *et al.*, 2013). For example, there may be a need to counter potential employee cynicism regarding the importance or relevance of the environmental issues for the organisation involved. Renwick *et al.* (2013) note that it may be important not only to develop training in environmental management, but also to assess the general effectiveness of training for its intended purposes.

These issues have been evident within the case organisation, and one of the key challenges at Mater was the need to harness staff support for sustainability initiatives. At the beginning of the organisation's sustainability journey (2010), focus groups and interviews were conducted with staff to gauge their support and identify ways to encourage ES practices. The results of these interviews showed that staff were willing to engage with ES, but were concerned that engagement in sustainability initiatives would result in additional work on top of already high work demands. Staff also raised the issue that there needed to be support for any initiative from the highest levels of the organisation. The key recommendations from the research included:

- improve organisational communication of sustainability strategies;
- ensure congruence between sustainability message and organisational action;

- ensure visual top management support for sustainability; and
- harness employee ownership of environmental sustainability.

These recommendations were acted upon, with a particular focus on developing employee knowledge and empowerment. Three key initiatives were put in place: (1) a sustainability focused communication strategy; (2) behaviour change interventions and campaigns; and (3) data collection on environmental knowledge across the organisation. Each of these initiatives is discussed in turn.

Sustainability-focused communication strategy

Working closely with the marketing department, the Director of Environmental Sustainability developed a communication strategy that included creation of an identifying icon and theme for all communications (*Sustainability at Mater*), and the following aims and objectives. The target audience is staff across the organisation, including clinical and non-clinical staff. It was noted that some audiences needed different messages because of their different work environments across the clinical and non-clinical areas.

As a result of the collaborative research and the support from the marketing department, a number of initial communication mechanisms were created. These included: a sustainability-focused staff intranet webpage, a hospital internet page devoted to environmental sustainability, regular articles in the staff newsletters and other relevant publications, posters placed in different areas of the hospital with sustainability messages, and a suite of presentations that have been delivered in multiple contexts across the organisation.

The sustainability intranet page was created and provided a central repository for a wide range of information available to staff under broad headings of "What are we doing?" and "What else is happening?" plus a communication tab, as well as some general information areas to share information about sustainability in the wider community. The page is continually updated and is available to all staff that have access to a hospital-based computer. Initial attempts to include the ES message on the health service internet site were not successful; however, the requirement to meet a then existing piece of state legislation that required businesses to publically state their energy-saving initiatives proved to be the "push" to include this area of intent in information intended for the external community.

In order to communicate the *Sustainability at Mater* message and progress, there was also a need to communicate with staff who do not have regular access to a computer. In the hospital setting, many staff work in non-administrative positions in which they are not able to access a computer regularly. In order to communicate with these staff, 15-minute face-to-face in-service presentations are delivered in clinical departments. While this is particularly time consuming for the Director Environmental Sustainability, it is a clear demonstration of the commitment from the organisation's leadership to the importance of sustainability. This initiative continues to date, and it has thus far proved to be a very effective tool to deliver the *Sustainability at Mater* programme results to a wide audience across the organisation.

Behaviour change interventions and campaigns

The second mechanism that has been introduced to engage staff is through behaviour change interventions and targeted campaigns. A large suite of interventions has been put in place across the organisation, but three have been particularly effective.

The first initiative was a campaign designed to reduce energy usage in administrative areas (see Russell *et al.*, 2016 for a full description of this action research initiative). The *Turn it Off* campaign used posters featuring executive members modelling the targeted behaviours and sticker prompts to encourage staff to use less energy in their everyday workplace behaviours. The campaign was successful and resulted in significantly less waste of electricity in the form of standby power for computing equipment. It was particularly successful for behaviours with a strong element of individual responsibility, such as turning off computer monitors and hard drives. The intervention was not successful in changing behaviours that are collectively orientated, such as turning off lights.

The second campaign encouraged staff to purchase and use a refillable coffee cup. On reusing their cups, staff are given a small discount on each cup of coffee purchased. This campaign has been successful, with over 4,000 staff purchasing a cup and reusing them rather than using disposable cups. This is a cost-neutral initiative, as the cups are bought with a bulk discount and then sold to staff with a free cup of coffee when purchased. Over 65,000 refills have been utilised since this cup was launched. When the cups were launched, a cup was provided to each member of the executive team to again model the behaviour that was being targeted.

The third campaign was a staff pledge that was launched on World Environment Day 2012 (see Mater Health Services, 2016b). This campaign encouraged staff to sign up to a pledge and commit to engaging in up to 17 behaviours to reduce their environmental impact across the themes of energy, water, waste, and transport. A target of 2,500 staff participants (33 per cent of all staff) was achieved over a two-year time-frame, in addition to 27,019 personal behaviours, which validated the communication poster messaging that "Individual behaviours can make a difference". Further employee engagement was also demonstrated by 30 per cent of those who committed to the pledge also committing to becoming sustainability supporters in their own work area.

This campaign has continued with promotion during monthly corporate orientation, face-to-face presentations, and within dedicated education programmes. To June 2016, 3,330 staff have pledged to 37,282 behaviours, improving their sustainability performance by changing their actions.

Data collection on environmental knowledge

The third approach aimed to gauge awareness and support for staff across the organization was as part of an annual all-of-staff survey in 2011. Annual staff surveys have been coordinated through the HR division for a number of years, and in 2011 questions about ES were added to the all-of-staff survey. Results showed that approximately 50 per cent of staff were aware of sustainability initiatives and activities. A follow up to the survey was conducted in 2015 in order to measure any change in awareness as a result of the staff engagement campaigns and education delivered to date. The results were positive and showed an increase in staff perceptions for four key indices, and no change in the fifth index. The results from the total Mater cohort of staff responses showed a 12.8 per cent increase in staff awareness of the *Sustainability at Mater* programme.

In addition to the three key interventions, the organisation has also engaged in a suite of additional interventions, including:

- 2010 October – national ride to work day
- 2011 March – "Turn it Off" campaign launched
- 2011 June – reusable cups – over 4000 to date – reduces waste and raises awareness
- 2011 October – national ride to work day
- 2011 December – five environmental sustainability questions included in the all-of-staff survey
- 2012 June – ES pledge of behaviours launched on World Environment Day
- 2012 October – national ride to work day
- 2012 November – national recycling week 2012 – Over 600 kilos collected during a "Friday file fling"

- 2013 March – mobile phone recycling initiated, with four permanent collection points now on site
- 2013 October – national ride to work day
- 2013 November – national recycling week – over 5000 kilos collected during the "Friday file fling"
- 2014 June – World Environment Day photo competition
- 2014 July – ES pledge reached target of 2500 staff and collated 27,019 behaviours and, as at June 2016, has reached 3,330 staff and 37,282 behaviours
- 2014 October – national ride to work day – 60 participants
- 2014 November – sustainability at work staff suggestions
- 2015 January – launch of Mater car pool database
- 2015 May – five follow up ES questions included in all-of-staff survey
- 2015 October – *Transport Access Guide* launched on national ride to work day
- 2015 November – "What happens to waste at Mater?" launched in national recycling week
- 2016 June – *Sustainability at Mater* – video photomontage of staff involvement with initiatives.

Leadership

Evidence suggests that strong leadership and supervisory support can lead to more effective sustainability outcomes (Egri and Herman, 2000). In general, there is very strong leadership support for sustainability initiatives at Mater, as evidenced by senior managers modelling behaviour in the "Turn it Off" campaign (Russell *et al.*, 2016), and support of the many on-going initiatives. Senior staff and the leadership team have also engaged effectively with research to identify the organisational response to environmental issues. Interviews from the research identified divergent perspectives on the fit between organisational values and sustainability priorities. What this highlighted, however, was the need to align the sustainability agenda and initiatives with multiple perspectives and viewpoints.

In 2010, a series of interviews was conducted with senior executives and board members of the organisation. During these interviews, participants were asked about the values of the organisation and the fit between Mater values and sustainability. Divergent perspectives were raised, with some participants suggesting that sustainability is embodied within current values whereas other participants reported that sustainability was secondary to the organisation's values and potentially in competition with values of patient care. This divergent perspective was a challenge for the progression of sustainability initiatives at the senior executive level.

A follow up was conducted in 2013 and results showed that the perspectives of the senior executives were less divergent. Most participants agreed that ES was compatible with the values of the organisation. However, it was also acknowledged that environmental initiatives were considered along with all other projects. In this way, the value of environmental initiatives needed to be evaluated in the same way that other projects and priorities are evaluated within the organisation. For example:

> This is an organisation that's been around for 100 years and it's going to be here for hundreds of years into the future. It needs to refresh and strengthen itself and sustainability is a fundamental part of all that.
>
> Yes, it's respect and maybe that's one to build on. We talk about respect for human beings. There has to be an element of respect for the Earth.
>
> (Extracts from two interviews given by senior executives at Mather in 2013)

Although almost all participants suggested that the values of the organisation are compatible with sustainability, but there was still evidence of the competing priorities within the organisation. For example, as one participant put it, ES "[doesn't] have a priority" and that there were "some pretty big priorities that need to be managed first":

> So, we have things like for example patient safety, which is critically important; customer engagement; environmental sustainability, so there are lots of different strategies that the organisation needs to consider. It's like I said, it's about having a balanced approach so you're not just focusing on one area and letting others fall away. So, it's about I guess keeping all the balls in the air.

Motivation

The second key element of the AMO model is motivation. Motivation can be influenced by extrinsic (for example, financial) and intrinsic (for example, interesting work) rewards, performance reviews, feedback, career development, employment security, and work–life balance. The key focus of the motivation component of the AMO model is to ensure motivation and commitment through practices such as contingent rewards and effective performance management. In their application of the AMO theory to a sustainability context, Renwick *et al.* (2013) identify the key needs for motivation in GHRM as: (1) performance management and appraisal; and (2) pay and reward systems.

Performance management and appraisal

As part of performance development plans for all Mater staff, a key goal to deliver operational efficiency also included a number of behaviours from the ES pledge as options that staff could select from to make their personal contribution to increasing Mater's operational margin.

The pledge was successful, as it focused on giving staff alternatives to current practices for some of the behaviours and encouragement to participate at different levels according to their preferences. These behaviours were translated into performance indicators across the organisation. Within performance reviews, employees can choose behaviours most relevant to their work area and role. Examples included:

- energy behaviours that were linked back to the successful "Turn it Off" campaign or with some cross promotions with the dieticians during health Weight Week, which encouraged employees to "take the stairs instead of the lift";
- water behaviours were linked to encourage staff to use a refillable water bottle which was the most popular behaviour and Mater has produced a wide variety of water bottles promoting a multitude of health-related projects or departments; similarly, previous water saving initiatives such as installation of sensor activation were linked to turning off the water flow as an opportunity when washing your hands;
- alternative transport behaviours from individual car use have grown over the organisation's sustainability journey and these behaviours are well supported with days that encourage staff to ride to work, the promotion of bicycle-user groups, a carpooling database, and a comprehensive travel access guide that was introduced in 2015 to show staff the many opportunities to travel to work without driving every day; and
- waste behaviours, particularly, in non-clinical areas, the removal of under desk waste bins and their replacement with a small eco-desk top bin, along with centralised general and comingled waste bins which has seen a large increase in recycling and, in clinical areas, the replacement of large 240 litre clinical waste bins with a smaller

more mobile 64 litre bin supported by increased waste segregation education, which has shown a large decrease in clinical and related waste; staff are encouraged to continue to reduce waste in all aspects of their role.

Pay and reward systems

Within the motivation element of the model, Mater has emphasised performance management and appraisal, with much less emphasis on pay and reward systems. This, however, may be an effective mechanism to improve the GHRM practices of the organisation. The only initiative to date that links to employee pay is the ability for eligible staff to salary package their public transport costs as a before-tax deduction. This is only utilised by a minority of staff, as this benefit falls within the same benefits category as mortgage and rent payments in which the vast majority of staff already utilise the maximum allowance.

Opportunity

Wider employee participation in organisational practices is often seen as crucial to the success of organisational outcomes. Opportunity is influenced by employee involvement in initiatives, team working, and communication (Applebaum *et al.*, 2000). In application to GHRM, opportunity involves two key issues that are particularly relevant to the Mater case study, namely: (1) involvement of employees in the identification of opportunities for improved sustainability performance (Henriques and Sadorsky, 1999; Renwick *et al.*, 2013); and (2) a supportive organisational culture (Russell and McIntosh, 2011). Renwick *et al.* (2013) suggest that these two criteria are important elements of providing the opportunity for employee participation in GHRM practices. Each is addressed in turn.

Employee engagement

There was a concerted effort at the beginning of this journey to implement easy wins and changes that staff and management could "see" and "touch" and that were relatively inexpensive or provided a quick return on investment. These initiatives were put in place to ensure employee engagement across the organisation and to develop a culture of small wins to subsequently harness support for potential future larger-scale changes. The small changes that were implemented at the beginning of the organisation's sustainability journey included mandating duplex printing in non-clinical areas (over 12.5 million pages saved), installing water tanks (24 on site), installing secure cages to park bicycles (three cages and 90 spaces and lockers available), and implementing printer cartridge recycling.

The first large financial investment was with a lighting project in one of the Mater car parks to replace nearly 3,000 T8 fluorescent tubes with more energy effective T5 fittings. This proof of concept delivered a 32.4 per cent energy reduction and was a less than two-year return on investment that also attracted funding from the Energy Provider as part of their peak load reduction project (see Mater Health Services, 2016a). The success from this financial and environmental improvement has facilitated financial investment support from the Chief Financial Officer and further lighting projects have been conducted that have delivered similar and better results, through installation of energy efficient lighting options. These quick-win outcomes showcased to staff at all levels of the organisation that minimal individual effort can make a difference and this has underpinned the on-going messages to staff that support consumption reduction to provide increased financial benefits to patients.

Engagement with external partnerships has also enhanced opportunities for staff engagement across the organisation. An early partnership was formed with an external carbon management company in 2008–2009 to measure Scope 1 and 2 emissions along with easy to measure Scope 3 emissions. Over this time, data collection internally has greatly improved and for comparative examples a base line of 2010–2011 has been accepted as the beginning benchmark for future years. As part of this service, a number of recommendations to reduce emissions are included in the yearly carbon report and, at the end of the 2014–2015 financial year, 31 have been implemented out of a total of 34. A number of these recommendations were already in place or in progress; however, the external input into the progression of change supported existing priorities. From 2015–2016, the data is now collected in a specialised sustainability software solution and full "go live" is due in 2016–2017 for all Mater sites so that carbon reporting can be managed in house.

Research collaborations have formed a key element on which the *Sustainability at Mater* strategy has been based. Complementing the internal efforts from the Director Environmental Sustainability and the Environmental Sustainability committee, an external research partnership was formed in 2010 through a business relationship with senior academics. A number of environmental behaviour studies were conducted that encourage ES practices (see, for example, Russell *et al.*, 2016).

Supportive organisational culture

At the start of Mater's sustainability journey, there was no identified sustainability culture. A number of awareness-raising initiatives including education and communication strategies have been delivered and the results clearly show that this culture is growing within Mater. While the initial approach to promote ES was coordinated and delivered by a separate ES position, there have been, and still are, a number of HR-related support functions that have assisted with the embedding of this thinking into normal business practices. Results of the all-of-staff survey clearly show an increase in staff awareness, which is an indicator or artefact of a growing sustainability culture (Russell and McIntosh, 2011).

Current position and priorities

To March 2016, the environmental agenda had been led by the one full-time equivalent position of the Director Environmental Sustainability. The efforts to advocate, influence, and engage employees in change at all levels of the organisation have been successful across the breadth of the Mater. However, given the breadth of opportunities to engage with across business, there are many prospects to further embed environmental considerations into current activities. The organisation has recently employed another part-time employee to focus on sustainability, and it is likely that this will further enhance Mater's capacity to integrate and raise awareness of sustainability within the organisation.

Staff engagement continues to be a major focus for the organisation. The release of a *Sustainability at Mater* photo video montage of staff from across the organisation from different management levels, disciplines, and roles, including representatives from all of the hospitals in the Mater group demonstrates that there are now a large number of initiatives that have become part of business as usual in all areas of the hospital. Released on World Environment Day 2016, it is also the first campaign from any part of the hospital that will showcase the breadth of work already achieved in the three key areas of health, education, and research.

The first Environmental Management Plan (2015–2019) with clear targets for achievement for the next three years was endorsed by the ES committee and approved by the Group Executive in late 2015. This sets clear key performance indicators that Mater is targeting and will continue to require strong top management support to implement.

Conclusions

Mater's progress in embedding ES into business practice has been achieved through incremental change across a wide variety of themes and initiatives. Mater continues to try to create change by embedding ES in HRM practices, with the aim of changing current business-as-usual processes. Continued top management support from the senior executive and board members along with HRM support to promote accepted behaviours and stewardship considerations are key to embedding environmental sustainability into business-as-usual activities. The focus on HRM initiatives has been growing in tandem with diverse initiatives to address the major themes of energy, water, waste, procurement, facilities design, transport, and stakeholder engagement, and will continue to be a focus for future successes. The Mater case is a clear demonstration of how one organisation continues to embed ES into the organisation and, in doing so, addresses the key HRM components of ability, motivation, and opportunity.

References

Applebaum, E., Bailey, T., Berg, P., and Kalleberg, A. (2000) *Manufacturing advantage: Why high-performance work systems pay off*. Ithaca, NY: Cornell University Press.

Bailey, T. (1993) *Disrectionary effort and the organization of work: Employee participation and work reform since Hawthorne*. Paper prepared at Columbia University for Sloan Foundation.

Bansal, P., and Roth, K. (2000) "Why companies go green: A model of ecological responsiveness", *Academy of Management Journal*, vol. 43, no. 4, pp. 717–736.

Chen, L., Marsden, J. R., and Zhang, Z. (2012) "Theory and analysis of company-sponsored value co-creation", *Journal of Management Information Systems*, vol. 29, no. 2, pp. 141–172.

Egri, C. P., and Herman, S. (2000) "Leadership in the North American environmental sector: Values, leadership styles, and contexts of environmental leaders and their organizations", *Academy of Management Journal*, vol. 43, no. 4, pp. 571–604.

Henriques, I., and Sadorsky, P. (1999) "The relationship between environmental commitment and managerial perceptions of stakeholder importance", *Academy of Management Journal*, vol. 42, no. 1, pp. 87–99.

Kaifeng, J., Lepak, D. P., Jia, J. U., and Baer, J. C. (2012) "How does human resource management influence organizational outcomes? A meta-analytic investigation of mediating mechanisms", *Academy of Management Journal*, vol. 55, no. 6, pp. 1264–1294. DOI: 10.5465/amj.2011.0088.

Mater Health Services. (2016a) *Case study: Energy savings – parking lot lighting*. Retrieved 16 July 2016, from http://greenhospitals.net/wp-content/uploads/2014/11/Mater-Health-Services-case-study-ESpledge-Leadership.pdf.

Mater Health Services. (2016b) *Case study: Leadership*. Retrieved 16 July 2016, from http://greenhospitals.net/wp-content/uploads/2014/11/Mater-Health-Services-case-study-ES-pledge-Leadership.pdf.

May, D. R., and Flannery, B. L. (1995) "Cutting waste with employee involvement teams", *Business Horizons*, vol. 38, pp. 28–38.

McNiff, J., and Whitehead, J. (2001) *Action research: Principles and practice* (Second Edition). London: Falmer Press.

Renwick, D., Redman, T., and Maguire, S. (2013) "Green human resource management: A review and research agenda', *International Journal of Management Reviews*, vol. 15, no. 1, pp. 1–14.

Roy, M.-J., and Therin, F. (2008) "Knowledge acquisition and environmental commitment in SMEs", *Corporate Social Responsibility and Environmental Management*, vol. 15, pp. 249–259.

Russell, S. V., and McIntosh, M. (2011) "Changing organizational culture for sustainability". In N. M. Ashkanasy, C. P. M. Wilderom and M. F. Peterson (Eds), *Handbook of Organizational Culture and Climate* (Second Edition), pp. 393–412. Thousand Oaks, CA: Sage.

Russell, S. V., Evans, A., Fielding, K. S., and Hill, C. (2016) "Turn it off: An action research study of top management influence on energy conservation in the workplace", *Frontiers in Psychology*, vol. 7, DOI: 10.3389/fpsyg.2016.00389.

Thompson, F., and Perry, C. (2004) "Generalising results of an action research project in one work place to other situations: Principles and practice", *European Journal of Marketing*, vol. 38, no. 3, pp. 401–417.

5 Enabling green spillover

How firms can benefit from employees' private green activism

Susanne Blazejewski, Anja Gräf, Anke Buhl and Franziska Dittmer

Introduction

Research on Green Human Resource Management (GHRM) has advanced considerably over the last decade. Authors have conceptually and empirically provided important insights into the dimensions and antecedents of employee green behavior (EGB) (Norton *et al.*, 2012; Ones and Dilchert, 2012; Paillé and Boiral, 2013; Temminck *et al.*, 2013) and on how firms can actively enable and support EGB through the design and implementation of GHRM instruments (Jackson and Seo, 2010; Ehnert and Harry, 2012; Taylor *et al.*, 2012; Renwick *et al.*, 2013). Firms should develop training schemes, appraisal and reward systems, employee participation programs and, more generally, a greener corporate culture that motivates EGB and that better aligns this behavior with the respective corporate sustainability or environmental strategies. In the GHRM literature, this prevalent notion of "motivation" and "alignment" of employees who need to be "greened" (Wehrmeyer, 1996), seems to imply a persistent focus on employees who are not yet sufficiently familiar with, and intrinsically engaged in, environmental activities at their workplaces. While this still may well describe the majority of the workforce, there is also a considerable and growing group of employees who are intrinsically motivated to behave pro-environmentally – at home and at work. In Germany, for instance, recent studies have disclosed that 14 percent of the population is "sustainability-oriented" in their lifestyle (UBA, 2015) and literature on the 'spillover' phenomenon suggests that it is likely that green behavior in one area can spill into another one (Tudor *et al.*, 2007; Andersson *et al.*, 2012).

This chapter therefore focuses on green "committed activists" or "green change agents" (Wright *et al.*, 2012) i.e., employees who, based on their public and private green activism, are also intrinsically motivated to engage in green behavior at work. In line with the 'Green work–life balance' approach (Muster and Schrader, 2011; Schrader and Harrach, 2013), we propose that these green activists-cum-employees do require different support structures, and another approach of GHRM than that currently suggested in the literature. So far, the literature on GHRM does not differentiate between different types of – more or less green – employees and their potentially heterogeneous needs concerning enabling structures and support for EGB. This chapter seeks to contribute to closing this gap by delineating (1) whether privately and publicly green activists are in fact willing to transfer their attitudes, behaviors and initiatives to their workplaces; (2) which barriers and/or supportive HRM structures are important to them; and (3) how firms' current HRM tools and structures do – more or less adequately – respond to their perceived support needs. The chapter draws from data collected in interviews with public and private activists in Germany on their green initiatives in their respective work environment between 2014 and 2016. The individual-level data is complemented by organizational-level data on GHRM structures and instruments in 14 large and medium-sized firms where we interviewed HR professionals and works council representatives as well as sustainability managers who were personally involved in green initiatives undertaken by green employees. In this way, we are able to triangulate the employees' perceptions of barriers and supportive structures for their green initiatives with respective organizational perspectives. The empirical material helps us to better understand the needs of intrinsically motivated green activists-cum-employees and to draw implications for the design of GHRM instruments directed at this particular group.

The chapter contributes to the current debates on GHRM in three ways. First, while the GHRM literature so far tends to focus exclusively on EGB at the workplace, we seek to better understand the relationship between private green activism and EGB, i.e., spillover processes, and how GHRM needs to respond to employees' life–work spillover attempts. Second, while the dominant GHRM literature seems to maintain that employees' "environmental attitudes and behavior at work are mainly seen as results of corporate environmental activities" (Muster and Schrader, 2011, p. 143), i.e., they are triggered and conditioned mainly by corporate training or recognition and reward schemes, we demonstrate that a particular group of green employees is willing to engage in "high-intensity" (Ciocirlan, 2016) EGB even in the absence of corporate support. In line with Norton *et al.* (2015), we refer to EGB as a workplace-specific form of pro-environmental behavior and, in following Ciocirlan (2016), we call high-intensity EGB those behaviors that involve green extra-role initiative-taking which is characterized by, for example, uncertainty regarding the outcomes, high visibility, and high organizational or individual costs, such as loss of reputation, demotion, or firing. Third, we contribute to a more fine-grained discussion on GHRM by identifying an important sub-group of green activists-cum-employees who differ from other employees in their responses to and their needs regarding GHRM instruments. In particular, we show that employees willing to spill over their green initiatives from 'life' to 'work' are often more competent on sustainability issues than their organizations at large and that they respond rather sensitively to corporate feedback and recognition schemes for their green initiatives. In both instances, standard GHRM tools may turn out to be counterproductive and effectively crowd out employees' motivation to perform high-intensity EGB.

This chapter is structured as follows. In the first section, we review the ongoing discussion on pro-environmental spillover processes. We propose here that individuals developing a strong green identity through public and/or private green activism hold a strong motivation also to engage in high-intensity EGB. Our second section discusses the influence of the perceived organizational context on green employees' willingness and ability to spill over their private green activism to their workplaces. We propose that individuals who hold a strong green identity do engage in high-intensity EGB even in exclusionary contexts, i.e., in the absence of supportive GHRM tools and structures. The third section presents results from a qualitative study on green employees and their spillover experiences at work. Finally, we draw out implications for the design and implementation of GHRM tools in view of the needs and preferred strategies of 'green' employees for their green initiatives at work.

Life–work spillover processes as a basis for green initiative taking

We argue that GHRM needs to better understand and respond more adequately to the diverse needs of different types of employees. In particular, we suggest that individuals with a strong propensity to engage in high-intensity EGB respond differently to GHRM structures and instruments offered by their employer and require a different kind of support to unfold their full potential. In our study, this intrinsic motivation to undertake green extra-role initiatives at work is rooted in green activism in the individual's life outside of the workplace, e.g., in environmental movements or groups (Greenpeace, Friends of the

Earth), or as an active prosumer (e.g., solar plant ownership or as a member of a renewable energy cooperative). This transfer of environmental attitudes, behavior, and competences across life domains has recently received growing attention in research on spillover effects in environmental psychology (Thøgersen and Crompton, 2009; Truelove et al., 2014) and on green work–life balances in the HRM research community (Muster, 2011; Muster and Schrader, 2011; Schrader and Harrach, 2013). The investigation of green life–work spillover processes enables us to better understand how and why individuals are willing and able to engage in high-intensity EGB and what their particular needs and interests are with regard to organizational support of their green initiatives. As we will demonstrate below, these green activists tend to see themselves as eco-pioneers and green experts in the firm and therefore respond rather reluctantly to corporate attempts to educate them on environmental issues, or to standard feedback and recognition and reward routines. We propose that their divergent needs for HRM instruments and organizational support on green issues are largely conditioned by processes of spillover and identity work emanating from their private and public environmental activism.

In the environmental psychological literature, research on spillover effects across domains, i.e. from the life domain to the work domain or vice-versa, is still scarce. While Andersson et al., (2012) show how the implementation of environmental management systems at work supports recycling behavior of employees at home, other authors (Lee et al., 1995; Tudor et al., 2007) demonstrate that recycling behavior at home also has positive effects on recycling behavior at the workplace – provided that the necessary infrastructure is available (e.g., bins for waste separation). While psychological research thus has successfully established that spillover occurs – at least regarding recycling behavior – the underlying processes as well as the influence of the organizational context beyond the mere physical infrastructure is less well understood. Here, the psychological literature on in-domain spillover (i.e., inside the life domain but across behaviors such as recycling, food and energy consumption, mobility) provides more advanced insight. Whereas negative spillover effects such as the rebound effect are well explained by concepts of moral licensing (e.g., Mazar and Zhong, 2010; Klöckner et al., 2013), researchers have found promising evidence for the important role of identity as an explanatory factor for positive spillover effects (Whitmarsh and O'Neill, 2010; van der Werff et al., 2013). Self-identity is found to be an "independent predictor of environmental activism intentions indicating that the stronger participants' sense of themselves as environmental activists, the greater their intentions to engage in this behavior" (Fielding *et al.*, 2008, p. 323). So far, it remains unclear whether the identity effect holds for spillover across domains, particularly in view of the influence of the organizational context at work that effectively delimits the individual's scope for EGB. A meta-analysis (Lo *et al.*, 2012) did not find any study that included environmental identity as antecedent of EGB (see Ciocirlan, 2016).

The literature on green work–life balance (Muster and Schrader, 2011) also remains scant on the role of identity for spillover processes. While it does provide fundamental insights into the interactional relationship between EGB and pro-environmental behavior at home, it so far remains largely at a conceptual stage (Muster and Schrader, 2011). In addition, it focuses on consumptive behavior only (Muster, 2011, 2012; Schrader and Harrach, 2013) whereas we seek to draw attention to spillover effects involving high-intensity EGB such as extra-role green initiative-taking. Also, the concept so far concentrates on the harmonization between domains but does not delineate situations where green employees with spillover intentions might be stuck in a non-supportive organizational context (Ciocirlan, 2016). As we will show below, for employees with a strong environmental identity, a non-supportive work context does not result in inaction but in a diversion of high-intensity green engagement to other, more welcoming niches in or outside the firm. A narrow focus on mutual enforcement or alignment through GHRM tools might deter from a closer investigation of green employees' actual needs and spillover strategies-in-use which might, with proper support, develop into crucial elements of green transformation in their respective organizations. On the basis of our prior discussion we propose the following:

Proposition 1: Individuals holding a strong and salient environmental identity are more likely to engage in spillover activities involving high-intensity EGB, even in non-supportive organizational contexts.

Individuals who develop a strong environmental identity through public and private environmental activism (Stürmer and Kampmeier, 2003; Fielding *et al.*, 2008; Dono *et al.*, 2010) are willing to activate this identity also in their working contexts. As we will show below, they do engage in high-intensity EGB even in unfavorable conditions. Since their behavior is associated with and conditioned by their private engagement and their personal and social identity as 'an environmentalist', their engagement at work might involve a different form or quality than when their green behavior would be triggered and structured by the organization. First, employees disclosing their private engagement and a strong green identity in the working context might be more vulnerable to deprecatory remarks by peers and supervisors less attuned towards the green movement. At the same time, since their green extra-role initiatives at work are grounded in their environmental identity which, in turn, draws from a long-term, tightly-knit, green social network in the private domain, they can receive support for their engagement at work from sources outside the workplace. Creed, DeJordy, and Lok (2010) show for the case of gay and lesbian priests how their identity and the social support in the queer community can serve as a strong psychological resource for demanding situations at their workplaces. Still, so far it remains unclear whether green employees require more or less support from colleagues and supervisors in their workplaces in order to successfully conduct their high-intensity EGB. Second, in their private and public engagement, green activists develop substantial skills and knowledge bases, both regarding social competences (e.g., networking, communication) and expertise (e.g., on solar technology, e-mobility). This might lead to a situation where the green expertise of engaged employees is more advanced than that of their colleagues and/ or the organization at large. The offer of standard sustainability training by the company might thus be perceived as inadequate or even as offensive. Third, employees with a green identity are intrinsically motivated to engage in EGB. Standard GHRM appraisal schemes such as monetary rewards for green behavior could then lead to crowding out (Frey and Osterloh, 2002) since they might be perceived as implying that the behavioral impulse derives from individual interests rather than an identification with the 'good cause' (e.g., the Energiewende [energy transition]):

Proposition 2: Individuals holding a strong environmental identity pursue different strategies and require a different kind of organizational support to successfully engage in pro-environmental spillover processes than employees without such an identity anchor.

Enabling EGB: the role of GHRM and supportive structures

Whether employees effectively engage in high-intensity EGB does not only depend on their willingness but also on their ability to do so in the context of their respective workplace. The literature on EGB or related concepts such as EWB (environmental work behavior, see Ciocirlan,

2016) provide different conceptualizations of the organizational context. Since they are often based on the Theory of Planned Behavior or Framing Theory (Fielding *et al.*, 2008; Steg and Vlek, 2009; Greaves *et al.*, 2013; Steg *et al.*, 2014), proponents from the environmental psychology field rarely look at the specific constitution of the context as such but rather focus on the individual's assessment regarding his/her self-efficacy in general. When considered at all, the conceptualization of the environment is reduced to the provision of the required infrastructure, e.g., for recycling behavior (Lee *et al.*, 1995). The conceptualization of the organizational environment features more prominently in research in the OCBE (organizational citizenship behavior for the environment) perspective (Boiral, 2009; Daily *et al.*, 2009; Boiral *et al.*, 2015; Paillé and Raineri, 2015). Here, authors emphasize two dimensions of the organizational context: Organizational concern for the environment (e.g. as formalized in CSR/sustainability policies) and organizational support, most importantly supervisory support (Ramus and Steger, 2000; Paillé and Raineri, 2015; Raineri and Paillé, 2015). More recently, Paillé and colleagues (2014) have broadened their perspective by integrating 'strategic human resource management' as an antecedent of employee OCBE. Their empirical data reveals that, in firms with a strong environmental concern, strategic human resource policies can contribute considerably to an increase in OCBE (Paillé *et al.*, 2014). How specific human resource practices might impact OCBE is so far not covered in this stream of literature. This is, in turn, the focus of much of the GHRM literature. Renwick *et al.* (2013) maintain that three key areas need to be addressed with GHRM practices in order to enable EGB: Selection and training, feedback and appraisal, and green culture and leadership. Regarding selection and training, proponents of the GHRM concept delineate that active recruitment and development of environmental knowledge and competences of corporate employees do substantially contribute to the successful implementation of environmental management systems (Daily *et al.*, 2012; Teixeira, Jabbour and de Sousa Jabbour, 2012). Regarding appraisal schemes, authors demonstrate, for instance, how rewards and recognition practices need to be adjusted in order to motivate employees to engage in EGB (Govindarajulu and Daily, 2004; Wagner, 2013). A green corporate culture and green supervisory support are crucial to socialize employees according to the organizational sustainability values (Harris and Crane, 2002) and to encourage them, also through role-modeling, to engage in EGB. Supervisory support is repeatedly identified as the single most important antecedent of EGB (Ramus and Steger, 2000; Zibarras and Ballinger, 2011; Robertson and Barling, 2013).

While the GHRM literature does not systematically address the question of whether employees with a strong green identity and a background of private/public green activism respond differently to these HRM practices, the Green work–life balance concept (Muster and Schrader, 2011) does explicitly focus on spillover processes. Muster and Schrader (2011) identify GHRM practices that should foster the transferal of green behavior from the private domain to the workplace. These include information-based (brochures, lectures, intranet informing about green behavior), service-based (green concierge, canteen, and mobility services at work) and finance-based (discounts for green company offers such as job tickets) instruments (Muster and Schrader, 2011).

This review of the literature reveals three limitations that we address with our study. First, GHRM research predominantly focuses on low-intensity green behavior: Whereas Muster and Schrader (2011) explicitly concentrate on green consumption on the job, other authors limit their attention to less demanding, adaptive behavioral types (Ones and Dilchert, 2012) such as conserving or preventing harm (re-use, re-cycle) and/or working sustainably (confirming to environmental management system, choosing responsible behavioral alternatives). High-intensity EGB (Ciocirlan, 2016) such as pro-environmental intrapreneurship (initiative taking) and eco-helping (educating others) which put higher demands on the organization (e.g., with respect to required resources and associated risks) and on the individual initiator (regarding required competences, time and stamina) are so far under-researched in the GHRM literature. They do feature prominently in the OCBE literature, which, however, as discussed above, does not provide a differentiated conceptualization of GHRM practices. Second, proponents in the GHRM field assume that companies need to align employee behavior to their green policies and values. This seems to imply an asymmetric situation in which employees are always less motivated to engage in and less knowledgeable about green issues and green behavioral options than the corporation, i.e., its upper echelon. A configuration in which employees are ahead of the organization with regard to green development issues awaits further investigation. We could expect, for instance, that the influence of supervisory support and training schemes becomes less important when employees are intrinsically motivated green activists. Third, the dominant notion of alignment in the GHRM literature seems to go hand in hand with a passive conceptualization of the employee. Employees are presented as recipients of corporate support, rewards, and information on green issues who will adapt their behavior to the structures and instruments on offer. This perspective would consequently maintain that contexts in which support is missing (i.e., exclusionary contexts, see Ramarajan and Reid, 2013) preclude

EGB. In line with the work–life balance model by Ramarajan and Reid (2013), we argue, however, that exclusionary contexts do not prevent action but lead actors to change their strategies in response. These authors suggest that, particularly for individuals with inclusionary preferences (e.g., rooted in an integrative identity structure), unfavorable contextual conditions are associated with strategies such as concealing (hidden action), resisting, or inverting (attempts to overcome the exclusionary pressure) and not with inaction. Although the model by Ramarajan and Reid (2013) focuses on the work–life family balance phenomenon, we suggest that it is useful also for a better understanding of the actor–structure relationship in green spillover processes. Based on this model, we can expect that individuals holding a strong green identity do actively and strategically – and not adaptively – react to the organizational context and GHRM instruments in place. For the case of social issue selling, Sonenshein, DeCelles, and Dutton (2014) have demonstrated that not only do committed activists act strategically but that they also effectively construct their own context depending on the interests and initiatives pursued. In their final discussion, the authors tentatively suggest that highly motivated actors (such as strongly identified green activists) might actually work more effectively in a non-aligned context. Although they do not pursue this route of argumentation further, we might prolong it for the case investigated here: Individuals with a strong environmental identity might deliberately disregard or circumvent green organizational support structures when they can thus maintain coherence regarding their self-concept. Thus:

> Proposition 3: Individuals holding a strong green identity actively construct a context that allows them to engage in high-intensity EGB even in exclusionary organizations.

In the following section, we use our empirical data to explore and further elaborate these propositions. In particular, in order to better account for the contextual impact on green work–life spillover of the green activists-cum-employees in focus here, we explore (1) how their green identity impacts on their willingness and ability to initiate high-intensity EGB, and (2) how they perceive and actively handle (construct) an organizational context that allows for green extra-role initiative taking, even in exclusionary contexts. In the discussion section, we derive implications for GHRM practices which help to make use of the potential for green transformation offered by green activists at work.

Findings

From data that has been collected for a larger research program, we present some exploratory results from our investigation of the EGB of green activists-cum-employees. Data analysis reveals different angles to themes that are currently addressed in GHRM research. Looking more closely at green activists-cum-employees, we are able to identify important factors that need to be taken into account when high-intensity EGB is addressed: (1) employees' green identity and the willingness to spill over; (2) their strategies for high-intensity EGB; and (3) the overcoming of barriers to high-intensity EGB. The following table gives an overview of green activists-cum-employees, their jobs, and the industries they work in.

The interviewees in Table 5.1 have different backgrounds to their motivation to engage in high-intensity EGB. For example, one of the interviewees has a degree in environmental studies. Others are active in associations and act as promoters for renewable energy. One is a Greenpeace activist. Another interviewee has a very impressive account of private green projects: Besides building several photovoltaic installations, he was also a driver for renewable energies and was head of several associations in the field of wind and solar energy.

Table 5.1 Interviewees

Interviewee*	Private green activity or education	Job	Industry
Ann	Master's degree in Environmental Management and Policy	Environmental manager	Mining
Peter	Renewable energy projects (solar and wind power), starting RE** cooperatives, member of several RE associations	Controller	Automotive
Sara	Greenpeace activist	Accountant	Production
Max	Environmental movement activist since 1980s, RE projects	Environmental manager	Telecommunication
Tim	Vice-chairman of a club for solar energy	Civil servant	Federal government department

Notes
** All names are pseudonyms.
** RE stands for renewable energy.

In the following section, we present the three key insights from our data: (1) a strong green identity leads to high-intensity EGB, even when the context is averse to high-intensity EGB; (2) green activists-cum-employees who encounter barriers to high-intensity EGB develop strategies to overcome these; and (3) green activists-cum-employees create contexts in which their high-intensity EGB can be successful despite a generally adverse environment.

Employees' green identity and willingness to spill over

Data analysis shows that green activists-cum-employees present a strong green identity connected with a high intrinsic motivation to engage in green activism at work as well as in their private lives. As can be seen from their private green activities described above, they are motivated to do their share in promoting environmental protection:

> Limits to growth. [...]. That's the basic motive, actually a small contribution, I don't overestimate myself, I know that it is a small contribution and I cannot save the world alone. I would feel stupid, if I didn't do that. Really. I have to do that and the information I have is also a mandate.
>
> (Max)

> Since 1986, so since Chernobyl, it became clear to me that it cannot go on like that.
>
> (Peter)

These green activists frequently ("10 to 15 hours a week" [Sara]) and on a long-term basis ("for 20 years" [Tim]) engage in green activism in non-governmental organizations, renewable energy and other public environmental activities.

The intrinsic motivation to engage in green activism also extends to the working sphere. One interviewee even changed his job in order to get into a position at work where he would be able to do more for the environment – despite detrimental effects for himself:

> [...] then a colleague called me ... there is a job ad regarding environmental protection, are you interested? And then I had to make a decision, either career and money or environmental protection.
>
> (Max)

Barriers for EGB

Green activists in our data have considerable experience in pro-environmental initiatives in the private domain and through public and private projects have become quite knowledgeable, e.g., in the field of renewable energy. As a consequence, they perceive a strong knowledge asymmetry with regard to their workplace context. The interviewees identify themselves as experts and pioneers and stress the considerable gap between their personal competences regarding green issues and those of the organization they work for:

> Actually, what I learned at the university [about environmental protection measures]. I have got the feeling, nothing sinks in here … well, very, very little at most.
>
> (Ann)

> I was one of the first in the company, who also had a railnet card [...] I traveled to the single factories and I didn't travel by car, but by rail. That was a small revolution, of course.
>
> (Peter)

> They [colleagues] keep trying yet again; when our boss says, "Well, we would like white paper," then I say, it's like this and that and explain it. And then [they answer] "yes, true yes." And then they start thinking and then they also say, "I look for envelopes made from recycled paper." That's when I notice, it bears fruit. Small, but still.
>
> (Sara)

Related to their concept of themselves as experts on green issues vis-à-vis a company that is far less competent – at least in their view – is the notion of being one-of-a-kind, an 'exotic' and 'pioneer' in the organizational context. Several interviewees report that they feel quite isolated sometimes and also link this perception to a barrier to EGB in their workplaces.

> Some think I am a weirdo.
>
> (Sara)

> Whoever is committed exposes themselves and, therefore, takes a risk. That can offer chances to find recognition as pioneer, as expert, as innovator – maybe to be able to actually achieve something – but there are also risks. Some may consider you a wise guy, an exotic, or a disturber.
>
> (Tim)

> He [supervisor] supports my general work. But when I have some exotic ideas – which are somehow exotic to him – then I am laughed at.
>
> (Ann)

Although green activists-cum-employees seem to be predestinated for high-intensity EGB, they often perceive the context as unfavorable. During the interviews, they describe their organizations as adverse environments where green activities are not welcome, or are completely disregarded. The lack of support, however, does not result in inaction. Instead, it is met with an ongoing willingness to bring in new green ideas even if they will not produce change soon. Moreover, despite difficulties these employees are found to be persistent in their high-intensity EGB. Interviewees refer to situations where official management statements emphasize the corporate green policy while, from the employees' point of view, actual support for implementing environmental activities is minimal:

> When you ask around, doesn't matter to whom, environmental protection, do you like it? Then everybody always says "yes." Nobody says anything against environmental protection. But when you ask then, what are you ready to pay? Or how many hours would you provide, what are you doing for it? Then the numbers dwindle very fast.
>
> (Max)

Apart from the lack of operative green engagement, interviewees refer to inadequate organizational instruments or processes, which do not provide "proper" support for their green initiatives. In particular, financial incentive schemes for green employee behavior are described as ineffective and unnecessary. Also, standard suggestion schemes are deemed inadequate for their specific initiatives, because ideas will generally be evaluated by colleagues less knowledgeable or interested in green projects.

> Why do [green] suggestions fail? That can have different reasons. I think: The level of knowledge of the person who will judge and evaluate the suggestions is the main reason, and that was very little in our organization. Then another department, property management, got involved and my impression was: There it was even smaller.
>
> (Tim)

For me, this [suggestion scheme] is absolutely not attractive. And how it is handled, you can just abolish it. Well, maybe it is for people who work in the mines or in the factory – they are, absolutely massively, after the prizes.

(Ann)

The quotes demonstrate that financial incentives for green ideas and initiatives are not the focus of our interviewees. For them, being rewarded by accomplishing a green project or positive feedback on green issues from colleagues is much more important than financial rewards or formal acknowledgement.

Employees' strategies for high-intensity EGB

Green activists-cum-employees develop particular strategies to tackle organizational barriers to EGB and engage in high-intensity EGB. Engaging in high-intensity EGB is described as a "marathon" (Max) and something that needs to be "tried again and again" (Sara), so patience and a long-term perspective are crucial to cope with barriers and lack of support:

[It was] far more important to hang on in the company. That's in my opinion the main message, to hang on, including when the structures are constantly changing and when people let you bounce off. A marathon aspect, an endurance-run aspect, or having a lot of staying power, that's the decisive point.

(Max)

I will try this again and again. Because it is my personal conviction. And as long as I can influence this, I will do that.

(Sara)

Other green activists work around an unfavorable environment by stretching their competences in order to force change, despite the lack of supportive structures. Max explains:

So I went a little over my competences now. […] But complying with the [company] rules doesn't work; if you stick to all the formalities, nothing ever gets done. […] If you really comply with how everything is written, that's actually worth nothing.

(Max)

Frustrated green activists-cum-employees also resort to hidden behavior. In one case, an interviewee who sensed an opportunity simply switched to a green electricity supplier without informing her supervisors – so far, her behavior remains undisclosed and she has decided to keep silent about it.

Contextual constructions for high-intensity EGB

Since existing instruments such as suggestions schemes are often considered inappropriate for high-intensity EGB, green activists-cum-employees create their own networks or niches in which their green ideas can take hold more easily:

> I think I won't hand in official suggestions any more. When I have ideas, I will pass them on to single persons, so as to bring them into certain circles.
>
> (Tim)

Our data analysis further shows that they deliberately build up networks with like-minded colleagues. They help them to cope with the lack of support from supervisors or to find general support for high-intensity EGB in an unfavorable environment. Ann describes how she felt before she started networking with two like-minded colleagues in her company:

> … before there was this connection to Kate and Lisa, I had been thinking intermittently: 'No, no, after the probation period, I'll be gone.' […] Because you get crazy. When you have such a position of a lone fighter, and you don't know, somehow, 'Whom can I tell what to', and there is no exchange, and you feel somehow completely lost, right?
>
> (Ann)

> [It is] mainly about hanging on and to take those along of course who are interested or, let's say, those where you notice, they are interested in supporting it too, and that they also do something. That was very important.
>
> (Max)

Inside the niches or lateral networks thus created, interviewees were then able to find feedback, support, and understanding for their EGB projects, which helped them to keep up their engagement over longer periods of time and against barriers inside the organization.

Discussion: clearing the way for green work–life spillover with GHRM

Our interview data demonstrates that green activists are willing to spill over their engagement and their green identity to their workplaces and that they pursue green initiatives even in non-supportive contexts, albeit with unusual or undercover strategies. This finding is in line with the more general perspective of Ramarajan and Reid (2013), who argue that strong personal preferences bring forth different behavioral strategies in exclusionary contexts than in supportive, inclusionary settings. This should not lead us to the deceptive conclusion that firms could dispense with their efforts to supply supportive structures and cultures for EGB because green employees do not rely on them anyhow. Instead, we can learn from the green activists' strategies how they actually engage with the organizational context they encounter and what their needs are in constructing a context in which their green initiatives can flourish. These insights can help us then to design GHRM tools that actually respond to the strategies preferred by green activists-cum-employees.

Based on the empirical findings, we can identify four areas where the actual needs of these particular employees deviate from those we would expect in view of the assumptions implicit in the GHRM literature so far:

1   Regarding leadership – a key element of the GHRM portfolio – green activists-cum-employees also suffer when they do not receive adequate support from their supervisors. A lack of support does not, however, result in inaction. Instead, people build up their own lateral support networks. These typically include other single green activists-cum-employees across functions and hierarchies whom they have recognized as allies in spirit. These networks help to push green projects through other routes when the activists' own supervisor blocks the initiative. Decentral social niches also provide encouragement when the activists' initiative turns into a frustrating, year-long marathon or when colleagues from their own teams continue to belittle their efforts.

2   Because their engagement is related to their personal and social identity, green activists react differently to green support structures that might be totally adequate for other less green colleagues. While, for instance, employee suggestion schemes can be successfully employed to encourage and incentivize green ideas, green activists tend not to use them. This is due to the fact that suggestion

schemes are usually designed so that, after positive evaluation of an idea, the responsible department takes over the realization of the idea (e.g., an employee's e-mobility idea is implemented by the transport department/fleet management). Whereas ordinary employees might be happy to hand over their idea to the specialists and get on with their actual job, green activists hold a strong personal attachment to their ideas and also consider themselves the "experts" in that field. They prefer to keep the development of their idea under their control and thus seek paths outside formal suggestion schemes.

3 For green activists-cum-employees, the reward for their substantial efforts lies in the successful implementation of their green initiatives. We take from our findings that they are not activated by or likely to respond to e.g., monetary rewards for EGB, nor do they present a need for formal recognition rituals. However, they want the opportunity to engage in high-intensity EGB. More than other employees, they fear to compromise their identity and their intrinsic motivation if their engagement is linked to incentives or formal praise provided by persons or organizations that do not match their personal moral standards regarding sustainability and climate protection (see Muster and Schrader, 2011, p. 152).

4 Green activists consider themselves 'experts' and 'pioneers' on green issues; regarding green expertise, they see themselves often as being ahead of their organization and colleagues. Since this notion is part of their concept of self, it is particularly stable. Consequently, they are often the ones who provide information and try to educate their colleagues on green issues, even though this is not their formal role. In this way, they also seek to enlarge the green network they eventually rely on to continue with their green extra-role initiatives, i.e., they strategically invest in the creation of their own supportive contexts, at least in niches.

These observations from an admittedly limited empirical study do provide preliminary support for the propositions formulated above. Green activists, at least in this sample, actively seek to spill over their green identity and their initiatives to their workplaces. They do engage in high-intensity EGB, even in unsupportive contexts. And they do strategically engage in the construction of a context that allows them to pursue their green ideas and thus to contribute to the transformation of their respective organizations from the bottom up. The propositions thus form a helpful basis for further empirical research.

For the design of GHRM tools and processes in practice, our findings also provide some interesting implications: Whereas the Green HRM literature tends to focus on the necessary support for EGB by supervisors, our findings suggest that, for green activists, facilitation of lateral or horizontal green support structures is much more important. In large organizations, this network building can be eased through intraorganizational social media networks such as the Telekom Social Network at Deutsche Telekom: It provides a virtual platform where employees can post company-related issues but also communicate about private interests and thus, for instance, connect with other like-minded employees among the workforce.

Regarding incentives, it is much more important for green activists to keep ownership of their own project than to gain recognition and rewards. Here, companies should develop systems for the recognition of high-intensity EGB that provide time rather than monetary rewards for green extra-role initiative-taking. Time could be provided in the form of Corporate Volunteering programs (employees can pursue their green private or public projects full time for a limited time period) or as a percentage of their weekly working time (e.g., 10 percent for their green projects). Finally, green activists-cum-employees are willing to engage in role-modeling and educating others. Through job enrichment schemes, firms could actively encourage employees to readjust their formal job assignments. A qualification format called 'Energiescouts' in Germany enables employees to take over green project work (in this case related to climate protection and the energy transition) on a voluntary basis alongside their ordinary jobs. They can choose the focus of their project work (e.g. mobility, renewable energy supply, facilities, production, etc.) according to their personal competences and interests (which often derive from their private green engagement). Each energy-scout can dedicate 10 percent of his/her working time to green projects. In addition, they can recruit a team of two or three further employees to help them develop and implement such initiatives. Thus, this instrument not only encourages spillover behavior and acknowledges the expert knowledge of green activists in their respective field of interest, but also recognizes the need of green activists to build up supportive green niches to help them to avoid and cope with frustrations.

Conclusions

The contributions of this chapter are threefold. First, we drew attention to a specific group of employees formerly underrepresented in the GHRM literature. In particular, we were able to delineate that green activists-cum-employees use different strategies and hold divergent preferences regarding the constitution of a supportive context for EGB than other employees. Second, based on our qualitative data, we confirmed that identity (as a 'green activist', as an 'environmentalist') does play an important role in motivating spillover behavior and high-intensity EGB. This finding should encourage further research on identity work and its relationship to EGB. Third, we have provided preliminary ideas as to how the divergent needs of green activists and their particular identity structure impact the design of adequate GHRM instruments such as reward systems and training schemes. Although they are clearly a highly idiosyncratic minority, this group of employees does warrant further attention since they are motivated to engage in high-intensity EGB although it often resembles a 'marathon', work around frustrations, and also share their green expertise with others. In doing so, green activists could develop into important role models and ambassadors for the future green transformation of their respective organizations.

References

Andersson, M., O. Eriksson and C. von Borgstede (2012) "The effects of environmental management systems on source separation in the work and home settings," *Sustainability*, vol. 4, no. 6, pp. 1292–1308.

Boiral, O. (2009) "Greening the corporation through organizational citizenship behaviors," *Journal of Business Ethics*, vol. 87, no. 2, pp. 221–236.

Boiral, O., P. Pallié and N. Raineri (2015) "The nature of employees' pro-environmental behaviors." In Robertson, J. L. and Barling, J. (Eds.). *The psychology of green organizations: The nature of employees' pro-environmental behaviors*, pp. 12–32. Oxford University Press: Oxford.

Ciocirlan, C. E. (2016) "Environmental workplace behaviors definition matters," *Organization & Environment*, Online first February 2, pp. 1–20.

Creed, W. D., R. DeJordy and J. Lok (2010) "Being the change: Resolving institutional contradiction through identity work," *Academy of Management Journal*, vol. 53, no. 6, pp. 1336–1364.

Daily, B. F., J. W. Bishop and N. Govindarajulu (2009) "A conceptual model for organizational citizenship behavior directed toward the environment," *Business & Society*, vol. 48, no. 2, pp. 243–256.

Daily, B. F., J. W. Bishop and J. A. Massoud (2012) "The role of training and empowerment in environmental performance: A study of the Mexican maquiladora industry," *International Journal of Operations & Production Management*, vol. 32, no. 5, pp. 631–647.

Dono, J., J. Webb and B. Richardson (2010) "The relationship between environmental activism, pro-environmental behaviour and social identity," *Journal of Environmental Psychology*, vol. 30, no. 2, pp. 178–186.

Ehnert, I. and W. Harry (2012) "Recent developments and future prospects on sustainable human resource management: Introduction to the special issue," *Management revue*, vol. 23, no. 3, pp. 221–238.

Fielding, K. S., R. McDonald and W. R. Louis (2008) "Theory of planned behaviour, identity and intentions to engage in environmental activism," *Journal of Environmental Psychology*, vol. 28, no. 4, pp. 318–326.

Frey, B. S. and M. Osterloh (2002) *Managing motivation*. Gabler: Wiesbaden.

Govindarajulu, N. and B. F. Daily (2004) "Motivating employees for environmental improvement," *Industrial Management & Data Systems*, vol. 104, no. 4, pp. 364–372.

Greaves, M., L. D. Zibarras and C. Stride (2013) "Using the theory of planned behavior to explore environmental behavioral intentions in the workplace," *Journal of Environmental Psychology*, vol. 34, pp. 109–120.

Harris, L. C. and A. Crane (2002) "The greening of organizational culture: Management views on the depth, degree and diffusion of change," *Journal of Organizational Change Management*, vol. 15, no. 3, pp. 214–234.

Jackson, S. E. and J. Seo (2010) "The greening of strategic HRM scholarship," *Organization Management Journal*, vol. 7, no. 4, pp. 278–290.

Klöckner, C. A., A. Nayum and M. Mehmetoglu (2013) "Positive and negative spillover effects from electric car purchase to car use," *Transportation Research Part D: Transport and Environment*, vol. 21, pp. 32–38.

Lee, Y.-J., R. De Young and R. W. Marans (1995) "Factors influencing individual recycling behavior in office settings. A study of office workers in Taiwan," *Environment and Behavior*, vol. 27, no. 3, pp. 380–403.

Lo, S. H., G. J. Y. Peters and G. Kok (2012) "A review of determinants of and interventions for proenvironmental behaviors in organizations," *Journal of Applied Social Psychology*, vol. 42, no. 12, pp. 2933–2967.

Mazar, N. and C.-B. Zhong (2010) "Do green products make us better people?," *Psychological Science*, vol. 21, pp. 494–498.

Muster, V. (2011) "Companies promoting sustainable consumption of employees," *Journal of Consumer Policy*, vol. 34, no. 1, pp. 161–174.

Muster, V. (2012) "Negative influences of working life on sustainable consumption," *International Journal of Consumer Studies*, vol. 36, no. 2, pp. 166–172.

Muster, V. and U. Schrader (2011) "Green work–life balance: A new perspective for green HRM," *German Journal of Research in Human Resource Management*, vol. 25, no. 2, pp. 140–156.

Norton, T. A., H. Zacher and N. M. Ashkanasy (2012) "On the importance of pro-environmental organizational climate for employee green behavior," *Industrial and Organizational Psychology*, vol. 5, no. 4, pp. 497–500.

Norton, T. A., Parker, S. L., Zacher, H., and Ashkanasy, N. M. (2015) "Employee green behavior: A theoretical framework, multilevel review, and future research agenda," *Organization & Environment,* vol. 28, no. 1, pp. 103–125.

Ones, D. S. and S. Dilchert (2012) "Environmental sustainability at work: A call to action," *Industrial and Organizational Psychology*, vol. 5, no. 4, pp. 444–466.

Paillé, P. and O. Boiral (2013) "Pro-environmental behavior at work: Construct validity and determinants," *Journal of Environmental Psychology* vol. 36, no. 1, pp. 118–128.

Paillé, P. and N. Raineri (2015) "Linking perceived corporate environmental policies and employees eco-initiatives: The influence of perceived organizational support and psychological contract breach," *Journal of Business Research*, vol. 68, no. 11, pp. 2404–2411.

Paillé, P., Y. Chen, O. Boiral and J. Jin (2014) "The impact of human resource management on environmental performance: An employee-level study," *Journal of Business Ethics*, vol. 121, no. 3, pp. 451–466.

Raineri, N. and P. Paillé (2015) "Linking corporate policy and supervisory support with environmental citizenship behaviors: The role of employee environmental beliefs and commitment," *Journal of Business Ethics*, vol. 137, no. 1, pp. 129–148.

Ramarajan, L. and Reid, E. (2013) "Shattering the myth of separate worlds: Negotiating nonwork identities at work," *Academy of Management Review*, vol. 38, no. 4, pp. 621–644.

Ramus, C. A. and U. Steger (2000) "The roles of supervisory support behaviors and environmental policy in employee 'ecoinitiatives' at leading-edge European companies," *Academy of Management Journal*, vol. 43, no. 4, pp. 605–626.

Renwick, D. W. S., T. Redman and S. Maguire (2013) "Green Human Resource Management: A review and research agenda," *International Journal of Management Reviews*, vol. 15, no. 1, pp. 1–14.

Robertson, J. L. and J. Barling (2013) "Greening organizations through leaders' influence on employees' pro-environmental behaviors," *Journal of Organizational Behavior*, vol. 34, no. 2, pp. 176–194.

Schrader, U. and C. Harrach (2013) "Empowering responsible consumers to be sustainable intrapreneurs." In U. Schrader, V. Fricke, D. Doyle and V. W. (Eds.). *Enabling resonsible living*, pp. 181–192. Thoresen: Berlin.

Sonenshein, S., K. DeCelles and J. Dutton (2014) "It's not easy being green: Self-evaluations and their role in explaining support of environmental issues," *Academy of Management Journal*, vol. 57, no. 1, pp. 7–37.

Steg, L., J. W. Bolderdijk, K. Keizer and G. Perlaviciute (2014) "An integrated framework for encouraging pro-environmental behaviour: The role of values, situational factors and goals," *Journal of Environmental Psychology*, vol. 38, pp. 104–115.

Steg, L. and C. Vlek (2009) "Encouraging pro-environmental behaviour: An integrative review and research agenda," *Journal of Environmental Psychology*, vol. 29, no. 3, pp. 309–317.

Stürmer, S. and C. Kampmeier (2003) "Active citizenship: The role of community identification in community volunteerism and local participation," *Psychologica Belgica*, vol. 43, no. 1–2, pp. 103–122.

Taylor, S., J. Osland and C. P. Egri (2012) "Guest editors' introduction: Introduction to HRM's role in sustainability: Systems, strategies, and practices," *Human Resource Management*, vol. 51, no. 6, pp. 789–798.

Teixeira, A. A., C. J. C. Jabbour and A. B. L. de Sousa Jabbour (2012) "Relationship between green management and environmental training in companies located in Brazil: A theoretical framework and case studies," *International Journal of Production Economics*, vol. 140, no. 1, pp. 318–329.

Temminck, E., K. Mearns and L. Fruhen (2013) "Motivating employees towards sustainable behaviour," *Business Strategy and the Environment*, vol. 24, no. 6, pp. 402–412.

Thøgersen, J. and T. Crompton (2009) "Simple and painless? The limitations of spillover in environmental campaigning," *Journal of Consumer Policy*, vol. 32, no. 2, pp. 141–163.

Truelove, H. B., A. R. Carrico, E. U. Weber, K. T. Raimi and M. P. Vandenbergh (2014) "Positive and negative spillover of pro-environmental behavior: An integrative review and theoretical framework," *Global Environmental Change*, vol. 29, pp. 127–138.

Tudor, T., S. Barr and A. Gilg (2007) "A tale of two locational settings: Is there a link between pro-environmental behaviour at work and at home?," *Local Environment*, vol. 12, no. 4, pp. 409–421.

UBA, B. (2015) *Umweltbewusstsein in Deutschland 2014 Ergebnisse einer repräsentativen Bevölkerungsumfrage.*

van der Werff, E., L. Steg and K. Keizer (2013) "The value of environmental self-identity: The relationship between biospheric values, environmental self-identity and environmental preferences, intentions and behaviour," *Journal of Environmental Psychology*, vol. 34, no. 1, pp. 55–63.

Wagner, M. (2013) "'Green' human resource benefits: Do they matter as determinants of environmental management system implementation?," *Journal of Business Ethics*, vol. 114, no. 3, pp. 443–456.

Wehrmeyer, W. (Ed.) (1996) *Greening people: Human resources and environmental management.* Greenleaf: Sheffield,

Whitmarsh, L. and S. O'Neill (2010) "Green identity, green living? The role of pro-environmental self-identity in determining consistency across diverse pro-environmental behaviours," *Journal of Environmental Psychology*, vol. 30, pp. 305–314.

Wright, C., D. Nyberg and D. Grant (2012) "'Hippies on the third floor': Climate change, narrative identity and the micro-politics of corporate environmentalism," *Organization Studies*, vol. 33, no. 11, pp. 1451–1475.

Zibarras, L. and C. Ballinger (2011) "Promoting environmental behaviour in the workplace: A survey of UK organisations." In D. Bartlett, *Going green: The psychology of sustainability in the workplace*, pp. 84–90. The British Psychological Society.

Part II

Contextualising GHRM – from GHRM to sustainability?

6 Employee control, ethics and politics – GHRM in context

Luca Carollo and Marco Guerci

Introduction

For business organizations, being responsible towards the natural environment is today considered a moral imperative, as concerns about environmental protection are growing in public opinion in several countries, as documented by the most recent reports from Eurobarometer (for example, Special Eurobarometer, 2014). These concerns have been reinforced by the continuous emergence of well-known environmental-related company scandals, such as the software installed at Volkswagen in diesel engines that detected when they were being tested. As a result, company behaviours are more and more under public scrutiny, so that environmental management is now considered as a mega-trend to be faced by any business organization (Lubin and Esty, 2010).

Management studies have been informed by this trend and today environmental management is a developed stream of research to which the most reputable management journals devote special issues and editorials (for example, George *et al.*, 2015). Not surprisingly, the human resource management (HRM) discipline has devoted growing attention to this topic, advancing the idea that an effective environmental management system should also include HRM practices and systems, called green HRM (GHRM) (Renwick *et al.*, 2013). Two recent contributions are particularly illustrative in this sense. The first contribution is a conceptual paper in which renowned scholars in the HRM field have extended the current theorizations about strategic HRM, showing how the HRM practices and systems implemented by business organizations affect multiple stakeholders within and outside the company, among which is the natural environment (Jackson *et al.*, 2014). The second contribution is a state-of-the-art paper in which the authors review the extant empirical literature on relationships between HRM and environmental management, showing how several HRM practices have been found associated with superior environmental performance (Renwick *et al.*, 2013). In parallel with these research developments, HRM practice has also recently started to be informed by the principles of environmental management, as witnessed by several contributions developed by the leading HRM professional associations (for example, SHRM, 2012).

Notwithstanding such recent knowledge advancements, a key point seems to be underdeveloped in extant GHRM research and practice, as it is only partially recognized that GHRM does not exist in a vacuum, but is always embedded in a social system. The contextualization of GHRM could improve our understanding of the phenomenon, as it could show how it is commonly embedded in a web of tensions. Some examples can help to understand what we mean here. A first example is the case of Ilva, an Italian iron and steel company which has recently attracted the attention of both scholars and politicians (Vagliasindi, 2015). The Italian authorities found the major plant of this company not to be compliant with current environmental regulations and demonstrated that the company's lack of environmental responsibility had caused severe damage to local human and animal health. As a result, the owners and the managers of the company were charged with several crimes and arrested. In parallel, the Italian judiciary imposed the precautionary seizure of most of the equipment of the plant. That decision caused the major economic collapse of the company, which led to the need to radically cut the number of people employed in the plant. However, the plant is located in an economically depressed area, traditionally characterized by high unemployment rates. In order to handle the economic and social consequences of this decision, and as a response to a strong protest from the local employees and their representatives, the Italian Government allowed the plant to continue operations, despite the judicial decision. A second well-known example concerns the American retailer Wal-Mart. In an influential piece, Pfeffer (2010) highlighted that Wal-Mart, which is trying to radically reduce its footprint on the natural environment, has exploitative organizational practices which dramatically hurt its employees and their families. This evident contradiction led the author to write provocatively: 'We should care as much about people as we do about polar bears' (p. 43).

The two examples just reported show how, in environmental management, there are different and potentially conflicting issues at stake, as well as a large set of actors involved; specifically, the cases reveal that a fair balance between the right to health and the protection of environment, the right to have decent work and the production needs, could be very difficult to achieve. Moreover, what emerges from the cases is that environmental management systems are always embedded in a web of tensions, which may easily result in ethical and political issues. Accordingly, the extant literature on environmental management has started addressing these issues. For example, business ethics research is debating the ethical underpinnings of environmental management systems in business organizations (for example, Becker, 2012), showing that those systems are often affected by amoralization (Crane, 2000). Similarly, critical scholars have shown that environmental sustainability is often serving the economic interests of shareholders, as it is often conceived as merely eco-efficiency (Banerjee, 2011) and it transforms the social good of the environment into a market commodity (Nyberg and Wright, 2013).

It seems that, so far, the research stream on GHRM has dedicated less attention to those ethical and political issues, which remain largely unexplored. That is somehow surprising, given that HRM research has traditionally paid significant attention to the analysis of how firms manage their employment relations from an ethical perspective (for example, Greenwood, 2013; Jack *et al.*, 2012) and from a politically aware perspective too (see Delbridge and Keenoy, 2010). In parallel, HRM education has been recently more and more reflexively critical about its ethical and political assumptions (Bratton and Gold, 2015).

In this context, the present chapter has the broad aim of contextualizing green HRM in its ethical and political contexts, specifically addressing in the following sections three issues in GHRM, namely how it balances control and commitment, its political meanings, and its ethical assumptions. Finally, a concluding section summarizes the implications of these issues for HRM researchers and practitioners.

Contextualization #1 – GHRM in the control/commitment dichotomy

The dichotomy between commitment and control has characterized the evolution of organization studies and of the HRM field in particular. Indeed, contributions on the history of HRM research and practice (for example, Kaufman, 2014) show how, originally, personnel management was meant to win commitment from employees, in accordance with human relations (Mayo, 1933) and human resources (Argyris, 1957; McGregor, 1960) schools of thought, and avoiding some of the control-centric employment practices promoted by scientific management (Taylor, 1903) and administrative theory (Fayol, 1949). Today, it is quite established that the objective of people management within business organizations is to gain control over and, at the same time, commitment from the workers (Hyman, 1987). However, the rhetorical shift from personnel management to HRM is considered as an ideological reconfiguration of the field, which creates room for more sophisticated forms of managerial control (Keenoy, 2009).

Embedding GHRM in such a context requires us to go deeper into the very idea of employee control which, as anticipated, has radically evolved in the last decades. In fact, in the last years, new forms of managerial control have been identified, and empirical studies have demonstrated how these co-exist with more traditional forms of control, which have not disappeared (Thompson and van den Broek, 2010). Specifically, two broad forms of managerial control are today recognized in organization practices (Maguire, 2000). The first is managerial control through the work organization: this form of control is based on the idea that exploitation is a basic necessity in the capitalist economy and the drive for exploitation has created organizational structures to control workers (Braverman, 1974). Taylorism and neo-Taylorism are considered the organizational approaches which extensively apply this form of control over employees (Pruijt, 2003). Furthermore, this form of control is today implemented by increased employee surveillance made possible by the development of information and communications technology, as extensively happens in call centres (Taylor *et al.*, 2002). The second form of managerial control is the so-called 'soft control', where control is internalized by employees and does not require any direct supervision/surveillance by management. An exemplary contribution about this form of control is the paper by Willmott (1993), in which the author shows how external control is internalized by employees through the managerial measures aimed at establishing a strong organizational culture. In sum, whereas the first form of managerial control focuses on objective and behavioural aspects of the work performance, soft control targets employee minds and subjectivities through norms, emotions, beliefs and values that affect behaviour indirectly (Alvesson and Willmott, 2002). GHRM has potential to relate to both forms of control, as we will argue in the following paragraphs.

First, GHRM makes use of the first form of managerial control by establishing procedures and tools intentionally and explicitly aimed at controlling employee green-related behaviours. Interesting examples of these tools are smart meters and in-car GPS[1] devices, which allow organizations to promote employees' energy conservation behaviours through individual feedback and incentives. At the same time, a long tradition of employment studies warns organizations on the possible downsides of potentially 'invasive' procedures, which might produce privacy concerns in the employee, thus resulting in negative psychological states (Moore, 2000; Smith and Tabak, 2009; Thompson *et al.*, 2009; Zweig and Webster, 2002). An interesting study on this is the one by Bolderdijk, Steg and Postmes (2013), which explores the effects of electronic monitoring on the energy consumption of employees. Their findings show that work-floor energy conservation policies which rely on electronic monitoring of individual behaviour actually result in employee concerns about their privacy. Interestingly, that concern is more likely when employees anticipate that electronic monitoring will lead to negative consequences for them personally and is less likely when employees anticipate possible benefits. Similar findings are available in the organization and management literature about a wide set of electronic monitoring devices in the field of environmental management (for example, Bedwell *et al.*, 2014; Horne *et al.*, 2015). As a result of these considerations, we highlight here that GHRM, even if aimed at improving the environmental performance of firms – which might be socially considered as a 'praiseworthy' organizational outcome – can be perceived by employees as an organizational system which applies to new aspects of organizational life and traditional forms of managerial control.

A second consideration concerns the possibility that GHRM might imply soft control. Indeed, GHRM is aimed at stimulating employees' environmental sensitiveness by 'instilling' the culture and values of environmental sustainability in personnel. Mainstream contributions often affirm that environmental sustainability is primarily a question of *shared* values in organizations (for example, Florea *et al.*, 2013; Paillé *et al.*, 2014; Sidiropoulos, 2014; Williams and Schaefer, 2013). However, there are control-related concerns here because critical scholars have repeatedly indicated HRM to be a means of symbolic power that, exercising control over employees' conscience and subjectivity, *imposes* shared values within organizations (Alvesson and Kärreman, 2007). Therefore, the attempt to create and develop a common green-related culture in an organization through communication, training, teambuilding and other GHRM tools could be interpreted as a form of soft control over employees (Forbes and Jermier, 2002; Howard-Grenville, 2006). In a recent paper, for example, Costas and Kärreman (2013) analyse two consulting firms committed to social and environmental responsibility, showing that certain practices help to construct an idealized image of an ethically and ecologically responsible corporate self, which ties employees' aspirational identities to the organization. In particular, they found that the interviewed consultants could be divided into three categories, namely those who support

CSR/environmental initiatives (the 'believers'), those who hold an ambivalent attitude (the 'straddlers'), and those who distance themselves from CSR/environmental initiatives (the 'cynics'). However, none of the categories of consultants could completely resist the aspirational control, as:

> straddlers feel ambivalent about the corporate manufactured nature of CSR programs but do not question the idealized CSR self and cynics are wrapped up in the spectacle of cynical distancing, simultaneously supporting the status quo while also enjoying the illusion of autonomy produced through their awareness of its various shortcomings.
>
> (p. 411)

The above reported case represents a key resource for contextualizing GHRM in relation to the control/commitment dichotomy. Indeed, it shows how GHRM can be used as a lever for promoting soft control over employees.

A final consideration regards an outcome explored in several recent studies in the GHRM field, which is the concept of organizational citizenship behaviour towards the environment (OCBE). This construct, defined as 'individual and discretionary social behaviours that are not explicitly recognized by the formal reward system and that contribute to a more effective environmental management by organizations' (Boiral 2009, p. 223), has been more and more used in GHRM research because it was demonstrated that employees engaging in voluntary actions which extend above and beyond job requirements contribute to a more effective environmental management (for example, Boiral, 2009) and improve environment-related organizational and individual performances (for example, Daily *et al.*, 2009). Therefore, several studies have recently empirically tested whether GHRM is associated with higher OCBE from employees, finding support for this prediction (for example, Paillé and Boiral, 2013; Pinzone *et al.*, 2016; Zibarras and Coan, 2015). However, even if not specifically targeting OCBE, an interesting stream of management research is today challenging the very idea of organizational citizenship behaviours (OCBs), showing how they are in many cases not performed voluntarily (Bolino *et al.*, 2013). Indeed, it often happens within organizations that, when OCBs are performed regularly over time, what was once considered beyond the scope of formal job requirements gradually become part of employees' regular or expected duties and simply viewed as in-role job performance (Van Dyne and Ellis, 2004). If so, the statistically significant relationships between GHRM and OCBEs tested in several recent studies create room for interpreting GHRM as a form of organizational control which is directed to broaden the scope of organizational expectations on employee behaviours.

Contextualization #2 – GHRM in the political arena

A second contextualization effort is aimed at recognizing the embeddedness of GHRM in the political and institutional context in which the firm is situated. The strong relations between HRM practices and the firm's external context have been already fully recognized by the International HRM research community, which typically situates the study of HRM within wider economic, organizational, political and institutional settings (for example, Delbridge *et al.*, 2011). As a result, this stream of studies, and in particular comparative International HRM, has demonstrated how different contexts lead companies to the implementation of different HRM practices (for example, Brewster and Meyrhofer, 2012). However, if compared to the 'traditional' stream of HRM research, which includes HRM in socio-political contexts, the contextualization of GHRM is more complicated, as is shown by the literature on political corporate social responsibility (CSR) and corporate political activity (CPA).

Indeed, these literatures have shown that: (1) many CSR activities, in which the organization provides community services traditionally regarded as a preserve of the state, have intended and unintended political impacts (which are at the core of the idea of 'political CSR', for example, Frynas and Stephens, 2015); and that (2) companies often implement CSR practices as tools of their political activities (den Hond *et al.*, 2014), therefore intending CSR as part of the attempts to shape government policy in ways favourable to the firm (Lawton *et al.*, 2013). In this perspective, environmental management in general (intended as a key component of the company's CSR strategy and activities), and GHRM in particular (intended as a key component of the company's environmental strategy and activities), cannot be seen as politically neutral systems, but as powerful political tools, which shape and are shaped by the political and institutional environment in which the company is embedded.

The critical management studies community has deeply explored the political connotation of these systems, highlighting how the growing orientation of corporations towards environmental sustainability can be conceived as a hegemonic move (Newton, 2009; Nyberg and Wright,

2013; Nyberg *et al.*, 2013; Tregidga *et al.*, 2014). A key concept here is that of 'appropriation', employed by critical researchers to point at ways in which objects, ideas, concepts, symbols and meanings which are originally part of another group are absorbed or assimilated by particular individuals, groups or organizations (Stokes, 2011). In particular, critical scholars have pointed out how corporations appropriated the idea of environmental sustainability developed by other social actors (such as NGOs, political organizations, and cultural associations) so that it today permeates most of the corporates' strategic statements and public communications (Jermier *et al.*, 2006). Appropriation is aimed at sterilizing critique of corporations and of the broader system in which they are embedded, and is considered to have two main consequences. First, as it is used by companies for absorbing critique and maintaining their business as usual, it implicitly reproduces an instrumental conception of environmentalism which, following the bottom line, reframes corporate sustainability as eco-efficiency and escapes any consideration of conflict and ethical concerns (Banerjee, 2001, 2011). In this perspective, another interesting concept is that of de-coupling, intended as the 'gaps between (organizations') formal structures and their ongoing activities' (Meyer and Rowan, 1977, p. 341). Indeed, firms which instrumentally appropriate the idea of sustainability are likely to commit to it, but not to modify their conduct; this often leads them to release information to confuse external stakeholders (Graffin *et al.*, 2011), or to avoid closely monitoring the effects of their sustainability practices (King and Lenox, 2000). The second consequence of the corporate appropriation of the idea of environmental sustainability is purely political. Indeed, by this appropriation, corporations explicitly deny any political dimensions of environmental sustainability and reduce it to a merely technical issue to be addressed by corporations (Crane *et al.*, 2008). As a result, companies today are engaged through voluntary initiatives in the preservation of a common good (i.e. the environment), but at the same time continue to exercise political pressure for affecting regulatory changes in relation to environmental issues (Child and Tsai 2005; den Hond *et al.*, 2014). Therefore, there is the concrete possibility that companies take advantage of their voluntary efforts in regard to environmental sustainability for reducing the pressure of environmental regulation.

The debate on climate change in Australia recently reported by Nyberg and colleagues (2013) represents an interesting example of this. Australian companies have indeed tried to influence the debate on climate change and to orient the environment regulatory policies of the Australian state using two different strategies. First, companies opposed the political proposals of strict environmental regulations by undertaking traditional activities which can be intended as forms of CPA, such as, for example, 'corporate campaigning'. Specifically, companies set out their formal opposition to the proposed regulation, stressing its negative impacts on the broader national economy; lobby the government and involved ministers to influence their choices towards accommodating regulatory outcomes; and promote public campaigns using advertising activities to convince public opinion of the threats to jobs of the proposed regulation. Interestingly, this activity of 'campaigning' goes together with a more innovative set of actions, called by the authors 'exemplifying'. Through this set of actions, companies promoted themselves as responsible citizens who care about the environment and put in place voluntary initiatives able to make a real difference in regard to the environment. This set of activities included, for example, showing the implementation of progressive environmental management systems, partnering with green-concerned NGOs, adopting international standards for monitoring and disclosing their environmental performance. Therefore, companies on the one hand adopted the traditional measures for accommodating a favourable environmental regulation and, at the same time, expanded their consensus among Australian citizens, showing how much they care about the environment. This is not an isolated case, as Chatterij and Listokin (2007) derived similar conclusions in the study of voluntary reporting initiatives: companies tried to take advantage of their adoption of the UN Global Compact guidelines in order to avoid the political attempts to extend mandatory reporting.

In sum, we argue that GHRM – as a component of the company environmental system and as a key antecedent of firms' environmental performance – is not a politically neutral management system, but it is exposed to risks associated with its strategic use by companies in the political environment. For those involved in the field, therefore, it is important to be aware of the non-eliminable political dimension of GHRM. This warning is timely today, when the broad field of HRM research seems to be often unaware of its political connotations. Indeed, some authors have expressed concern about that. Recently, Thompson (2011) and Godard (2014), for example, put forward a harsh critique of the predominance in the HRM field of empirical studies placed at the individual level, as the prevalence of organizational behaviour theories and approaches downplays the possibility of developing critical and contextual visions of HRM. Similarly, Watson (2010) considers the inclusion of the broader social and institutional context a distinguishing aspect of a social science approach to HRM, whereas Delbridge and Keenoy (2010) affirm that 'contextualizing the practices of HRM within the prevailing socio-economic order of capitalism and its associated discourse of market individualism' (p. 807) represents the first point of a critical HRM research agenda.

Given these considerations, it seems urgent that there is reflection inside the community of GHRM scholars and, more generally, of those interested in studying employment relations about the political and contextual positioning of GHRM. This contextualization might cover, for example, issues related to how GHRM is linked to different social, economic, cultural and institutional environments; how it is linked with the existing socio-economic order and how it relates to the natural environment; and who is actually benefitting from the introduction of GHRM policies and practices in organizations.

Contextualization #3 – GHRM in the ethics debate

As recognized by Greenwood (2013), HRM research has started to consider the ethical component of managing people in organizations relatively late, as the first contributions aimed at an ethical analysis of HRM appeared in the late 1990s (for example, Legge, 1998; Winstanley *et al.*, 1996). Those seminal contributions generated a set of more specific contributions in the late 2000s (for example, Deckop *et al.*, 2006; Pinnington *et al.*, 2007) and the literature which explores HRM from an ethical perspective is today growing, as witnessed for example by a special issue of *Journal of Business Ethics* published in 2012 followed by several contributions recently published in ethics-related journals (for example, Marshall *et al.*, 2015; Zhang *et al.*, 2015). As a result of this growing interest in the intersections between HRM and ethics, HRM practices are today under ethical scrutiny, even though this ethical analysis of HRM can be based on a wide set of possible ethical assumptions (Jack *et al.*, 2012). Recognizing the plurality of the possible research approaches integrating HRM and ethics, Greenwood (2013) has proposed the idea of 'ethical HRM' research which, according to the author, is different from 'mainstream HRM' because of its focus on what is wrong/bad and right/good (mainstream HRM being focused on what is effective/not effective); and which is different from 'critical HRM', the latter being based on the idea of HRM as a control device, whereas ethical HRM is based on the idea that HRM is a moral activity with potential to enhance quality of life.

Although the interest in the ethical dimension of HRM is growing over time, contributions on the ethical aspects of GHRM are not (yet) available. Pragmatically, the contributions and insights provided by available business ethics literature on general HRM could be applied to GHRM. However, the intersection between GHRM and ethics is more complex because, as the literature is highlighting how HRM is ethically insidious, ethics-centred literature on environmental management is also showing several ethical traps. Therefore, an ethical analysis of GHRM can be difficult, as it should merge the ethical risks associated with HRM with the ethical risks associated with environmental management.

Indeed, a long-standing stream of research called environmental ethics has addressed the relation between humans and the natural environment, extending the anthropocentric view of ethics by providing moral standing to non-human entities also, including animals, plants and ecosystems (for example, Leopold, 1949). Today, business ethics is extending the focus of environmental ethics, introducing the broader idea of ethics of sustainability (for example, Becker, 2012; Florea *et al.*, 2013; Kilbert *et al.*, 2012). In this perspective, the firms' environmental responsibility towards the environment is conceived as part of a broad set of responsibilities the firms have towards a wide set of actors. As a consequence, ethics contributions point out the need (and the challenge) to simultaneously address 'the three justice dimensions of sustainability: intragenerational justice, intergenerational justice, and justice towards nature' (Stumpf *et al.*, 2015, p. 7444). Available literature, however, highlights several concerns about the predominance of the specific dimension of sustainability over the others, for example when environmentalism dominates *any* ethical concern of the organization (so-called 'Eco fascism', see Jermier and Forbes, 2016). Therefore, simultaneously dealing with those different moral obligations is recognized as a challenge for many business organizations, as trade-offs between them are likely to happen (Hahn *et al.*, 2010, 2016).

Those trade-offs are also likely to emerge in GHRM when it comes to balancing environmental performances with other organizational performances, as evidenced by the broader sustainability ethics perspective. Kramar (2014), Ehnert (2009), and Taylor, Osland and Egri (2012), for example, include GHRM among the various attempts to reform strategic HRM, and under the more general approach of sustainable HRM intended as a broad HRM approach aimed at simultaneously preserving, regenerating and developing the economic, environmental and social performance of the firm. Actually, potential trade-offs between social and environmental sustainability may be particularly problematic in an area such as HRM, which should have employee advocacy (and thus social sustainability) among its main objectives (Ulrich, 1997). This possibility has been acknowledged by Jackson, who called for a 'problem-focused agenda for research on workforce management and environmental sustainability' in order to recognize that 'HRM practitioners negotiate solutions that optimize results against multiple and sometime conflicting goals' (2012, p. 420).

An interesting case here is reported in a recent research work (Guerci and Carollo, 2016) in which the authors show how GHRM brings several tensions to the organization, deriving from the multiple dimensions of sustainability. Specifically, the authors found that orienting the HRM system of a firm towards environmental goals along with economic and social goals brings tensions into the organization. Indeed, fostering environmental plans might increase the possibility of financial shortages and thus be detrimental to other plans, for example those aimed at improving current employees' working lives. For example, in one of the companies under study, an open conflict emerged between environmental, social and financial sustainability. The company, active in the pharmaceutical industry, was investing in environmental sustainability (for example, internally promoting training in order to improve employee green behaviours) and at the same time laying-off a significant part of the marketing department of their headquarters. The co-existence of those choices raised protests from the workforce, so that the employees supported by their unions decided to make the case public through national newspapers. The outcome of that 'disclosure' was public concern about the ethics of the company, which resulted in strong political pressures from different actors as well as reputational costs for the organization. It is important to notice that the company did not face similar problems in other (even more radical) downsizing processes implemented in previous years, when the company reduced its workforce without, at the same time, investing in environmental management. That is a clue to how, in that case, several actors perceived that there was a clash between using the HRM system for pursuing economic and environmental objectives and social objectives (i.e. avoiding downsizing). Moreover, in general, the reported experience confirms that trade-offs among social, environmental and economic performances could affect the GHRM field.

In light of the above reported arguments and cases, it seems important to foster a reflection within HRM research and practice about the ethical contextualization of GHRM. This ethical contextualization might cover, for example, the risk of a 'primacy' of certain moral responsibilities over others (for example, the responsibility toward the natural environment over the responsibility toward current and future employees).

Implications and conclusions

The three issues discussed in this chapter present significant implications for researchers, practitioners and educators addressing GHRM. First, in terms of HRM research, we highlight the need for research designs that focus on GHRM while not overlooking relevant contextual variables. Specifically, we argue that a contextualized view of GHRM should adopt multi-level frameworks, which consider at the same time relevant individual, organizational, and societal variables. Indeed, we argue that GHRM research could provide practically relevant and theoretically insightful knowledge accounting for (1) the broad dynamics in which GHRM is embedded, which contribute to shape GHRM practices within business organizations; and (2) the intended and unintended (as well as short- and long-term) outcomes of GHRM practices at the three cited levels of analysis. We argue that this kind of GHRM research would not expose the field to the strong criticisms which have been recently put forward regarding the a-contextualized view of organizational practices adopted by extant HRM research (for example, Kaufman, 2015). In terms of HRM practice, the present contribution recommends organizational practitioners to develop a critical view of GHRM, refusing naïve views of the phenomenon. Indeed, given the diffuse social concern about environmental protection, the risk that GHRM could be interpreted by practitioners as a set of practices which are value-laden per se is rather concrete. On the contrary, we have shown here that – even if targeting a commendable outcome – GHRM practices are not free from negative consequences, which might concern its control orientation over employees, its 'use' for political reasons by the company, or conflicts between its inherent ethical dimensions. This consideration leads to our last set of implications, which regard HRM educators. In order to preserve future practitioners from an uncritical adoption of prescriptive and superficial approaches to GHRM, HRM education should deal with GHRM, contextualizing it within broad societal issues; that should result in the preparation of future HR managers sensitive to context, power and inequality and familiar with reflexive-critical thinking, as proposed by the theorists of critical HRM education (for example, Bratton and Gold, 2015; Van Buren III and Greenwood, 2013).

In conclusion, in this chapter we have made a first attempt at contextualizing GHRM in its ethical and political contexts, specifically addressing three key issues, namely how GHRM balances control and commitment, addresses its political meanings, and develops its ethical assumptions. Notably, this effort has been based on the integration of the literature about GHRM with three other streams of HRM literature, namely critical HRM (for example, Delbridge and Keenoy, 2010), ethical HRM (for example, Greenwood, 2013), and sustainable HRM (for example, Taylor *et al.*, 2012). Assuming that the relevance gap which often characterizes HRM research could be addressed by merging together streams of HRM research (Yeung, 2011), we conclude this chapter advancing the need for HRM contributions which integrate green, critical, ethical and sustainable HRM research, aspects which, even if dealing with similar issues, too often appear barely connected.

Note

1 Abbreviation for 'global positioning system', where signals are sent from satellites to a special device used to track the position of people/things on the Earth's surface accurately. Retrieved from: www.oxfordlearnersdictionaries.com/definition/english/gps?q=gps.

References

Alvesson, M., and Kärreman, D. (2007) 'Unravelling HRM: Identity, ceremony, and control in a management consulting firm', *Organization Science*, vol. 18, no. 4, pp. 711–723.

Alvesson, M., and Willmott, H. (2002) 'Identity regulation as organizational control: Producing the appropriate individual', *Journal of Management Studies*, vol. 39, no. 5, pp. 619–44.

Argyris, C. (1957). *Personality and the organization: The conflict between the system and the individual.* New York: Harper.

Banerjee, S. B. (2001) 'Managerial perceptions of corporate environmentalism: Interpretations from industry and strategic implications for organizations', *Journal of Management Studies*, vol. 38, no. 4, pp. 489–513.

Banerjee, S. B. (2011) 'Embedding sustainability across the organization: A critical perspective', *Academy of Management Learning & Education*, vol. 10, no. 4, pp. 719–731.

Becker, C. U. (2012) 'The challenges of sustainability ethics'. In C. U. Becker. *Sustainability ethics and sustainability research*, pp. 33–34. Utrecht: Springer,

Bedwell, B., Leygue, C., Goulden, M., McAuley, D., Colley, J., Ferguson, E., *et al.* (2014) 'Apportioning energy consumption in the workplace: A review of issues in using metering data to motivate staff to save energy', *Technology Analysis & Strategic Management*, vol. 26, no. 10, pp. 1196–1211.

Boiral, O. (2009) 'Greening the corporation through organizational citizenship behaviors', *Journal of Business Ethics*, vol. 87, no. 2, pp. 221–236.

Bolderdijk, J. W., Steg, L., and Postmes, T. (2013) 'Fostering support for work floor energy conservation policies: Accounting for privacy concerns', *Journal of Organizational Behavior*, vol. 34, no. 2, pp. 195–210.

Bolino, M. C., Klotz, A. C., Turnley, W. H., and Harvey, J. (2013) 'Exploring the dark side of organizational citizenship behavior', *Journal of Organizational Behavior*, vol. 34, no. 4, pp. 542–559.

Bratton, J., and Gold, J. (2015) 'Towards critical human resource management education (CHRME): A sociological imagination approach', *Work, Employment & Society*, vol. 29, no. 3, pp. 496–507.

Braverman, H. (1974). *Labor and monopoly capital: The degradation of work in the twentieth century*. New York: Monthly Review Press.

Brewster, C., and Mayrhofer, W. (Eds). (2012). *Handbook of research on comparative human resource management*. Cheltenham, UK: Edward Elgar Publishing.

Chatterji, A., and Listokin, S. (2007) 'Corporate social irresponsibility', *Democracy*, vol. 3, no. 52.

Child, J., and Tsai, T. (2005) 'The dynamic between firms' environmental strategies and institutional constraints in emerging economies: Evidence from China and Taiwan', *Journal of Management Studies*, vol. 42, no. 1, pp. 95–125.

Costas, J., and Kärreman, D. (2013) 'Conscience as control–managing employees through CSR', *Organization*, vol. 20, no. 3, pp. 394–415.

Crane, A. (2000) 'Corporate greening as amoralization', *Organization Studies*, vol. 21, no. 4, pp. 673–696.

Crane, A., Matten, D., and Moon, J. (2008) 'Ecological citizenship and the corporation: Politicizing the new corporate environmentalism', *Organization & Environment*, vol. 21, no. 4, pp. 371–389.

Daily, B. F., Bishop, J. W., and Govindarajulu, N. (2009) 'A conceptual model for organizational citizenship behavior directed toward the environment', *Business & Society*, vol. 48, no. 2, pp. 243–256.

Deckop, J., Giacalone, R., and Jurkiewicz, C. L. (2006). *Human resource management ethics*. Greenwich, CT: Information Age Publishing.

Delbridge, R., and Keenoy, T. (2010) 'Beyond managerialism?', *The International Journal of Human Resource Management*, vol. 21, no. 6, pp. 799–817.

Delbridge, R., Hauptmeier, M., and Sengupta, S. (2011) 'Beyond the enterprise: Broadening the horizons of international HRM', *Human Relations*, vol. 64, no. 4, pp. 483–505.

den Hond, F., Rehbein, K. A., de Bakker, F., and Kooijmans-van Lankveld, H. (2014) 'Playing on two chessboards', *Journal of Management Studies*, vol. 51, no. 5, pp. 790–813.

Ehnert, I. (2009). *Sustainable human resource management. A conceptual and exploratory analysis from a paradox perspective*. Heidelberg: Springer.

Fayol, H. (1949). *General and industrial management*. London: Pittman.

Florea, L., Cheung, Y. H., and Herndon, N. C. (2013) 'For all good reasons: Role of values in organizational sustainability', *Journal of Business Ethics*, vol. 114, no. 3, pp. 393–408.

Forbes, L. C., and Jermier, M. C. (2002) 'The institutionalization of voluntary organizational greening and the ideals of environmentalism: Lessons about official culture from symbolic organization theory'. In A. J. Hoffman and M. J. Ventresca (Eds). *Organizations, policy and the natural environment*, pp. 194–213. Stanford, CA: Stanford University Press.

Frynas, J. G., and Stephens, S. (2015) 'Political corporate social responsibility: Reviewing theories and setting new agendas', *International Journal of Management Reviews*, vol. 17, no. 4, pp. 483–509.

George, G., Schillebeeckx, S. J., and Liak, T. L. (2015) 'The management of natural resources: An overview and research agenda', *Academy of Management Journal*, vol. 58, no. 6, pp. 1595–1613.

Godard, J. (2014) 'The psychologisation of employment relations', *Human Resource Management Journal*, vol. 24, no. 1, pp. 1–18.

Graffin, S. D., Carpenter, M. A., and Boivie, S. (2011) 'What's all that (strategic) noise? Anticipatory impression management in CEO succession', *Strategic Management Journal*, vol. 32, pp. 748–770.

Greenwood, M. (2013) 'Ethical analyses of HRM: A review and research agenda', *Journal of Business Ethics*, vol. 114, no. 2, pp. 355–366.

Guerci, M., and Carollo, L. (2016) 'A paradox view on green human resource management: Insights from the Italian context', *The International Journal of Human Resource Management*, vol. 27, no. 2, pp. 212–238.

Hahn, T., Figge, F., Pinkse, J., and Preuss, L. (2010) 'Trade-offs in corporate sustainability: You can't have your cake and eat it', *Business Strategy and the Environment*, vol. 19, no. 4, pp. 217–229.

Hahn, T., Pinkse, J., Preuss, L., and Figge, F. (2016) 'Ambidexterity for corporate social performance'. *Organization Studies*, vol. 37, no. 2, pp. 213–235.

Horne, C., Darras, B., Bean, E., Srivastava, A., and Frickel, S. (2015) 'Privacy, technology, and norms: The case of Smart Meters', *Social science research*, vol. 51, pp. 64–76.

Howard-Grenville, J. A. (2006) 'Inside the "black box": How organizational culture and subcultures inform interpretations and actions on environmental issues', *Organization & Environment*, vol. 19, no. 1, pp. 46–73.

Hyman, R. (1987) 'Strategy or structure? Capital, labour and control', *Work, Employment & Society*, vol. 1, no. 1, pp. 25–55.

Jack, G., Greenwood, M., and Schapper, J. (2012) 'Frontiers, intersections and engagements of ethics and HRM', *Journal of Business Ethics*, vol. 111, no. 1, pp. 1–12.

Jackson, S. E. (2012) 'Building empirical foundations to inform the future practice of environmental sustainability'. In S. E. Jackson, D. S. Ones, and S. Dilchert (Eds). *Managing human resources for environmental sustainability*, pp. 416–432. New Jersey: Jossey-Bass.

Jackson, S. E., Schuler, R. S., and Jiang, K. (2014) 'An aspirational framework for strategic human resource management', *The Academy of Management Annals*, vol. 8, no. 1, pp. 1–56.

Jermier, J. M., and Forbes, L. C. (2016) 'Metaphors, organizations and water: Generating new images for environmental sustainability', *Human Relations*, vol. 69, no. 4, pp. 1001–1027.

Jermier, J. M., Forbes, L. C., Benn, S., and Orsato, R. J. (2006) 'The new corporate environmentalism and green politics'. In S. Clegg, C. Hardy, T. Lawrence, and W. R. Nord (Eds). *The SAGE handbook of organization studies*, pp. 618–650. London: Sage.

Kaufman, B. E. (2014) 'The historical development of American HRM broadly viewed', *Human Resource Management Review*, vol. 24, no. 3, pp. 196–218.

Kaufman, B. E. (2015) 'Evolution of strategic HRM as seen through two founding books: A 30th anniversary perspective on development of the field', *Human Resource Management*, vol. 54, no. 3, pp. 389–407.

Keenoy T. (2009) 'Human Resource Management'. In M. Alvesson, T. Bridgman, and H. Willmott (Eds). *The Oxford handbook of critical management studies*, pp. 454–472. Oxford: Oxford University Press.

Kilbert, C. J., Monroe, M. C., Peterson, A. L., Plate, R., and Thiele, L. P. (2012) *Working toward sustainability: Ethical decision-making in a technological world*. Chichester, UK : John Wiley.

King, A. A., and Lenox, M. J. (2000) 'Industry self-regulation without sanctions: The chemical industry's responsible care program', *Academy of Management Journal*, vol. 43, pp. 698–716.

Kramar, R. (2014) 'Beyond strategic human resource management: Is sustainable human resource management the next approach?', *International Journal of Human Resource Management*, vol. 25, no. 8, pp. 1069–1089.

Lawton, T., McGuire, S., and Rajwani, T. (2013) 'Corporate political activity: A literature review and research agenda', *International Journal of Management Reviews*, vol. 15, no. 1, pp. 86–105.

Legge, K. (1998) 'Is HRM ethical? Can HRM be ethical?' In M. Parker (Ed.). *Ethics and organization*, pp. 150–172. London: Sage.

Leopold, A. (1949). *A Sand County almanac*. Oxford: Oxford University Press.

Lubin, D. A., and Esty, D. C. (2010) 'The sustainability imperative', *Harvard Business Review*, vol. 88, no. 5, pp. 42–50.

Maguire, S. (2000) 'The discourse of control'. In P. Tittle (Ed.). *Ethical issues in business: Inquiries, cases, and readings,* pp. 216–224. Peterborough, ON: Broadview Press.

Marshall, A. J., Ashleigh, M. J., Baden, D., Ojiako, U., and Guidi, M. G. (2015) 'Corporate psychopathy: Can "search and destroy" and "hearts and minds" military metaphors inspire HRM solutions?', *Journal of Business Ethics*, vol. 128, no. 3, pp. 495–504.

Mayo, E. (1933). *The human problems of an industrial civilization*. New York: Macmillan.

McGregor, D. (1960). *The human side of enterprise*. New York: McGraw-Hill.

Meyer, J. W., and Rowan, B. (1977) 'Institutionalized organizations: Formal structure as myth and ceremony', *American Journal of Sociology*, vol. 83, no. 2, pp. 340–363.

Moore, A. (2000) 'Employee monitoring and computer technology: Evaluative surveillance v. privacy', *Business Ethics Quarterly*, vol. 10, pp. 697–709.

Newton, T. J. (2009) 'Organisations and the natural environment'. In M. Alvesson, T. Bridgman, and H. Willmott, *The Oxford handbook of critical management studies*, pp. 125–143. Oxford: Oxford University Press.

Nyberg, D., and Wright, C. (2013) 'Corporate corruption of the environment: Sustainability as a process of compromise', *The British Journal of Sociology*, vol. 64, no. 3, pp. 405–424.

Nyberg, D., Spicer, A., and Wright, C. (2013) 'Incorporating citizens: Corporate political engagement with climate change in Australia', *Organization*, vol. 20, no. 3, pp. 433–453.

Paillé, P., and Boiral, O. (2013) 'Pro-environmental behavior at work: Construct validity and determinants', *Journal of Environmental Psychology*, vol. 36, pp. 118–128.

Paillé, P., Chen, Y., Boiral, O., and Jin, J. (2014) 'The impact of human resource management on environmental performance: An employee-level study', *Journal of Business Ethics*, vol. 121, no. 3, pp. 451–466.

Pfeffer, J. (2010) 'Building sustainable organizations: The human factor', *The Academy of Management Perspectives*, vol. 24, no. 1, pp. 34–45.

Pinnington, A., Macklin, R., and Campbell, T. (2007). *Human resource management: Ethics and employment*. Oxford: Oxford University Press.

Pinzone, M., Guerci, M., Lettieri, E., and Redman, T. (2016) 'Progressing in the change journey towards sustainability in healthcare: The role of "Green" HRM', *Journal of Cleaner Production*, vol. 122, pp. 201–211.

Pruijt, H. (2003) 'Teams between neo-Taylorism and anti-Taylorism', *Economic and Industrial Democracy*, vol. 24, no. 1, pp. 77–101.

Renwick, D. W., Redman, T., and Maguire, S. (2013) 'Green human resource management: A review and research agenda', *International Journal of Management Reviews*, vol. 15, no. 1, pp. 1–14.

Sidiropoulos E. (2014) 'Education for sustainability in business education programs: A question of value', *Journal of Cleaner Production*, vol. 85, pp. 472–487.

Smith, W. P., and Tabak, F. (2009) 'Monitoring employee e-mails: Is there any room for privacy?', *Academy of Management Perspectives*, vol. 23, pp. 33–48.

Society for Human Resource Management (2012). *HRM's role in corporate social and environmental sustainability*. Alexandria: SHRM. Available at: www.shrm.org/about/foundation/products/pages/sustainabilitypg.aspx.

Special Eurobarometer 416/Wave EB81.3 (2014) *TNS Opinion & Social*; http://ec.europa.eu/public_opinion/archives/ebs/ebs_416_en.pdf.

Stokes, P. (2011). *Critical concepts in management and organization studies: Key terms and concepts*. Basingstoke, UK: Palgrave Macmillan.

Stumpf, K. H., Baumgärtner, S., Becker, C. U., and Sievers-Glotzbach, S. (2015) 'The justice dimension of sustainability: A systematic and general conceptual framework', *Sustainability*, vol. 7, no. 6, pp. 7438–7472.

Taylor, F. W. (1903). *Shop management*. New York: Harper.

Taylor, P., Mulvey, G., Hyman, J., and Bain, P. (2002) 'Work organization, control and experience of work in call centres', *Work, Employment & Society*, vol. 16, no. 1, pp. 133–150.

Taylor, S., Osland, J., and Egri, C. P. (2012) 'Guest editors' introduction: Introduction to HRM's role in sustainability: Systems, strategies, and practices', *Human Resource Management*, vol. 51, no. 6, pp. 789–798.

Thompson, L. F., Sebastianelli, J. D., and Murray, N. P. (2009) 'Monitoring online training behaviors: Awareness of electronic surveillance hinders e-learners', *Journal of Applied Social Psychology*, vol. 39, pp. 2191–2212.

Thompson, P. (2011) 'The trouble with HRM', *Human Resource Management Journal*, vol. 21, no. 4, pp. 355–367.

Thompson, P., and Van den Broek, D. (2010) 'Managerial control and workplace regimes: An introduction', *Work, Employment & Society*, vol. 24, no. 3, pp. 1–12.

Tregidga, H., Milne, M., and Kearins, K. (2014) '(Re)presenting "sustainable organizations"', *Accounting, Organizations and Society*, vol. 39, no. 6, pp. 477–494.

Ulrich, D. (1997) *Human resource champions: The next agenda for adding value and delivering results.* Cambridge, MA: Harvard Business School Press.

Vagliasindi, G. M. (2015) 'Effective networking, formal versus substantial compliance, conflicting powers'. In M., Faure, P. De Smedt, and A. Stas (Eds). *Environmental enforcement networks: Concepts, implementation and effectiveness*, pp. 430–452. Cheltenham, UK: Edward Elgar Publishing.

Van Buren III, H. J., and Greenwood, M. (2013) 'Ethics and HRM education', *Journal of Academic Ethics*, vol. 11, no. 1, pp. 1–15.

Van Dyne, L., and Ellis, J. B. (2004) 'Job creep: A reactance theory perspective on organizational citizenship behavior as overfulfillment of obligations'. In J. A. M. Coyle-Shapiro, L. M. Shore, M. S. Taylor, and L. E. Tetrick (Eds). *The employment relationship: Examining psychological and contextual perspectives*, pp. 181–205. Oxford: Oxford University Press.

Watson, T. J. (2010) 'Critical social science, pragmatism and the realities of HRM', *The International Journal of Human Resource Management*, vol. 21, no. 6, pp. 915–931.

Williams, S., and Schaefer, A. (2013) 'Small and medium-sized enterprises and sustainability: Managers' values and engagement with environmental and climate change issues', *Business Strategy and the Environment*, vol. 22, no. 3, pp. 173–186.

Willmott, H. (1993) 'Strength is ignorance, slavery is freedom: Managing culture in modern organisations', *Journal of Management Studies*, vol. 30, no. 4, pp. 515–552.

Winstanley, D., Woodall, J., and Heery, E. (1996) 'The agenda for ethics in human resource management', *Business Ethics: A European Review*, vol. 5, no. 4, pp. 187–194.

Yeung, A. (2011) 'Celebrating 50 years: How robust and relevant is our HR knowledge?', *Human Resource Management*, vol. 50, no. 4, pp. 451–453.

Zhang, M. M., Bartram, T., McNeil, N., and Dowling, P. J. (2015) 'Towards a research agenda on the sustainable and socially responsible management of agency workers through a flexicurity model of HRM', *Journal of Business Ethics*, vol. 127, no. 3, pp. 513–523.

Zibarras, L. D., and Coan, P. (2015) 'HRM practices used to promote pro-environmental behaviour: A UK survey', *The International Journal of Human Resource Management*, vol. 26, no. 16, pp. 2121–2142.

Zweig, D., and Webster, J. (2002) 'Where is the line between benign and invasive? An examination of psychological barriers to the acceptance of awareness monitoring systems', *Journal of Organizational Behavior*, vol. 23, pp. 605–633.

7 Competing paradigms

Status quo and alternative approaches in HRM

*Brian Matthews, Lisa Obereder, Ina Aust
(was Ehnert) and Michael Müller-Camen*

Introduction

This chapter discusses the status quo paradigm in human resources management (HRM) and alternative approaches. Although the paradigm currently dominating HRM and performance has existed for several decades, it often fails in terms of sustainability aspects. Tackling environmental and social sustainability issues is one of the most important challenges facing humanity on an international scale and should therefore also be a priority for organisations and in particular their HR departments. If organisations want to survive in the long run and contribute to a sustainable environment, it is time for HRM to critically reflect on its current goals within and outside of an organisation. The dominating HRM paradigm – whether in its shareholder ('hard' HRM) or stakeholder-oriented ('soft' HRM) version – primarily aims at organisational performance in such forms as productivity and efficiency increases. In this chapter, we will outline the status quo of the HRM–performance debate; in the next section, we focus on the downsides of the dominating paradigm. We will further discuss whether the paradigm shift to a new sustainability paradigm in HRM will actually take place, as well as possible conflicts between prior and new paradigms.

The dominating HRM paradigm: the purpose of HRM is to increase financial performance

One of the major shifts in HRM paradigms was the development from an administrative-oriented understanding of people management as 'personnel management' to a strategic understanding of people management as 'human resource management (HRM)' (Guest, 1987; Kaufman, 2001). While 'personnel management' primarily emphasised the administrative role and personnel processes (such as compliance with legal labour market requirements), the strategic orientation of HRM recognised the value of employees as important resources for organisations (Beardwell *et al.*, 2004; Liu *et al.*, 2007; Van Buren *et al.*, 2011). This turning point was supported by two HRM models developed in the early 1980s known as the Harvard model (Beer *et al.*, 1984) and the Michigan model (Fombrun *et al.*, 1984). These now classic models both consider cost-effective HRM as a key to organisational success and survival (Beer *et al.*, 2015). The main differences between these models (Harvard vs. Michigan) are (1) a multi-stakeholder perspective vs a shareholder perspective, (2) a social systems perspective vs an individual perspective, (3) individual wellbeing, organisational effectiveness, societal wellbeing as outcomes ('soft' HRM approach) vs outcomes in relation to shareholders ('hard' HRM approach), and (4) different kinds of antecedents (Beer *et al.*, 2015).

Both models, Harvard and Michigan, shaped theoretical developments in HRM considerably (Ehnert, 2009). For example, the question of whether HRM should be 'soft' or 'hard' (Truss *et al.*, 1997) or both (Legge, 2005) was debated frequently. While 'hard' approaches traditionally understood HRM as a function to contribute to organisational performance objectives, 'soft' approaches interpret HRM as a function to compensate negative externalities from corporate business activities. The underlying competing rationalities of 'developmental humanism' vs 'utilitarian instrumentalism' (Hendry and Pettigrew, 1990) show an important area of paradoxical tensions in which HRM practitioners need to operate on a daily basis (Ehnert, 2009). HR practitioners find themselves trapped between competing objectives which cannot easily be combined, especially if investments in HRM activities, which do not directly contribute to better financial performance or employee wellbeing, are considered to be economic disadvantages in a competitive global market.

Although the Harvard model considered long-term consequences of HRM activities and a multi-stakeholder perspective, the main focus in HRM research in the last 30 years was on how organisational performance can be increased (Kaufman, 2015) – where performance was primarily interpreted as financial performance (Boselie *et al.*, 2005). In other words, for decades the debates of Strategic HRM scholars circled around the question of how decisions in HRM can positively influence shareholder value (Beer *et al.*, 2015). Research on the HRM–performance link (e.g. Becker and Gerhart, 1996; Boxall and Purcell, 2011; Delaney and Huselid, 1996; Delery and Shaw, 2001) has become the 'holy grail' of HRM and the assumption that the purpose of HRM is mainly to support the business strategy has been the dominant paradigm in HRM

(Greenwood, 2002). Four different modes of theorising in Strategic HRM research have formed our understanding of the HRM–performance link: the universalistic, contingency, configurational and contextual approaches (Martín-Alcázar *et al.*, 2005). First, the universalistic or 'best practice' approach assumes that best single or sets of HR practices contribute directly to better firm performance (Becker and Gerhart, 1996; Pfeffer, 1994). Second, the contingency or 'best fit' approach denies best practices and suggests that contingency variables moderate the link between HRM and performance (Delery and Doty, 1996). The Michigan model is one of the early fit models promoting the idea that a tight fit or alignment between strategy, structure and HRM policies increases organisational efficiency and effectiveness (Wright and McMahan, 1992). Later research identified several relevant types of 'fit' (Wood, 1999) but there has also been much criticism, for example, regarding the approach's 'strategic determinism' (Brewster and Hegewisch, 1994). Third, the configurational or 'best bundles' approach focuses on identifying HRM patterns or systems which influence organisational performance, assuming that these HRM systems should be both internally coherent and consistent with the external environment of an organisation (Martín-Alcázar *et al.*, 2005). Research on the HRM–performance link from universalistic, contingency and configurational approaches primarily seeks explanations of how, why and under what conditions investments in HRM influence business performance (Ferris *et al.*, 1999). First and foremost, the dependent variables and outcomes of these studies are financial indicators, such as stock performance, share price, return on investment or return on assets (Beer *et al.*, 2015). Assessing wider environmental or societal impact is not part of these approaches to theorising on HRM. However, the fourth approach to theorising on HRM, the contextual approach, considers both internal facets of HRM and its cultural, social, institutional, political, competitive, etc. context (Brewster, 1999; Paauwe, 2004). The contextual approach to HRM has therefore paved the way for exploring the impact of HR strategies on an organisation's external environments; however, a relatively small number of HRM scholars use it.

The dominant approaches used for theorising on the HRM–performance link, also influence HRM metrics used to measure success in HRM. In the universalistic approach, the use of 'natural, meaningful metrics' (Becker and Gerhart, 1996, p. 791) is not surprising, since they emphasise outcomes for shareholders in the concept of performance and underline the strategic position of HRM (Paauwe and Boselie, 2005). The interest in developing HRM metrics that assess the value of HRM investments is based in particular on human capital theory. This theory views employees as a form of capital, arguing that costs for workforce training and development constitute an investment when linked to a corresponding increase in productivity (Becker *et al.*, 1998). While universalist scholars assume that the relationship between HRM practices and performance outcomes is linear, scholars from the other three approaches have challenged the idea of a direct causal relationship between HRM practices and organisational financial success. Contingency studies have included strategic variables (fit between HR and corporate strategy), organisational variables (e.g. size, technology, structure) and environmental factors (e.g. competitive, technological, labour market context) (e.g. Jackson and Schuler, 1995). Dominant theoretical perspectives have been behavioural theories, the Resource Based View and the Capabilities Based View (Martín-Alcázar *et al.*, 2005).

Configurational studies also challenged linear relationships between HRM–performance and attempted to open the 'black box' of universalistic and contingency models by explaining the internal dynamics of the HRM function. For example, Ability–Motivation–Opportunity (AMO) theory has supported an indirect relationship between HR practices and performance via employees (Kaufman, 2015). According to this theory, performance is a function of ability, motivation and opportunity (e.g. Paauwe, 2009). Specific HRM systems, also called high-performance work systems, influence the ability and motivation of employees, which then contribute to organisational performance (Appelbaum *et al.*, 2000). Particularly in the US, larger corporations have used high-performance HRM practices such as job redesign, improved training opportunities and employee participation schemes to increase global business competitiveness (Delaney and Huselid, 1996). On the one hand, this competiveness comprises the generation of high value within the organisation and, on the other hand, the protection of this asset by creating attributes that are hard to copy (Huselid, 1995; Kaufman, 2015). The contextual approach has been an important extension of Strategic HRM theorising, with the objective of understanding the influence of HRM on the external context (Brewster, 1999), for example by including variables that the other approaches have neglected, such as the influence of public administration or trade unions and by considering a multi-stakeholder approach (Martín-Alcázar *et al.*, 2005). This links the contextual approach to the early Harvard model.

In recent years, scholars following a contextual approach have highlighted limitations of the dominant HRM paradigm that the most important purpose of HRM is to increase financial performance. For example, Boxall and Purcell (2011) have integrated social legitimacy as an important strategic goal for HRM in their theorising, as the viability of companies focusing on profit only cannot be ensured any more. Paauwe (2004) has proposed a context-based human resource theory integrating the tension of economic rationality versus relational rationality (legitimacy, fairness), serving as a basis for relationships with internal and external stakeholders. Although these recent developments are promising in relation to making HRM more sustainable, the assumption that the economic rationality should be dominant remains vastly unchallenged and the ecological dimension of external environments vastly unexplored. The following question arises:

> What is the problem with the dominating HRM paradigm and is it sustainable?

Until recently, there has long been optimism that HRM would meet the expectations regarding its initial role of advocating for employees and their welfare (Van Buren *et al.*, 2011). However, due to technological advances and a rapidly changing global workplace environment, HR managers have to deal with an ever-increasing number of conflicting interests, values and meanings (Giddens, 1991). This is especially true of the employee interest–profit conflict. In times of economic unbalance and uncertainty, organisations tend to place their trust in established conservative frameworks. As we have seen, HRM has a long tradition of adhering to a modernist and rationalist paradigm which aims to 'unleash human expertise in order to improve performance' (Swanson and Holton, 2001, p. 4). However, issues of increased rationalisation, deskilling and resource maximisation have unavoidably undermined the labour–HRM relationship on which organisational performance relies. A number of critical researchers have highlighted how HRM still proclaims, on the one hand, to have as its goal individual employee support, training and development, while, on the other hand, it acts to continually undermine personal agency and voice in the interest of 'resource units' which are easier to control and to align with corporate aims (Alvesson and Willmott, 2002; Townley, 1999). Others criticise HRM for neglecting its role in the advancement of human potential and talent and for its concentration on short-term economic goals (Garavan and McGuire, 2010).

A gap has thus developed between the humanistic, developmental rhetoric of HRM and actual workplace practices (Legge, 1999). People and their needs are no longer the central concern of HR managers, who are now preoccupied with the implementation of coercive business strategies and the rationalisation of work routines in the interests of higher productivity and task effectiveness (Lamm and Meeks, 2009). Nonetheless, a narrow rationalist perspective which views the 'human' in HRM as a negative attribute and something to overcome rather than something to be valued will, in the long term, hinder sustainability (Johnsen and Gudmand-Hoyer, 2010). According to Greenwood (2002), the term 'management' is often seen as a euphemism for 'use', and defining human beings as a resource is close to putting them in the same category as commodities such as 'furniture and computers' (p. 261). Alvesson and Willmott (2002) suggest that such paradigms of instrumentalist rationality simply act to regulate employee identities through 'discursive practices of teamwork and partnership' (p. 3) and are not sustainable in the long term (Ehnert, 2009). Hancock and Tyler (2001) go further and argue that HR practices are not only used to control and regulate employee behaviour, but are being increasingly and overtly applied to generate managerial control over employee 'mindpower and subjectivities' (Alvesson and Willmott, 1996, p. 192), and individual beliefs, values and attitudes (Rusaw, 2000).

McCracken and Wallace (2000) suggest that strategic HR practices in particular express an explicit prioritisation of economic goals over other outcomes, such as employee development or environmental protection. Although viewing human beings as strategic assets could be regarded as an ethical concern (Van Buren *et al.*, 2011; Waring and Lewer, 2004), applying an ethical sensitivity to theories, models and practices has so far been neglected in HRM (Janssens and Steyaert, 2012). Even if we judge ethical issues as irrelevant to business success, the assumption behind the HRM–performance paradigm is that employees act in alignment with HRM goals which they perceive to be in their shared interests. Research suggests that employees are beginning to lose trust and question the motivation behind strategic HRM decisions and are seeking alternative approaches more compatible to their actual workplace experiences (Wright and Nishii, 2006). As a result, to become and remain sustainable, HR will need to take into account the rights of employees and their interests as well as their personal and professional needs (Ehnert, 2009). Furthermore, one should not forget the importance of the relationship to external stakeholders. While it seems that HRM has to date mainly considered stakeholders within organisational boundaries (Ehnert, 2009; Janssens and Steyaert, 2009), researchers argue that HRM can no longer ignore the impact of HR policies on wider stakeholders such as the civil society, community, employees in the supply chain and the environment (Beer *et al.*, 2015; Müller-Camen and Elsik, 2014; Paauwe and Boselie, 2005; Renwick *et al.*, 2013).

It is therefore time to overcome such simplistic approaches and revive earlier humanistic multi-stakeholder philosophies, which have almost been forgotten in recent decades (Beer *et al.*, 2015). Janssens and Steyaert (2009) argue that HRM needs to be reframed through the introduction of 'alternative paradigms, perspectives and political value', and that only by the replacement of performance by a broader concept of outcome (including green behaviour and environmental performance) will HRM be able to consider its 'societal embeddedness and the long-term impact it has on different stakeholders in society' (p. 148). Similarly, Docherty, Forslin and Shani (2002) proposed that sustainability cannot be based on exploitation of both employees and the environment, and long-term organisational success cannot be achieved without a strategy incorporating social and environmental sustainability as well. Therefore, it is an economic, social and environmental necessity for organisations to start demonstrating genuine care about other stakeholders and their interests.

A first step for organisations would be to distance themselves from the shareholder approach and to bring in a more holistic perspective aimed at aligning organisational, societal and environmental values (Paauwe and Boselie, 2005). This would also suit future (more environmentally concerned) employees. Younger generations in particular have started to show both an increasing ethical and environmental awareness and a willingness to take ethically responsible decisions (Taylor, 2011). HR could play a leading role in promoting ethical awareness and behaviour across the workforce. It is suggested that a change towards more sustainable HR practices should go hand in hand with new ethical and corporate social responsibility rules of engagement (Cohen *et al.*, 2012). Rimanoczy and Pearson (2010) imply that HRM could achieve this by changing organisational culture towards more work floor democracy, which would encourage a regaining of employee trust and commitment in acceptance of a new sustainable green paradigm. There is general agreement that organisational goals need to be urgently redefined in terms of long-term sustainability. The recent global financial crisis helped expose the weaknesses of short-term capitalist thinking. In addition, the clarity about globally limited resources and also about environmental pollution is an increasing external pressure on organisations to meet the challenge of internal change in order to survive in the future (Ehnert and Harry, 2012).

For the present HRM paradigm, this means adapting to the current needs of building sustainable organisations, with HRM playing a vital role in implementing a 'sustainability mind-set' at all organisational levels (Ehnert and Harry, 2012, p. 232). It is thus time for organisations to replace their short-term based shareholder perspective with a multi-stakeholder approach taking into consideration economic, environmental and societal necessities. The mainstream HRM paradigm is not sustainable because it reflects a very narrow understanding of strategic success (dominance of financial performance), because it underestimates the importance of ethical HRM behaviour and because the impact of HRM on the natural environment and the link to regenerative actions needed to sustain resources for future business activities are absent. Sustainable HRM practices in general, and Green HRM (GHRM) in particular, need to move up organisational and HRM agendas, not least because more and more consumers, investors and even future employees are demanding that this happens (Taylor, 2011). In the next section, we will discuss an alternative approach to HRM with special regard to GHRM as a response to increasing internal organisational necessity and external environmental pressures.

Sustainability as the new HRM paradigm? The purpose of HRM is to increase ecological and social progress

An attempt to redesign the current HRM paradigm can be seen in organisational sustainability and its associated value debate about the future (Gollan and Xu, 2014). An organisation is required to:

> maintain itself and enhance its capacity to solve major problems; to maintain a decent level of support and welfare for present and future generations; and extend the productive life of organizations and to maintain high levels of efficiency and performance to add value to society.
>
> (Gollan and Xu, 2014, p. 227)

One approach that tries to meet these challenges is Sustainable HRM. There are different theoretical perspectives to Sustainable HRM, but one particularly relevant for GHRM is the resource regeneration and reproduction-oriented focus (Ehnert, 2009). It has different roots, which include Aristotle's understanding of a self-sustaining household, the notion of sustainability of old European forestry laws, a systemic corporate perspective (Luhmann, 1995) and co-evolution theory (Bateson, 1972). From this perspective, an organisation is sustainable if 'resource reproduction divided by resource consumption equals one' (Müller-Christ and Remer, 1999, p. 70, translated by the authors). In other words, companies have to balance resource consumption and reproduction. Reproduction occurs in organisational environments such as labour markets, education systems or families. As these are 'sources of resources', organisations have to invest actively in the survival of these environments (Müller-Christ, 2001) in order to have durable access to human and social resources (Müller-Christ and Remer, 1999).

Business organisations are under extreme pressure from a number of sides (political, economic and social) to change business practices to improve environmental responsibility and behaviour (Sarkis *et al.*, 2010). Expectations have increased that organisations will act towards achieving social and environmental goals as much as they do to achieving financial goals or goals of profitability (Moon *et al.*, 2005). It seems that, in addition to the increased need for legal compliance to stricter environmental and health and safety regulations, managers are beginning to recognise the competitive and economic advantages of a more efficient use of limited resources and the importance of regenerating them whenever possible. As a result, more and more organisations are implementing corporate sustainability strategies and policies. In many cases, HR departments have been allocated the responsibility of aligning these new green polices with traditional workplace processes, especially regarding pro-environmental behaviour among employees (Renwick *et al.*, 2013). Many researchers argue that the key to changing environmental performance will be the ability to promote individual behaviour (Uzzell and Moser, 2009). Some companies have actually adapted recruiting procedures to capture green attitudes among recruits (Ones and Dilchert, 2013), while others are redesigning training and development programmes to propagate green practices (Stalcup *et al.*, 2014). Through the introduction of environmental management systems (EMS) and a corresponding standardisation of practices and reporting procedures, legislators had expected improved environmental performance (Ronnenberg *et al.*, 2011). However, although an increasing number of organisations are complying and reporting on the negative environmental impact of workplace processes (Jackson, 2012), EMS alone has proved an ineffective tool in changing non-sustainable practices. Much research instead seems to underline the importance of GHRM, which is expressed by intensive HR practices of employee support, empowerment, and environmental training in establishing effective pro-environmental behaviour among staff. Leal Filho (2000) argues further that the concept of sustainability needs to be installed as a shared workplace meaning through socialisation HR practices focusing on environmentally friendly behaviour (Jackson, 2012). Research has shown that organisations which respect, encourage and engage employees in environmental management will be the most successful

(May and Flannery, 1995). Other research highlights key factors such as management commitment (Ramus 2002; Ronnenberg *et al.*, 2011), environmental initiatives and reward systems, and the introduction of problem-solving 'green teams' (Beard and Rees, 2000). The World Business Council for Sustainable Development suggested how key HR practices such as recruiting and retention, compensation and rewards, and talent management can be sustainably reframed (WBCSD, 2005). Despite an increased awareness of the need for change and a gradual move towards more green HR practices, some research seems to indicate that HR managers are still not effectively aligning the HR role with environmental sustainability nor having any major impact (Harris and Tregidga, 2012). Bierema (2009) criticised HRM for 'embracing performativity' and concentrating on short-term economic goals at the expense of badly needed sustainable reform (p. 92). HR managers will need to become more involved in corporate strategic decision making in order to prioritise green practices over economic ones and to turn green boardroom discourses into green workplace action (Andersen, 2007; Prasad and Elmes, 2005). Although HRM as a discipline has been slow in meeting the challenge of sustainability, and there is still limited research into the relationship between HR practices and sustainability (Ehnert *et al.*, 2016), there is no doubt as to the important role HR has to play in the implementation of green agendas (Jackson *et al.*, 2011).

Conflict as catalyst for a paradigm change?

As already indicated, there is increasing awareness but also conflict among business leaders over the fact that corporations which restrict themselves to an economic paradigm with a focus on short-term results will be confronted with major problems and organisational challenges in the long term (Dunphy and Griffiths, 1998). There is still wide disagreement about how to achieve strategic objectives, reduce costs and maintain competitiveness, while at the same time limiting negative environmental impact. This sustainability debate has led to an ongoing reassessment of the dominating paradigm. As a consequence, HRM has been increasingly allocated the important role of securing organisational sustainability by (1) increasing organisational economic performance through innovative capabilities, (2) enhancing social performance through effective employee diversity management and (3) increasing environmental performance through the development of green workplace practices and environmentally friendly products (Jabbour and Santos, 2008). Although the introduction of GHRM practices in particular would represent a major paradigm change by prioritising environmental issues over economic ones, data suggests that it would still have a number of economic and organisational benefits. These would include a gain in market share by reaching more environmentally aware customers (Ginsberg and Bloom, 2004), and an increase in stock-market share value and increased brand-value through the creation of a new green corporate image (Miles and Covin, 2000). Other researchers propose that organisations should actively reframe their economic policies to include social costs as part of the organisation's cost structure, thus reflecting the prevailing negative externalities of HRM practices (Mariappanadar, 2013). Despite these strong economic arguments, a mainly ideological conflict still remains between mainstream and alternative sustainability perspectives that is hindering the advancement of the GHRM agenda (Renwick *et al.*, 2013).

It seems that the core issue in the successful evolution of a new GHRM will be conviction amongst HR managers of the social, economic and organisational need to change conventional HR practices and systems (Guerci and Pedrini, 2014). A number of frameworks have been offered in order to facilitate HR strategists in their decision-making. Dubois and Dubois (2012), for example, suggest that a systems approach would be useful in bridging the gap between Strategic HRM and a new GHRM paradigm. Mariappanadar (2014) puts forward a 'stakeholder harm index' framework, stressing the impact of current HR practices on the external environment (p. 314). Regardless of which framework is chosen, successful integration of HRM with sustainability would require the development of interactive, multi-dimensional complementary competencies. Jabbour and Santos (2008) advocate GHRM procedures which, among other things, help select future employees with environmental values, evaluate performance based on environmental criteria, and support the emergence of an eco-friendly organisational culture. Current organisational appraisal systems could, for example, be adapted to link individual environmental behaviour with recognition, rewards and career advancement (Jackson *et al.*, 2011). One key HR element would also seem to be employee training and development (Stalcup *et al.*, 2014). Some insist that levels of environment knowledge among staff will be directly related to GHRM acceptance (Parker, 2011). Corporations in the UK have, for instance, redesigned management training to emphasise not only the indispensability of environmental business evolution in general, but also the significant role of managers in inspiring and engaging staff towards green behaviour (Feasby and Wells, 2011).

Although HR managers are beginning to rethink how their interactions with employees can influence attitudes and facilitate a green paradigm transition (Zibarras and Coan, 2015), most organisations will still need to do far more to create a climate of 'eco-mindfulness' inducive to a sustainable change (Anderton and Jack, 2011, p. 78). Of course, a major conflict between the two paradigms is the issue of aligning current corporate monetary goals and performance cultures with wider stakeholders' environmental aims and obligations. While some corporations have indeed recognised the value of environmental management and GHRM practices for employee outcomes such as employee job satisfaction and retention (Jackson *et al.*, 2011), most managers still remain loyal to the dominating status quo of the financially focused HRM–performance paradigm. Jackson (2012) suggests that more research will be needed to underline the pivotal relationship between HRM support and environmental employee convictions and behaviour.

However, some researchers suggest that the impulse will not come from management but from employees themselves (Bartlett and Bartlett, 2011), where moral convictions and the strong dynamics and emotions behind conflicting and contradicting viewpoints could actually be used as catalysts for change for the good. Internal pressures impacting on human capital sustainability, decreasing loyalty and reduced identification with corporate goals will encourage HR managers to more effectively align the needs of stakeholders and business. Others suggest that accumulating environmental consciousness and expanding employee awareness of the negative impact of company practices on the external environment could act to intensify pressure on HR managers to initiate a desirable and imperative paradigm change (Harvey *et al.*, 2013).

Conclusions

Due to dramatic changes in the international business environment, such as climate change and water scarcity, HRM has been challenged to react to the needs of multiple stakeholders and environmental pressures. The various dominating performance-driven HRM paradigms alone have proven ineffective and unsustainable. Global pressures will need to be met with global HRM solutions. Greenwood (2013) suggests that a number of multi-national corporations are expressing difficulty in changing established ways of thinking which have tended to neglect international workers' rights and global social responsibility, especially in developing countries. Ehnert, Harry and Zink (2014) argue that a sustainable HRM paradigm will need to take a very balanced approach, offsetting the needs of external stakeholders and customers with employee wellbeing, health and safety. While some researchers argue for radical change, others take a more conservative approach and wish to build on current paradigms. However, although researchers such as Schuler and Jackson (2014) have recently put forward a number of revised Strategic HRM models which move away from earlier contingency-based philosophies towards a multiple stakeholder approach, these models still fail to meet the challenges of economic, social and environmental sustainability and have simply not gained enough acceptance in either the academic or business domains to make a major impact.

It seems undeniable that, if alternative approaches are to be successful (especially a green paradigm), the discipline of HR will need to do far more to develop employee organisational commitment, participation and organisational citizen behaviour towards a sustainable agenda and implement procedures which accommodate both internal (employees) and external stakeholder (customers, health and environmental legislators) needs. Strategic HRM, which has traditionally focused on controlling undesirable behaviour and issues of absenteeism, entrenchment and human capital depletion, will be challenged to emphasise the development of positive workplace environments which adhere to increasingly rigorous laws of health and safety, human rights and environmental protection. However, widespread acceptance of GHRM in both the business and academic worlds will also require a commitment beyond legal compliance, ecological branding, and annual sustainable reporting. HR professionals will need to critically reassess and redesign their role as mere administrators and managers of human capital towards being authentic, trustful, convincing leaders and nurturers of real holistic organisational change.

References

Alvesson, M. and Willmott, H. (1996) *Making sense of management: A critical analysis*. London: Sage.

Alvesson, M. and Willmott, H. (2002) 'Identity regulation as organizational control: Producing the appropriate individual', *Journal of Management Studies*, vol. 39, no. 5, pp. 619–644.

Andersen, P. (2007) *What is Web 2.0? Ideas, technologies and implications for education*. Bristol, UK: JISC.

Anderton, K. and Jack, K. (2011) Green behaviour change: A case study of Eco Concierge. In Bartlett, D. (Ed.) *Going green. The psychology of sustainability in the workplace*. Leicester, UK: The British Psychological Society, pp. 76–83.

Appelbaum, E., Bailey, T., Berg, P. and Kalleberg, A. (2000) *Manufacturing advantage: Why high-performance work systems pay off*. Ithaca, NY: Cornell University Press.

Bartlett, J. E. and Bartlett, M. E. (2011) 'Workplace bullying: An integrative literature review', *Advances in Developing Human Resources*, vol. 13, no. 1, pp. 69–84.

Bateson, G. (1972) *Steps to an ecology of mind: Collected essays in anthropology, psychiatry, evolution, and epistemology*. Chicago: University of Chicago Press.

Beard, C. and Rees, S. (2000) 'Green teams and the management of environmental change in a UK county council', *Environmental Management and Health*, vol. 11, no. 1, pp. 27–38.

Beardwell, I., Holden, L. and Claydon, T. (2004) *Human resource management: A contemporary approach*. Fourth edition. London: Pearson Education Limited.

Becker, B. and Gerhart, B. (1996) 'The impact of Human Resource Management on organizational performance: Progress and prospects', *Academy of Management Journal*, vol. 39, no. 4, pp. 779–801. DOI:10.2307/256712.

Becker, C. L., DeFond, M. L., Jiambalvo, J. and Subramanyam, K. R. (1998) 'The effect of audit quality on earnings management', *Contemporary Accounting Research*, vol. 15, no. 1, pp. 1–24.

Beer, M., Boselie, P. and Brewster, C. (2015) 'Back to the future: Implications for the field of HRM of the multi-stakeholder perspective proposed 30 years ago', *Human Resource Management*, vol. 54, pp. 427–438.

Beer, M., Spector, B., Lawrence, P., Mills, D. Q. and Walton, R. (1984) *Human resource management: A general manager's perspective*. New York: Free Press.

Bierema, L. L. (2009) 'Critiquing human resource development's dominant masculine rationality and evaluating its impact', *Human Resource Development Review*, vol. 8, no. 1, pp. 68–96.

Boselie, P., Dietz, G. and Boon, C. (2005). 'Commonalities and contradictions in HRM and performance research', *Human Resource Management Journal*, vol. 15, no. 3, pp. 67–94.

Boxall, P. and Purcell, J. (2011) *Strategy and Human Resource Management*. Basingstoke, UK: Palgrave Macmillan.

Brewster, C. (1999) 'Strategic Human Resource Management: The value of different paradigms', *Management International Review*, vol. 39, no. 3, pp. 45–64.

Brewster, C. and Hegewisch, A. (1994) *Policy and practice in European Human Resource Management: The Price Waterhouse Cranfield survey*. London: Routledge.

Cohen, E, Taylor, S. and Müller-Camen, M. (2012) *HRM's role in corporate social and environmental sustainability*, SHRM Foundation's Effective Practice Guidelines Series, no. 55.

Delaney, J. T. and Huselid, M. A. (1996) 'The impact of human resource management practices on perceptions of organizational performance', *Academy of Management Journal*, vol. 39, no. 4, pp. 949–969.

Delery, J. E. and Doty, D. H. (1996) 'Modes of theorizing in Strategic Human Resource Management: Test of universalistic, contingency, and configurational performance predictions', *Academy of Management Journal*, vol. 39, no. 4, pp. 802–835.

Delery, J. E. and Shaw, J. D. (2001) 'The strategic management of people in work organisations: Review, synthesis, and extension', *Personnel and Human Resource Management*, vol. 20, pp. 165–197.

Docherty, P., Forslin, J. and Shani, A. B. (2002) *Creating sustainable work systems: Emerging perspectives and practice.* Abingdon, UK: Psychology Press.

Dubois, C. L. and Dubois, D. A. (2012) 'Strategic HRM as social design for environmental sustainability in organization', *Human Resource Management*, vol. 51, no. 6, pp. 799–826.

Dunphy, D. and Griffiths, A. (1998) *The sustainable corporation: Organisational renewal in Australia.* St Leonards, NSW: Allen & Unwin.

Ehnert, I. (2009) *Sustainable human resource management. A conceptual and exploratory analysis from a paradox perspective.* Berlin: Physica-Verlag.

Ehnert, I. and Harry, W. (2012) 'Recent developments and future prospects on sustainable human resource management: Introduction to the special issue', *Management Revue*, vol. 23, no. 3, pp. 221–238.

Ehnert, I., Harry, W. and Zink, K. J. (2014) *Sustainability and Human Resource Management.* Berlin: Springer.

Ehnert, I., Parsa, S., Roper, I., Wagner, M. and Müller-Camen, M. (2016) 'Reporting on sustainability and HRM: A comparative study of sustainability reporting practices by the world's largest companies', *International Journal of Human Resource Management*, vol. 27, no. 1, pp. 88–108.

Feasby, J. and Wells, K. (2011) 'Greening your organisation: The case of the Environment Agency'. In Bartlett, D. (Ed.) *Going green. The psychology of sustainability in the workplace.* Leicester, UK: The British Psychological Society, pp. 18–30.

Ferris, G. R., Hochwarter, W. A., Buckley, M. R., Harrell-Cook, G. and Frink, D. D. (1999) 'Human resources management: Some new directions', *Journal of Management*, vol. 25, no. 3, pp. 385–415.

Fombrun, C., Tichy, N. M. and Devanna, M. A. (1984) *Strategic Human Resource Management.* New York: Wiley.

Garavan, T. N. and McGuire, D. (2010) 'Human resource development and society: Human resource development's role in embedding corporate social responsibility, sustainability, and ethics in organizations', *Advances in Developing Human Resources*, vol. 12, no. 5, pp. 487–507.

Giddens, A. (1991) *Modernity and self-identity: Self and society in the late modern age.* Palo Alto, CA: Stanford University Press.

Ginsberg, J. M. and Bloom, P. N. (2004) 'Choosing the right green-marketing strategy', *MIT Sloan Management Review*, vol. 46, no. 1, pp. 79–84.

Gollan, P. J. and Xu, Y. (2014) 'Fostering corporate sustainability'. In Ehnert, I., Harry, W. and Zink, K. J. (eds) *Sustainability and Human Resource Management.* Berlin: Springer, pp. 225–245.

Greenwood, M. R. (2002) 'Ethics and HRM: A review and conceptual analysis', *Journal of Business Ethics*, vol. 36, pp. 261–278.

Greenwood, M. (2013) 'Ethical analyses of HRM: A review and research agenda', *Journal of Business Ethics*, vol. 114, no. 2, pp. 355–366.

Guerci, M. and Pedrini, M. (2014) 'The consensus between Italian HR and sustainability managers on HR management for sustainability-driven change – towards a "strong" HR management system', *The International Journal of Human Resource Management*, vol. 25, no. 13, pp. 1787–1814.

Guest, D. E. (1987) 'Human Resource Management and Industrial Relations', *Journal of Management Studies*, vol. 24, no. 5, pp. 503–521.

Hancock, P. and Tyler, M. (2001) 'Managing subjectivity and the dialectic of self-consciousness: Hegel and organization theory', *Organization*, vol. 8, no. 4, pp. 565–585.

Harris, C. and Tregidga, H. (2012) 'HR managers and environmental sustainability: Strategic leaders or passive observers?', *The International Journal of Human Resource Management*, vol. 23, no. 2, pp. 236–254.

Harvey, G., Williams, K. and Probert, J. (2013) 'Greening the airline pilot: HRM and the green performance of airlines in the UK', *The International Journal of Human Resource Management*, vol. 24, no. 1, pp. 152–166.

Hendry, C. and Pettigrew, A. (1990) 'Human Resource Management: An agenda for the 1990s', *International Journal of Human Resource Management*, vol. 1, no. 1, pp. 17–43.

Huselid, M. A. (1995) 'The impact of Human Resource Management practices on turnover, productivity, and corporate financial performance', *Academy of Management Journal*, vol. 38, pp. 635–672.

Jabbour, C. J. C. and Santos, F. C. A. (2008) 'The central role of human resource management in the search for sustainable organizations', *The International Journal of Human Resource Management*, vol. 19, no. 12, pp. 2133–2154.

Jackson, S. E. (2012) 'Portrait of a slow revolution toward environmental sustainability'. In Jackson, S. E., Ones, D. S., and Dilchert, S. (Eds) *Managing human resources for environmental sustainability*. San Francisco, CA: Jossey-Bass, pp. 3–20.

Jackson, S. E. and Schuler, R. S. (1995) 'Understanding human resource management in the context of organizations and their environments', *Annual Review of Psychology*, vol. 46, no. 1, pp. 237–264.

Jackson, S. E., Renwick, D. W., Jabbour, C. J. and Müller-Camen, M. (2011) 'State-of-the-art and future directions for green human resource management: Introduction to the special issue', *German Journal of Human Resource Management: Zeitschrift für Personalforschung*, vol. 25, no. 2, pp. 99–116.

Janssens, M. and Steyaert, C. (2009) 'HRM and performance: A plea for reflexivity in HRM studies', *Journal of Management Studies*, vol. 46, no. 1, pp. 143–155.

Janssens, M. and Steyaert, C. (2012) 'Towards an ethical research agenda for international HRM: The possibilities of a plural cosmopolitan framework', *Journal of Business Ethics*, vol. 111, no. 1, pp. 61–72.

Johnsen, R. and Gudmand-Hoyer, M. (2010) 'Lacan and the lack of humanity in HRM', *Organization*, vol. 17, no. 3, pp. 331–344.

Kaufman, B. E. (2001) 'The theory and practice of Strategic HRM and participative management: Antecedents in early Industrial Relations', *Human Resource Management Review*, vol. 11, no. 4, pp. 505–533.

Kaufman, B. E. (2015) 'Evolution of Strategic HRM as seen through two founding books: A 30th anniversary perspective on development of the field', *Human Resource Management*, vol. 54, no. 3, pp. 389–407.

Lamm, E. and Meeks, M. D. (2009) 'Workplace fun: The moderating effects of generational differences', *Employee Relations*, vol. 31, no. 6, pp. 613–631.

Leal Filho, W. (2000) 'Dealing with misconceptions on the concept of sustainability', *International Journal of Sustainability in Higher Education*, vol. 1, no. 1, pp. 9–19.

Legge, K. (1999) 'Representing people at work', *Organization*, vol. 6, no. 2, pp. 247–264.

Legge, K. (2005) *Human Resource Management: Rhetorics and realities*. Anniversary Edition. Basingstoke, UK: Palgrave Macmillan.

Liu, Y., Combs, J. G., Ketchen, D. J. and Ireland, R. D. (2007) 'The value of human resource management for organizational performance', *Business Horizons*, vol. 50, pp. 503–511.

Luhmann, N. (1995) *Social systems*. Palo Alto, CA: Stanford University Press.

Mariappanadar, S. (2013) 'A conceptual framework for cost measures of harm of HRM practices', *Asia-Pacific Journal of Business Administration*, vol. 5, no. 2, pp. 15–39.

Mariappanadar, S. (2014) 'Stakeholder harm index: A framework to review work intensification from the critical HRM perspective', *Human Resource Management Review*, vol. 24, no. 4, pp. 313–329.

Martín-Alcázar, F., Romero-Fernández, P. M. and Sánchez-Gardey, G. (2005) 'Strategic Human Resource Management: Integrating the universalistic, contingent, configurational and contextual perspectives', *International Journal of Human Resource Management*, vol. 16, no. 5, pp. 633–659.

May, D. R. and Flannery, B. L. (1995) 'Cutting waste with employee involvement teams', *Business Horizons*, vol. 38, no. 5, pp. 28–38.

McCracken, M. and Wallace, M. (2000) 'Towards a redefinition of strategic HRD', *Journal of European Industrial Training*, vol. 24, no. 5, pp. 281–290.

Miles, M. P. and Covin, J. G. (2000) 'Environmental marketing: A source of reputational, competitive, and financial advantage', *Journal of Business Ethics*, vol. 23, no. 3, pp. 299–311.

Moon, J., Crane, A. and Matten, D. (2005) 'Can corporations be citizens? Corporate citizenship as a metaphor for business participation in society', *Business Ethics Quarterly*, vol. 15, no. 3, pp. 429–453.

Müller-Camen, M. and Elsik, W. (2014) 'IHRM's role in managing ethics and CSR globally'. In Collins, D., Wood, G. and Caligiuri, P. (Eds) *Routledge companion to International Human Resource Management*. New York: Routledge, pp. 552–561.

Müller-Christ, G. (2001) *Nachhaltiges Ressourcenmanagement: Eine wirtschaftsökologische Fundierung*. Marburg: Metropolis-Verlag, pp. 69–87.

Müller-Christ, G. and Remer, A. (1999) 'Umweltwirtschaft oder Wirtschaftsökologie? Vorüberlegungen zu einer Theorie des Ressourcenmanagements'. In Seidel, E. (Ed.) *Betriebliches Umweltmanagement im 21. Jahrhundert*. Berlin: Springer, pp. 69–87.

Ones, D. S. and Dilchert, S. (2013) 'Measuring, understanding, and influencing employee green behaviors'. In Huffman, A. H. and Klein, S. R. (Eds) *Green organizations: Driving change with IO psychology*. New York: Routledge, pp. 115–148.

Paauwe, J. (2004) *HRM and performance: Achieving long-term viability*. New York: Oxford University Press.

Paauwe, J. (2009) 'HRM and performance: Achievements, methodological issues and prospects', *Journal of Management Studies*, vol. 46, no. 1, pp. 129–142.

Paauwe, J. and Boselie, P. (2005) 'HRM and performance: What next?' *Human Resource Management Journal*, vol. 15, no. 4, pp. 68–83.

Parker, R. (2011) 'Green organizational performance: Behavioural change interventions based on the theory of planned behavior'. In Bartlett, D. (Ed.) *Going green. The psychology of sustainability in the workplace*. Leicester, UK: The British Psychological Society, pp. 36–46.

Pfeffer, J. (1994) *Competitive advantage through people: Unleashing the power of the workforce*. Boston, MA: Harvard Business School Press.

Prasad, P. and Elmes, M. (2005) 'In the name of the practical: Unearthing the hegemony of pragmatics in the discourse of environmental management', *Journal of Management Studies*, vol. 42, no. 4, pp. 845–867.

Ramus, C. A. (2002) 'Encouraging innovative environmental actions: What companies and managers must do', *Journal of World Business*, vol. 37, no. 2, pp. 151–164.

Renwick, D., Redman, T. and Maguire, S. (2013) 'Green human resource management: A review and research agenda', *International Journal of Management Reviews*, vol. 15, no. 1, pp. 1–14.

Rimanoczy, I. and Pearson, T. (2010) 'Role of HR in the new world of sustainability', *Industrial and Commercial Training*, vol. 42, no. 1, pp. 11–17.

Ronnenberg, S. K., Graham, M-E. and Mahmoodi, F. (2011) 'The important role of change management in environmental management system implementation', *International Journal of Operations & Production Management*, vol. 31, no. 6, pp. 631–647.

Rusaw, C. A. (2000) 'Uncovering training resistance: A critical theory perspective', *Journal of Organizational Change Management*, vol. 13, no. 3, pp. 249–263.

Sarkis, J., Helms, M. M. and Hervani, A. A. (2010) 'Reverse logistics and social sustainability', *Corporate Social Responsibility and Environmental Management*, vol. 17, no. 6, pp. 337–354.

Schuler, R. and Jackson, S. E. (2014) 'Human resource management and organizational effectiveness: Yesterday and today', *Journal of Organizational Effectiveness: People and Performance*, vol. 1, no. 1, pp. 35–55.

Stalcup, L. D., Deale, C. S. and Todd, S. Y. (2014) 'Human resources practices for environmental sustainability in lodging operations', *Journal of Human Resources in Hospitality & Tourism*, vol. 13, no. 4, pp. 389–404.

Swanson, R. A. and Holton, E. F. (2001) *Foundations of Human Resource development*. Oakland, CA: Berrett-Koehler Publishers.

Taylor, S. (2011) *Contemporary issues in Human Resource Management*. London: Chartered Institute of Personnel and Development.

Townley, B. (1999) 'Practical reason and performance appraisal', *Journal of Management Studies*, vol. 36, no. 3, pp. 287–306.

Truss, C., Gratton, L., Hope-Hailey, V., McGovern, P. and Stiles, P. (1997) 'Soft and hard models of human resource management: A reappraisal', *Journal of Management Studies*, vol. 34, no. 1, pp. 53–73.

Uzzell, D. and Moser, G. (2009) 'Introduction: Environmental psychology on the move', *Journal of Environmental Psychology*, vol. 29, no. 3, pp. 307–308.

Van Buren, H. J., Greenwood, M. and Sheehan, C. (2011) 'Strategic human resource management and the decline of employee focus', *Human Resource Management Review*, vol. 21, no. 3, pp. 209–219.

Waring, P. and Lewer, J. (2004) 'The impact of socially responsible investment on human resource management: A conceptual framework', *Journal of Business Ethics*, vol. 52, pp. 99–108.

WBCSD (2005) www.wbcsd.org.

Wood, S. (1999) 'Human Resource Management and performance', *International Journal of Management Journal*, vol. 1, no. 4, pp. 367–413.

Wright, P. M. and McMahan, G. C. (1992) 'Theoretical perspectives for Strategic Human Resource Management', *Journal of Management*, vol. 18, no. 2, pp. 295–320.

Wright, P. and Nishii, L. (2006) 'Strategic human resource management and organizational behaviour: Integrating multiple levels of analysis', *Working Paper 06–05*, CAHRS, Cornell University, Ithaca, NY.

Zibarras, L. D. and Coan, P. (2015) 'HRM practices used to promote pro-environmental behavior: A UK survey', *The International Journal of Human Resource Management*, vol. 26, no. 16, pp. 2121–2142.

8 Implementing sustainable HRM

The new challenge of corporate sustainability

Cathy Xu, Paul J. Gollan and Adrian Wilkinson

Introduction

Within a fast-changing global economic, social and ecological environment for business, there is a consensus that corporate sustainable development has become more important, and some argue a likely resource leading to a firm's competitive advantage (Crifo *et al.*, 2016; Hart, 1997; Porter and Kramer, 2006, 2011; Porter and van der Linde, 1995). Corporate sustainability is achieved through a balanced integration of the triple bottom line of business encompassing economic benefits, environmental stewardship and social responsibilities (Elkington, 1997, 2001), whereby a complex system of renewal and regeneration is established (Wilkinson *et al.*, 2001).

Corporate sustainable development represents both a challenge and an opportunity for human resources management (HRM), with sustainable HRM being seen by some as the next phase to managing people after strategic HRM (SHRM) (de Souza Freitas *et al.*, 2011; Kramar, 2014). In this phase, HRM is at the centre of the corporate sustainable development initiative. HR policies and practices are aligned with the strategic directions of an organization, contributing to the organization's sustainable development outcomes (de Souza Freitas *et al.*, 2011; Jabbour and Santos, 2008).

Sustainable HRM identifies the broader purposes for HRM, through its recognition of the complexities of workplace dynamics and the need to address the negative impacts of HRM practices on, for example, employees and the natural environment (Harris and Tregidga, 2012; Kramar, 2014). A body of knowledge on sustainable HRM continues to develop; however, the real challenge lies in how to integrate this into management practice in the workplace (Gollan and Xu, 2014; Kramar, 2014).

To address this challenge, we will in this chapter first examine the role HRM can play in achieving corporate sustainability and then briefly discuss to what extent sustainable HRM is a new people management approach transcending SHRM and its key underlying dimensions; next, we will explore two selected approaches to implementing sustainable HRM, with one based on an integrated diagnostic framework, and the other underpinned by complexity theory and complex adaptive system (CAS) thinking. The chapter will conclude with implications and directions for future research.

HRM and sustainability

The sustainable development concept referred to in this chapter is in line with the definition in the Brundtland Report (World Commission on Environment and Development (WCED), 1987), although our analysis is at the organizational level.

The Brundtland Report identifies three equally important pillars of sustainable development: economic, social and environmental (WCED, 1987). Applying the Brundtland approach to business management and drawing on stakeholder theory, it is proposed that corporate sustainable development requires three integrated organisational outcomes: economic performance, social and ecological/environmental impacts (Elkington, 1997, 2001). These three pillars underpinning sustainability are concerned with the major stakeholders of business, such as shareholders, employees, customers and the planet, both internal and external to an organisation (Elkington, 1997, 2001). Corporate sustainability also considers both the short- and longer-term impacts on these stakeholders.

Corporate sustainable development represents both a challenge and an opportunity for HRM, and HRM can play a valuable role, because:

> (a) human resource is a function which presents greater potential to include the postulates of sustainability in the organizational scope (M. R. Vickers, 2005); (b) modern human resource management and sustainable organizations require a long-term focus and actions which extrapolate the search for an exclusively economic performance (Wilkinson et al., 2001); (c) stimulating organizational sustainability is the current paradigm of human resource management (Boudreau and Ramstad, 2005); and (d) modern human resource management has to be effective in order to meet the needs of the multiple stakeholders of a company (Colakoglu, Lepak and Hong, 2006).
>
> (Jabbour and Santos, 2008, p. 2134)

Under the agenda of corporate sustainability, the entrenched approaches in management practice and underpinning theories, such as agency theory and economic liberalism assumptions, are re-evaluated (Gollan and Xu, 2014). The slash and burn strategies and established management approaches of downsizing have eroded the base of human resources in general (Gollan, 2000; Wilkinson, 2005). These entrenched management practices with the aim of maximizing profit have profound effects on employees, physiologically (e.g. health, even mortality) and psychologically (e.g. lowered self-confidence and increased stress), especially on those disadvantaged groups such as older workers and workers with disabilities (Pfeffer, 2010; Vickers, 2010). Furthermore, corporate sustainability requires a shift in HR management to allow the needs and aspirations of individuals to be placed at the heart of the workplace (Gollan, 2005). Challenges also arise from the need for HRM to shift its role in an organization from a functional department to a partner involved in strategic planning (Dunphy *et al.*, 2003; Jabbour and Santos, 2008). In reality, there is a clear gap: a survey on HR's role in corporate sustainability conducted by the Society for Human Resource Management (the world's largest association of HRM, representing about 250,000 members in over 140 countries) revealed a significant disconnection between HR's involvement in creating and in implementing sustainability strategy – only 6 per cent of HR was involved in the strategic planning of sustainability programs, whereas 25 per cent was involved in the implementation of strategy (Society for Human Resource Management, Business for Social Responsibility and Aurosoorya, 2011 p. 30).

Theoretically, the traditional theory of agency and economic liberalism assumes individuals are opportunistic and one-dimensional economic units, rather than social beings 'having social obligations where decision-making may be based on solidarity, and that trust may be the binding norm' (Huse, 2003 p. 218). The assumptions of agency theory lead to 'short-termism' – longer-term relations are seen as most efficiently governed by 'social contracts' underpinned by the legal system with self-intrinsic motivation reinforced under share price and management financial incentives (Kochan, 2003). By contrast, the integrated nature of sustainability requires management behaviour to be based on pro-social intrinsic preferences. We follow an acknowledgment of interdependency and the importance of having a strategic balance of knowledge and skills. But most significantly, we argue for the importance of knowing how to mobilize this mix of skills and knowledge to achieve not only profitability, but also social and environmental objectives. Knowledge management systems are ultimately transmitted in human networks based on human capability. The challenge is not only to make these networks effective but to influence the development of a more holistic system for the creation and diffusion of knowledge (Gollan and Xu, 2014; Wilkinson *et al.*, 2001).

Therefore, the central challenge for HRM will be to move organizations to adopt sustainable principles, practices and structures towards different organizational strategies and create a climate whereby employees' potential can be released under a shared value of sustainability. Thus, HR policies and practices need to be integrated for sustainable business performance and positive employee outcomes of equity, development and well-being. Importantly, the role that the HR function should play is as a strategic partner of business (Dunphy, 2003) and HRM is the centre of corporate sustainability (Jabbour and Santos, 2008).

In response to the above-mentioned challenge for HRM theory and practice, the past two decades saw a number of terms being used to link sustainability (or its environmental dimension) and HRM practices (see also Kramar, 2014). These include green HRM (GHRM) (Daily and Huang, 2001; Haddock-Millar *et al.*, 2016; Renwick *et al.*, 2016; Sanders, 2009), sustainable work systems (Docherty *et al.*, 2002), HR sustainability (Gollan, 2000; Wirtenberg *et al.*, 2007), and sustainable leadership and sustainable HRM (Ehnert, 2009a; Mariappanadar, 2003, 2012). Despite the differences in the extent to which these terms attempt to reconcile the economic performance of organizations with desirable human/social impacts and environmental outcomes, they are all concerned with the role of HRM and recognise the impact HR outcomes have on the overall organizational agenda of sustainability (Kramar, 2014). We thus consider all of the above terms are conceptually under the umbrella term of sustainable HRM used in this chapter.

Understanding sustainable HRM

The term sustainable HRM has been coined in the literature for more than a decade, although 'the literature is piecemeal, diverse and fraught with difficulties. There is no one precise definition of the term and it has been used in a variety of ways' (Kramar, 2014, p. 1075). Kramar (2014) modifies Ehnert's (2009b) initial definition to define sustainable HRM as 'the pattern of planned or emerging HR strategies and practices intended to enable the achievement of financial, social and ecological goals while simultaneously reproducing the HR base over a long term' (Kramar, 2014, p. 1084).

Sustainable HRM is thus perceived as a new people management approach beyond SHRM (Ehnert, 2009a; Gollan and Xu, 2014;

Kramar, 2014). Different from the SHRM approach in which HR practices primarily serve as mediating factors between financial outcomes and business strategy, sustainable HRM aims to simultaneously enhance a variety of outcomes, and for their own sake (Kramar, 2014, p. 1083).

There are various ways to differentiate organizations according to their sustainable development initiatives and HRM practices. Under the framing model of sustainable HRM, which was extended from Ehnert's (2009a) study, Kramar (2014) acknowledges that sustainable HRM can include aspects of SHRM and personnel management (PM) as an integral part in practice, just as SHRM includes the operational activities of PM. Taking an inclusive approach, Gollan and Xu (2014) propose a typology of sustainable HRM based on the two defining dimensions: (1) level of organizational commitment to sustainability (from compliance to an intrinsic case); and (2) level of HR involvement in strategic planning for corporate sustainability (from primarily focused on implementation to being extensively involved in strategic planning). Four groups thus emerge as: Compliance Personnel, High-involvement HRM, Responsible Personnel and Transcended HRM. Depending on its knowledge, ambition and ability, an organization may adopt any of these corporate sustainability strands and HRM practices, and may also choose to change at any time and at any desired pace, either gradual or radical. For example, Interface Carpet led by Ray Anderson (a progressive leader in corporate sustainability) has adopted an approach to corporate sustainable development, in which 'people have always been at the center of Interface's approach to sustainability' and HR is consistently involved in strategic planning at the firm level (Porter, 2008; Society for Human Resource Management *et al.*, 2011, p. 73). Whereas in Alcatel-Lucent, although there is also a high level of commitment to sustainable development, HR's role is primarily implementing rather than formulating the firm's corporate sustainability strategy (Society for Human Resource Management *et al.*, 2011, p. 70). In the following section, we will discuss two management tools selected to implement sustainable HRM for rationales we discuss.

Implementing sustainable HRM through integrative and dynamic approaches

We contend that all HRM strategies and practices aligned with organizational sustainability objectives come under the broad sustainable HRM umbrella. However, with different organizational strands in sustainability and a mixed HRM approach, because of their varied underlying ideology, awareness, ambition and ability, effective management tools or approaches to implementation can be quite different. Below, we present two applicable approaches, with the first one based on an integrated diagnostic framework and the second based on complexity theory and CAS thinking. This analysis builds on the authors' earlier studies of Gollan (2000), Wilkinson *et al.*, (2001) and Gollan and Xu (2014).

An integrated diagnostic framework and its implementation

Corporate sustainable development requires organizations to take a more holistic and integrated approach to people management. Previous studies have attempted to identify management tools for HR to have an influence on the outcome of corporate sustainability. For instance, Ehnert (2009b, p. 54) has identified the following instruments as relevant: HR development, design of reward systems, consideration of sustainability in the company's goals, strategies and organizational culture, as well as recruitment, HR marketing, HR care (e.g. job security, health promotion), HR deployment (e.g. flexible working time models, work–life balance, sabbaticals), and trust-sensitive, participative leadership. Jabbour and Santos (2008) focus on the central role of HRM in the search for organizational sustainability and suggest that HRM could contribute simultaneously to innovation management, the consolidation of cultural diversity and the improvement of performance in environmental management though developing organizational change in such things as value, competencies and organizational ethics, and aligning functional dimensions through recruitment, training, performance evaluation, reward and so on.

Gollan (2000) and Wilkinson *et al.* (2001) developed an integrated framework incorporating the major factors, influences and outcomes of sustainable HRM. Gollan and Xu (2014) amended the framework by including additional outcomes important to sustainable HRM study, such as equity, development and well-being outcomes from an employees' perspective, and the impact of sustainable HRM on external stakeholders such as the natural environment and the community. By adding these external factors into the model as drivers, the framework extended its initial scope beyond the boundary of an organization and was enabled to take into account changes required by regulations, market, technology and the natural environment (Gollan and Xu, 2014).

As shown in Figure 8.1, the model identifies five major factors in the debate about HRM contributing to corporate sustainability, namely organizational change (e.g. value and behaviour), workplace institutions

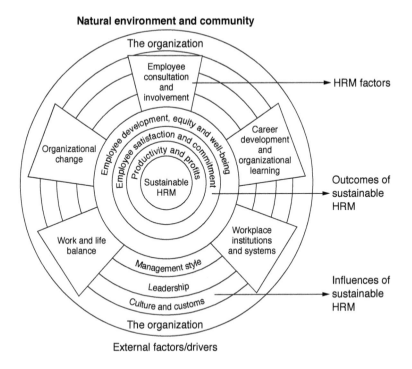

Figure 8.1 Factors, influences and outcomes of sustainable HRM – an integrated framework.

Source: Gollan and Xu (2014) which was adapted from Gollan (2000, p. 60).

and systems (e.g. recruitment and reward policies), career development and organizational learning (e.g. training and capability enhancement), employee consultation and involvement (e.g. innovation), and work–life balance.

Essentially, the model defines sustainable HRM in terms of the capacity of organizations to create value within their structure and systems, thereby having the ability and capacity to regenerate value and renew wealth through the application of HR policies and practices. This will entail investment in human knowledge through continuous learning, and the application and development of such knowledge through employee participation and involvement. In addition, the model identifies three main drivers (culture and customs, leadership, and management style) for organizations adopting sustainable HRM strategies and examines their impact on employee satisfaction and commitment and on the traditional organizational objectives of increased productivity and profits. Importantly, the model suggests that, to achieve the goal of corporate sustainability, HR policies and practices need to be integrated for sustained business performance and the positive employee outcomes of equity, development and well-being.

Applying Porter's (2008) interpretive approach to the implementation of corporate sustainability, we argue that this integrated diagnostic framework can work as a systems model for the inquiry and execution of sustainable HRM. Different from a linear model, the above framework views sustainable HRM as a process which typically proceeds in 'iterative, cyclical and non-linear' fashion (Gioia and Pitre, 1990, p. 588).

This integrative framework can be used by organizations pursuing sustainable HRM as a diagnostic tool for identifying the most acute issues where HRM may make a valuable contribution. The implementation of this approach requires firstly that the organization diagnose rather than immediately solve sustainable HRM issues, through an ongoing dialogue with its multiple stakeholders. A continuous process will then emerge, consisting of examination, learning, reframing and action, based on a shared understanding of issues and processes to address them. For instance, in Hitachi's case, 'social innovation' has been identified as the focus of its corporate sustainable development strategy, and hence became the focus of the company's sustainable HRM. Applying the diagnostic framework, sustainable HRM factors influencing innovative capability, such as career development, organizational learning, employee consultation and involvement, should be areas of top priority (Society for Human Resource Management *et al.*, 2011).

Furthermore, Gollan and Xu (2014) suggest that organizations taking more progressive stances in relation to corporate sustainability may find management tools based on complexity theory and CAS thinking more effective for the implementation of sustainable HRM. We discuss this next.

Complexity theory, CAS and its application

Complexity theory has its roots in hard science (later known as cybernetics), and was not long ago synonymous with bottom-up computer simulation (Espinosa and Porter, 2011). However, over the past decade there is an increasing acknowledgement of the profound philosophical implications of complexity thinking and the value of qualitative methodologies to the understanding of complex organizational problems, such as organizational transforming, corporate strategy, organization design and SHRM (Colbert, 2004; Richardson, 2007; Van Uden, 2005).

Complexity theory contends that, within complex systems, 'many agents, elements, and subsystems interact in densely connected networks' (Espinosa and Porter, 2011 p. 56). Different from the conventional linear systems or merely complicated systems, complex systems are non-reductive and indivisible into smaller units – the whole cannot be understood by being divided into parts (Espinosa and Porter, 2011; Richardson, 2008; Wulun, 2007). Mitleton-Kelly (2011) refers to organizations as 'complex evolving systems' that are organic, non-linear and require holistic approaches to their management, in which relations within interconnected networks are the order of the day.

There are several core dimensions/principles to complex systems, as summarized by Porter and Kramer (2011, pp. 66–67): self-organization (signifies a spontaneous and bottom-up process), nonlinear feedback and coevolution of agents, emergence (of novel patterns, structures and properties), path dependence (hence context and history matters) and emergent adaptations likely to occur at micro-sites or 'fitness frontiers' – the edge of chaos as some call it. Adding to this, Mitleton-Kelly (2011) has also noted the multi-dimensional nature (e.g. social, cultural, physical, economic, technical, political) of a complex system, and therefore suggests that focusing only on a single dimension is not sufficient (Mitleton-Kelly, 2011).

It is worth noting, however, that not every complex system is adaptive, and not every emerging adaptation increases the system's chances of survival – it does so only when the emergent order enhances the functioning or 'fitness' of the entire system and the system is thus a CAS (Espinosa and Porter, 2011 p. 57; Kauffman, 1993; Rihani, 2002).

An emerging stream in the corporate sustainability/CSR literature suggests viewing organizational sustainability through the lens of CAS, given the consistent underpinning philosophy or understanding of the world (eco- or human systems) as an ever evolving cyclic process of renewal and regeneration, during which interactions and exchange of information take place at multiple facets (Benn and Baker, 2009; Espinosa and Porter, 2011; Mitleton-Kelly, 2011; Norberg and Cumming, 2008; Porter, 2008). For instance, Benn and Baker (2009) identified shortcomings in the earlier versions of organizational development approaches, such as action research and team building approaches, as a result of their focus on the dualistic relationship between nature/employee, employee/organization etc. Considering the complex reality of the focal phenomena, the many contingency factors involved and their interrelatedness, they propose to view an organization as a complex adaptive system within which reality is portrayed as a living system, in which all components are interconnected and interdependent, and life is seen as continuous, rather than composed of discrete elements (p. 386). They also demonstrate the application of this CAS approach using a case example of a long-running environmental dispute.

Apart from using a CAS approach to understanding and managing firms' environmental initiative and business performance, CAS is suggested as being equally applicable to the studies of SHRM and the social dimension of corporate sustainability or CSR (Colbert, 2004; Espinosa and Porter, 2011; Porter, 2008). In his study on SHRM, Colbert (2004) argues that 'Pursuing a line of research in SHRM that focuses on coherence in the HR system, infused with a living-systems perspective, could help to inform the way organizations are studied and to improve the way they are managed.' We see this approach as particularly useful for a process involving transformational change, such as in the case of CSR and sustainable HRM (see also Seo *et al.*, 2004).

More discussion on complexity theory and CAS is available elsewhere in the context of organization studies (Anderson, 1999; Richardson, 2008; Rihani, 2002; Wulun, 2007), CSR (Benn and Baker, 2009; Espinosa and Porter, 2011; Porter, 2008) and SHRM (Colbert, 2004). Such knowledge, especially that gained from the CSR literature and SHRM, is transferrable to the context of sustainable HRM, a subset, and ultimately the centrality of CSR.

The CAS approach is particularly relevant and useful for organizations demonstrating intrinsic commitment to sustainability, where HR is extensively involved in strategic planning. In such organizations, sustainability strategy is embedded in all aspects and at all levels; HRM is a partner of strategic planning and people here are change agents. Importantly, the organization and not just its HR systems is expected to experience a transformational change and radical shifts in its way of working, thinking and relating, as suggested by Mitleton-Kelly (2011). Within such complex systems, people are seen as valuable assets/resources of an organization and society: they interact, are interrelated and co-evolve with other actors within and outside the organization. According to the resource-based view (RBV) (Barney, 1991; Wernerfelt, 1995), such resources may lead to innovations and the competitive advantage of a firm.

Within the CSR context, Espinosa and Porter (2011, p. 58) contend that CAS is mainly applied to organizations seeking radical change under the new circumstances in which they must operate to improve organizational adaptability and sustainability. Under such circumstances:

> CAS is a systems framework characterized by continual change and development, ongoing feedback across all levels, coevolving

bottom-up and top-down development, and by a growing focus on processes replacing some of the single-minded myopia over performance. It is not a static model, and in its profound dynamism are found the key issues and the keys to solutions for enhancing sustainability.

(Espinosa and Porter, 2011, p. 58)

Related to sustainable HRM are all three primary principles guiding CAS management methods, highlighted by Porter (2008, p. 403): building and empowering small groups and teams (the bottom of the conventional organizational hierarchy); stimulating adaptive learning at all levels of an organization, especially at the line level; and supporting innovation at the most decentralized, local sites where internal and external stakeholders have direct, ongoing contact and information exchange.

Table 8.1 lists some major HRM interventions required by core CAS principles, as identified in Gollan and Xu (2014). For example, the self-organization principle of CAS requires HR policy/incentives to enable greater autonomy and encourage staff to try out ideas locally and to explore the space of possibilities by experimenting with alternative procedures and processes to improve the patient journey; while the nonlinear feedback principle calls for HRM intervention to bridge the tight boundaries between specialities through, for instance, employee consultation and involvement.

An earlier discussion by Colbert (2004) on applying the complex RBV theory to SHRM suggests that future studies examine the effects of applying an complexity approach to HR management through case studies involving 'comparator companies, who occupy relatively equal strategic positions in the same industry, and collect[ing] qualitative schemes, along with supporting documentation' (Colbert, 2004, p. 356). However, cases where CAS has been thus applied to sustainable HRM are rare.

For the purpose of exemplifying, Gollan and Xu (2014) draw upon the longitudinal case studies by Mitleton-Kelly (2011) on two London hospitals: one teaching hospital and one District General Hospital. Briefly, the two hospitals were pushed by their 'health ecosystem' to a critical point at which they could 'no longer operate under their existing regime using established norms and procedures' (Mitleton-Kelly, 2011, p. 51). Options for them were either to do things radically differently along the CSR path or to go into decline. They therefore needed to explore their space of possibilities and develop new ways of working, thinking and relating. Adopting Espinosa and Porter's (2011) approach

Table 8.1 HRM interventions required by core CAS principles

Complexity principle	Required HRM intervention
Self-organization	HR policy/incentives to enable greater autonomy and encourage staff to try out ideas locally and to explore the space of possibilities by experimenting with alternative procedures and processes to improve the patient journey
Nonlinear feedback	Bridge the tight boundaries between specialities through, for instance, employee consultation and involvement
Edge of chaos	HR system and policy to enable and encourage productive energy to shift to key problems
Coevolution	HR policy or reward system to facilitate the reciprocal influence resulting in changes in the reciprocating entities
Emergence	Facilitating the bottom-up process of idea generation, through HR policy, reward system, career development and organizational learning, as well as employee consultation and involvement
Path dependence	HR policy or reward system to facilitate sharing of experience and knowledge at various levels and interfaces, so that the underlying reasons of success are understood and shared

Source: Gollan and Xu (2014).

of applying CAS, Gollan and Xu (2014) demonstrate how, in practice, operationalization of CAS dimensions through sustainable HRM contributes to organization sustainability. They do so by examining whether the managerial interventions (see Table 8.1) required by the six core principles of CAS within the context of sustainable HRM existed in the case and how that led to success or failure of a transformational change (for more detailed analysis see Gollan and Xu, 2014).

The case analysis shows how things dramatically altered when the hospital recognized that 'change is not about spelling out what everyone has to do, but in creating the right enabling environment' (Mitleton-Kelly, 2011, p. 50). In line with the CAS theory and its requirements of management intervention as listed in Table 8.1, the hospital started encouraging exploration of the possibilities, working better as a team, supporting each other and acknowledging their interdependence. A different way of thinking and learning was developed which enabled people to work with the independent sector. Management and staff also developed new patterns of connectivity, internally and externally. They were then ready to redeploy staff and to encourage role extension, while at the same time meeting the financial targets. Culturally, the organization accepted the challenge and responded to it. In short, they developed a new way of thinking, working and relating and management interventions were in line with the six CAS principle (Mitleton-Kelly, 2011). Within such an organization, CAS systems experience of both successes and failures was shared within a learning environment. Noticeably, all these interventions that are focused on people are within the regime of HRM for the ultimate goal of organization sustainability. Indeed, what worked in the above case was full engagement of the staff at all levels. 'Major sustainable improvement can only be achieved and persist if there is active involvement of employees, and innovation flourishes if the application of their distributed intelligence is encouraged' (Mitleton-Kelly, 2011, p. 52).

Importantly, the path-dependent nature of CAS determines that success (or failure) cannot be readily copied, but if 'why' it worked in that context and what would have stopped it working, i.e. the underlying principles, are understood, then they are more likely to be successfully adopted in a new context (Mitleton-Kelly, 2011, p. 46). Therefore, the above list of HRM interventions is neither exhaustive, nor generalizable to all cases. Applications to other contexts need to focus on identifying appropriate interventions required by the six core principles of CAS theory.

The application of complexity theory and the CAS approach to HR and organizational management is emerging in practice in various forms

(Colbert, 2004; Gollan and Xu, 2014). Among others, the self-management approach implemented at companies such as Zappos (Reingold, 2016) closely resembles the approach of sustainable HRM through applying complexity theory and CAS thinking. Apart from Zappos, a range of companies have also moved in this direction including Morning Star, a maker of tomato products; Valve, a developer of video games and gaming platforms; and W. L. Gore, a highly diversified manufacturer (Bernstein *et al.*, 2016). Again, noticeable variations exist on the self-organization theme, but the best known and most fully specified of these systems is holacracy, the self-management approach implemented at Zappos.

Zappos is an online shoe and clothing retailer founded in 1999 and then bought by Amazon in 2009 when the company had grown its business to over $1 billion in annual gross merchandise sales (Hsieh, 2015). The company states that it has a strong focus on organizational culture and a clear strategic commitment to sustainability: 'At Zappos, we believe that sustainability is crucial to our business and the planet' and:

> our sustainability efforts are woven into all of our business units. Our projects and initiatives are championed by the Campus Operations and Sustainability teams as well as the L.E.A.F. team, a grass-roots, employee-driven movement to promote environmental issues and awareness throughout the company.
>
> (Zappos.com, 2016)

The holacracy approach to people management at Zappos is consistent with CAS and includes self-organization into circles (i.e. teams), nonlinear feedback and coevolution of agents, emergence (of novel patterns, structures, and properties) and the edge of chaos. As Bernstein *et al.* (2016) describe it, the fundamental difference between the new forms, such as holacracy, and traditional organizations is that: 'If traditional organizations strive to be machines governed by Newtonian physics, precisely predicting and controlling the paths of individual particles, then self-managing structures are akin to biological organisms, with their rapid proliferation and evolution' (Bernstein *et al.*, 2016, p. 5).

At self-managed organizations, teams are essential blocks of the organization with middle management removed. After Zappos implemented holacracy, 150 departmental units evolved into 500 circles. The modularity allows for more plug-and-play activity across the enterprise than in a system where teams sit squarely in particular units and departments. Under holacracy, teams design and govern themselves following a constitution – a living document outlining and explaining the rules, in a broad-brush way, by which circles (teams) are created, changed and removed (Bernstein *et al.*, 2016). Thus, the organization is responsive to the requirements of the work rather than to the directives of any powerful individual. Self-managed organizations use structuring processes (rather than a fixed structure) to maintain order and clarity (Bernstein *et al.*, 2016).

These people management practices are aligned to the major sustainable HRM intervention required by core CAS principles as listed in Table 8.1, yet the outcomes of them are too early to judge in these real-life cases. It is worth noting, though, that a great deal of piecemeal adoption is already happening in practice. For example, Procter & Gamble operates a complex matrix organization in order to integrate its many brand categories, geographies and functions. But it also has a vast open-innovation program, in which teams of people external to P&G organize themselves to solve problems for the company. For decades, employees at Google and 3M have been encouraged to devote a percentage of their time to self-directed work – 'a volunteer economy that exists alongside the managerial hierarchy's more directed economy' (Bernstein *et al.*, 2016, p. 17). These business trends are interesting to observe and also offer a potentially fruitful way forward for sustainable HRM research.

Future research and implications for practitioners

Sustainable HRM represents a new approach to people management under the agenda of CSR and will continue to develop in the future. The current conceptualization of sustainable HRM:

> takes an explicit moral position, requires a multidisciplinary approach and needs to be informed by theories which enable an understanding of ambiguity, feedback between action and outcomes and complexity. Critical processes will involve iterative and emergent processes, stakeholder management and a recognition of the interdependence of processes at a number of levels.
>
> (Kramar, 2014)

Our effort here is focused on the approaches to executing sustainable HRM. To implement sustainable HRM, we argue that approaches can be quite different for organizations with a different level of commitment to sustainability and/or varied characteristics of HRM involvement. We thus propose two approaches for implementation: an

integrated diagnostic framework, which is more in line with the interpretive systems thinking; and the CAS approach, based on complexity
theory. We suggest that the former is more useful for organizations
where either the radical change required by CSR is not yet part of the
organizational strategy or HRM is not extensively involved in strategic
planning. For these organizations, the proposed integrative framework
can be used as a diagnostic tool for identifying the most acute issues and
areas in which HRM may have a valuable contribution to make within
the constrained organizational commitment to sustainability and/or
HRM involvement. In organizations that are more advanced in corporate sustainable development and where HR is extensively involved in
strategic planning, however, an approach based on complexity theory
and CAS thinking can be more effective. That is because of the consistency in their underpinning ideology, such as their viewing the world as
a complex, self-regulating and self-renewal system that is ever evolving
in a cyclical and non-linear fashion.

The application of complexity theory and CAS to organizational
study is an emerging research area, and it is even more so for their
application to the context of CSR and sustainable HRM. Drawing on a
number of studies, we have exemplified the application of CAS to sustainable HRM. The depth and scope of the discussion is limited by the
lack of primary data from a study specifically designed for sustainable
HRM and CAS application. However, this chapter provides some
guidance to both academics and managers interested in the usability and
applicability of complex systems theories.

It is worth noting also that there are various perspectives to complexity theories and hence different approaches (Colbert, 2004; Espinosa
and Porter, 2011; Gollan and Xu, 2014). Future research in applying
complexity theories to sustainable HRM might also look into and
compare how various approaches based on complexity theories work
individually and together.

In practice, HR has been identified as potentially making great contributions to sustainability in the areas of leadership development, training and development, diversity and multiculturalism, ethics and
governance, talent management and workforce engagement. On the
other hand, HR needs to do more to support the core qualities in the
areas of change management, collaboration and teamwork, creating and
inculcating values, and health and safety (Kramar, 2014; Renwick *et al.*,
2016; Wehling *et al.*, 2009).

This chapter has offered HRM practitioners management tools to
implement sustainable HRM. These approaches are not static. Essential
for the implementation of sustainable HRM with the CAS approach is

the focus on management (HRM or other) interventions required by the six core principles of CAS, and thus the creation of an enabling environment (Espinosa and Porter, 2011; Mitleton-Kelly, 2011). For managers intending to use this approach, what should be borne in mind is that success cannot be copied, but if the underlying principles are understood, then they can be adopted in a new context (Mitleton-Kelly, 2011).

Managing people and organizations with new approaches such as the holacracy approach at Zappos requires the readiness of individual employees to cooperate (Bernstein *et al.*, 2016). How the differences in employees' readiness and mindset affect the effective implementation of the management tools for sustainable HRM is another area worthy of future research attention.

Finally, future capabilities in an organization and, as a consequence, improvement in performance are premised on the belief that it is necessary to develop a new workplace culture which emphasizes the role of employees as assets rather than merely as a costly factor of production. There is no one best way for all organizations, only organic processes based on situational characteristics which satisfy the aims and objectives for the organization and its employees in a sustainable way.

References

Anderson, P. (1999) 'Complexity theory and organization science', *Organization Science*, vol. 10, no. 3, pp. 216–232.

Barney, J. (1991) 'Firm resources and sustained competitive advantage', *Journal of Management*, vol. 17, no. 1, pp. 99–120.

Benn, S. and Baker, E. (2009) 'Advancing sustainability through change and innovation: A co-evolutionary perspective', *Journal of Change Management*, vol. 9, no. 4, pp. 383–397.

Bernstein, E., Bunch, J., Canner, N. and Lee, M. (2016) 'Beyond the holacracy HYPE', *Harvard Business Review*, vol. 94, no. 7/8, pp. 38–49.

Boudreau, J. W. and Ramstad, P. M. (2005) 'Talentship, talent segmentation, and sustainability: A new HR decision science paradigm for a new strategy definition', *Human Resource Management*, vol. 44, no. 2, pp. 129–136.

Colakoglu, S., Lepak, D. P. and Hong, Y. (2006) 'Measuring HRM effectiveness: Considering multiple stakeholders in a global context', *Human Resource Management Review*, vol. 16, no. 2, pp. 209–218.

Colbert, B. A. (2004) 'The complex resource-based view: Implications for theory and practice in strategic human resource management', *Academy of Management Review*, vol. 29, no. 3, pp. 341–358. DOI:10.5465/AMR.2004.13670987.

Crifo, P., Diaye, M. A. and Pekovic, S. (2016) 'CSR related management practices and firm performance: An empirical analysis of the quantity–quality trade-off on French data', *International Journal of Production Economics*, vol. 171, pp. 405–416. DOI:10.1016/j.ijpe.2014.12.019.

Daily, B. F. and Huang, S. C. (2001) 'Achieving sustainability through attention to human resource factors in environmental management', *International Journal of Operations & Production Management*, vol. 21, no. 12, pp. 1539–1552.

de Souza Freitas, W. R., Jabbour, C. J. C. and Santos, F. C. A. (2011) 'Continuing the evolution: Towards sustainable HRM and sustainable organizations', *Business Strategy Series*, vol. 12, no. 5, pp. 226–234. DOI:10.1108/175156311111 66861.

Docherty, P., Forslin, J., Shani, A. and Kira, M. (2002) 'Emerging work systems: From intensive to sustainable'. In P. Docherty and J. S. Forslin (Eds), *Creating sustainable work systems, emerging perspectives and practice* (pp. 3–14). London: Routledge.

Dunphy, D. (2003) 'Tomorrow's people', *HR Monthly* (June), p. 10.

Dunphy, D., Griffiths, A. and Benn, S. (2003). *Organisational change for corporate sustainability*. London: Routledge.

Ehnert, I. (2009a) 'Sustainability and human resource management: Reasoning and applications on corporate websites', *European Journal of International Management*, vol. 3, no. 4, pp. 419–438.

Ehnert, I. (2009b) *Sustainable Human Resource Management: A conceptual and exploratory analysis from a paradox perspective. Contributions to management science.* Heidelberg: Physica, Springer.

Elkington, J. (1997) *Cannibals with forks: The triple bottom line of 21st century business*. Stony Creek, CT: New Society Publishers.

Elkington, J. (2001) *The chrysalis economy: How citizen CEOs and corporations can fuse values and value creation.* Oxford: Capstone/AJ Wiley.

Espinosa, A. and Porter, T. B. (2011) 'Sustainability, complexity and learning: Insights from complex systems approaches', *The Learning Organization*, vol. 18, no. 1, pp. 54–72.

Gioia, D. and Pitre, E. (1990) 'Multiparadigm perspectives on theory building', *Academy of Management Review*, vol. 15, no. 4, pp. 584–602.

Gollan, P. J. (2000) 'Human resources, capabilities and sustainability'. In D. Dunphy, J. Benveniste, A. Griffiths and P. Sutton (Eds), *Sustainability – The corporate challenge of the 21st century* (pp. 55–77). Sydney: Allen and Unwin.

Gollan, P. J. (2005) 'High involvement management and human resource sustainability: The challenges and opportunities', *Asia Pacific Journal of Human Resources*, vol. 43, pp. 18–33. DOI:10.1177/1038411105050305.

Gollan, P. J. and Xu, Y. (2014). 'Fostering corporate sustainability: Integrative and dynamic approaches to sustainable HRM'. In K. Zink, W. Harry and I. Ehnert (Eds), *Managing human resources sustainability* (pp. 225–245). Heidelberg: Springer Publishing.

Haddock-Millar, J., Sanyal, C. and Müller-Camen, M. (2016) 'Green human resource management: A comparative qualitative case study of a United States multinational corporation', *International Journal of Human Resource Management*, vol. 27, no. 2, pp. 192–211. DOI:10.1080/09585192.2015.1052087.

Harris, C. and Tregidga, H. (2012) 'HR managers and environmental sustainability: Strategic leaders or passive observers?' *International Journal of Human Resource Management*, vol. 23, no. 2, pp. 236–254. DOI:10.1080/09585192.2 011.561221.

Hart, S. L. (1997) 'Beyond greening: Strategies for a sustainable world', *Harvard Business Review*, vol. 75, no. 1, pp. 66–76.

Hsieh, T. (2015). *Why I sold Zappos*. Retrieved from www.inc.com/magazine/ 20100601/why-i-sold-zappos.html May 27th, 2015.

Huse, M. (2003) 'Renewing management and governance: New paradigms of governance?', *Journal of Management and Governance*, vol. 7, no. 3, pp. 211–221. DOI:10.1023/A:1025004111314.

Jabbour, C. J. C. and Santos, F. C. A. (2008) 'The central role of human resource management in the search for sustainable organizations', *International Journal of Human Resource Management*, vol. 19, no. 2, pp. 2133–2154.

Kauffman, S. (1993). *The origins of order: Self-organization and selection in evolution*. New York: Oxford University Press.

Kochan, T. A. (2003) 'Restoring trust in American corporations: Addressing the root cause', *Journal of Management and Governance*, vol. 7, no. 2, pp. 223–231. DOI:10.1023/A:1025049223409.

Kramar, R. (2014). 'Beyond strategic human resource management: Is sustainable human resource management the next approach?', *International Journal of Human Resource Management*, vol. 25, no. 8, pp. 1069–1089. DOI:10.1080/09585192.2 013.816863.

Mariappanadar, S. (2003) 'Sustainable human resource strategy: The sustainable and unsustainable dilemmas of retrenchment', *International Journal of Social Economics*, vol. 30, no. 8, pp. 906–923. DOI:10.1108/03068290310483779.

Mariappanadar, S. (2012) 'The harm indicators of negative externality of efficiency focused organisational practices', *International Journal of Social Economics*, vol. 39, pp. 209–220.

Mitleton-Kelly, E. (2011) 'A complexity theory approach to sustainability: A longitudinal study in two London NHS hospitals', *The Learning Organization*, vol. 18, no. 1, pp. 45–53.

Norberg, J. and Cumming, G. (2008) *Complexity theory for a sustainable future*. Columbia University Press.

Pfeffer, J. (2010) 'Building sustainable organizations: The human factor', *Academy of Management Perspectives*, vol. 24, no. 1, pp. 34–45.

Porter, M. E. and Kramer, M. R. (2006) 'Strategy and society: The link between competitive advantage and corporate social responsibility', *Harvard Business Review*, vol. 84, no. 12, pp. 78–92.

Porter, M. E. and Kramer, M. R. (2011) 'Creating shared value', *Harvard Business Review*, vol. 89, no. 1/2, pp. 62–77.

Porter, M. E. and van der Linde, C. (1995) 'Green and competitive: Ending the stalemate', *Harvard Business Review*, vol. 73, no. 5, pp. 120–134.

Porter, T. B. (2008) 'Managerial applications of corporate social responsibility and systems thinking for achieving sustainability outcomes', *Systems Research and Behavioral Science*, vol. 25, no. 3, pp. 397–411. DOI:10.1002/sres.902.

Reingold, J. (2016) 'The Zappos experiment', *Fortune*, vol. 173, no. 4, pp. 206–214.

Renwick, D. W. S., Jabbour, C. J. C., Müller-Camen, M., Redman, T. and Wilkinson, A. (2016) 'Contemporary developments in Green (environmental) HRM scholarship', *International Journal of Human Resource Management*, vol. 27, no. 2, pp. 114–128. DOI:10.1080/09585192.2015.1105844.

Richardson, K. A. (2007) 'Systems theory and complexity: Part 4. The evolution of system thinking', *Emergence: Complexity & Organization*, vol. 9, no. 1/2, pp. 150–166.

Richardson, K. A. (2008) 'Managing complex organizations: Complexity thinking and the science and art of management', *Emergence*, vol. 10, no. 2, pp. 13–26.

Rihani, S. (2002) *Complex systems theory and development practice*. New York: Zed Books.

Sanders, T. (2009) 'How HR can green up your company', *Employment Relations Today (Wiley)*, vol. 35, no. 4, pp. 17–23.

Seo, M., Putnam, L. L. and Bartunek, J. M. (2004) 'Dualities and tensions of planned organisational change'. In M. S. Poole and A. H. Van de Ven (Eds), *Handbook of organisational change and innovation* (pp. 73–107). Oxford: Oxford University Press.

Society for Human Resource Management, Business for Social Responsibility and Aurosoorya (2011) *Advancing sustainability: HR's role*. Retrieved from www.shrm.org/Research/SurveyFindings/Articles/Documents/11-0066_AdvSustainHR_FNL_FULL.pdf.

Van Uden, J. (2005) 'Using complexity science in organization studies: A case for loose application', *Emergence: Complexity & Organization*, vol. 7, no. 1, pp. 60–66.

Vickers, M. (2010) 'From the editor-in-chief's desk: Continuing the discussion on sustainability and work', *Employee Responsibilities and Rights Journal*, vol. 1, pp. 1–4.

Vickers, M. R. (2005) 'Business ethics and the HR role: Past, present, and future', *Human Resource Planning*, vol. 28, no. 1, pp. 26–32.

Wehling, C., Guanipa Hernandez, A., Osland, J., Osland, A., Deller, J., Tanure, B. and Sairaj, A. (2009) 'An exploratory study of the role of HRM and the transfer of German MNC sustainability values to Brazil', *European Journal of International Management*, vol. 3, no. 2, pp. 176–198.

Wernerfelt, B. (1995) 'The resource-based view of the firm: Ten years after', *Strategic Management Journal*, vol. 16, no. 3, pp. 171–174.

Wilkinson, A. (2005) 'Downsizing, rightsizing or dumbsizing? Quality, human resources and the management of sustainability', *Total Quality Management and Business Excellence*, vol. 16, no. 8/9, pp. 1079–1088. DOI:10.1080/14783360500163326.

Wilkinson, A., Hill, M. N. S. and Gollan, P. J. (2001) 'The sustainability debate', *International Journal of Operations and Production Management*, vol. 21, no. 12, pp. 1492–1502.

Wirtenberg, J., Harmon, J., Russell, W. and Fairfield, K. (2007) 'HR's role in building a sustainable enterprise: Insights from some of the world's best companies', *Human Resource Planning*, vol. 30, pp. 10–20.

World Commission on Environment and Development (WCED) (1987) *Our common future*. Oxford: Oxford University Express.

Wulun, J. (2007) 'Understanding complexity, challenging traditional ways of thinking', *Systems Research and Behavioral Science*, vol. 24, pp. 393–402.

Zappos.com. (2016) Zappos sustainability webpage. Retrieved from www.zappos.com/leed.

9 Future directions of Green HRM

Redefining Human Resource Management to humans really matter

Ante Glavas

> Always recognize that human individuals are ends, and do not use them as means to your end.
>
> *Immanuel Kant*

Immanuel Kant's quote above is still relevant today and can be applied to Human Resource Management (HRM). As Matthews and colleagues (this volume) put forward, organizational performance has become the predominant end in HRM. In this process, the actual individual has been overlooked (Weiss and Rupp, 2011). A central question of this chapter is what would Green HRM (GHRM) look like if the starting point was the individual and not the performance – whether performance is organizational and/or environmental/societal.

Prior work on environmental sustainability (ES) – broadly defined as a focus on the well-being of stakeholders, which includes the planet – has mostly focused on individuals as the means and not the end. In other words, scholars have explored how HRM can contribute to organizations improving their own ES. This work is important because it deals with the crucial issue of improving the well-being of the planet and species on it. There has been great work done in this area. A review is beyond the scope of this chapter: for those interested in an overview of the extant literature, see a review of GHRM (Renwick *et al.*, 2013), an edited volume on sustainability and HRM (Jackson *et al.*, 2012), and an edited volume on the contribution of Industrial–Organizational Psychology to ES (Huffman and Klein, 2013). The point of this chapter is not to refute that work, but rather to complement it by also exploring ES as an antecedent to HRM rather than an outcome. In this way, the individual is not overlooked. Moreover, I will propose that such an approach is cyclical, in that, when ES is embedded into HRM, it will also lead to improved ES.

The approach in this chapter was inspired by two elements often used as the starting point for process approaches used in HRM and organizational change (see Brown, 2008; Cooperrider and Fry, 2010). HRM often uses such approaches for the organization, but what would HRM look like if these approaches were applied to HRM itself? The first element is that the approach is human-centered. So, the question is what would HRM look like if we started with the needs of the individual first? The second element is that the questions we ask make all the difference. Rather than asking how we can achieve organizational performance, the question I ask in this chapter is "how can HRM inspire individuals, organizations, and society/the planet to thrive?" Although seemingly subtle, the question and initial focal point make a huge difference. This is important because the focus on the needs of individuals is not new (see Kristof, 1996, for a review). In other words, the premise of the chapter is that HRM could expand its gestalt from management of resources to one in which it is a vehicle through which individuals, and the planet, could thrive. In such a gestalt, HRM stands for "humans really matter," hence the title of this chapter.

To summarize, in this chapter, I explore the following three questions: what would HRM look like (1) if ES is an antecedent, (2) there is a focus on the needs of the individual, and (3) the end goal is for all to thrive – the individual first, then the organization, and society/the planet. The chapter is structured as follows. I first present a holistic model of what HRM might look like when ES is embedded. Then I put forward the theoretical implications for HRM when a holistic model is employed. Finally, I illustrate with a few examples what such a view of GHRM might look like in practice as well as explain a few potential implications for individuals, organizations, and society/the planet. I would also like to note that I wrote this chapter for both academic and non-academic audiences.

Holistic model of HRM

HRM models have focused on individual-level elements such as tasks and jobs as well as organizational-level elements such as performance management systems, labor issues, and legal matters. An argument can be made that every aspect of HRM is multilevel as seen with HR planning, recruitment, training, and development. HRM involves an interaction of organizational strategies and policies with the individual employee.

When the question is asked what HRM would look like if ES were embedded in HRM, then a gap becomes apparent in the multilevel models of HRM – they are in fact two-level models that involve the individual and organization, but not society/the planet. The implication of including a third level (i.e., external stakeholders, society, and the environment) shifts the dynamic of the two-level model approach to HRM. As an example, from another field but related to how a three-level model of GHRM might look, Aguinis and Glavas (2017) put forward how meaningfulness differs in a two-level model (i.e., individual–organization) and three-level model (i.e., individual–organization–society/planet). The authors take the example of the job characteristics model (Hackman and Oldham, 1975), in which meaningfulness has traditionally been limited to the task. However, when ES is introduced as a third level, meaningfulness changes. Employees now can find meaning not just in their tasks but also from working for an organization that cares for the well-being of external stakeholders. To extrapolate to HRM, such a three-level model has numerous implications. Take for example the issue of values in the workplace. Aspects of HRM are often built around finding a fit between (prospective) employees and the organization, which in turn influences how organizations approach processes of recruitment, selection, career development, performance management, retention, etc. An underlying assumption is that employees with greater values alignment will be more committed, more satisfied in their job, and less likely to leave (Kristof-Brown *et al.*, 2005). However, values alignment in a two-level model (i.e., employee–organization) runs the risk of being just words in a brochure while only organizational performance is what is valued. In a three-level model in which the organization is truly enacting its values through its strategies and actions towards stakeholders, society, and the planet, employees could perceive the values to be more genuine and as a result find greater alignment.

As a hypothetical example (based on actual companies but names are omitted), imagine that Company A and B have the same values, which are caring for stakeholders, integrity, responsibility, empathy, respect for the individual, and making the world a better place. In company A, a two-level model is implemented in which performance management systems are based on rewarding contributions to organizational performance (i.e., measured primarily through financial metrics as well as intangibles which lead to improved financial performance). In company A, most employees might not even be aware of the values and, if they are, they only see them in annual reports, internal presentations, and sometimes in training. As Glavas and

Godwin (2013) put forward, in such situations, there might even be a negative effect on employees through lower organizational identification. This is even more pronounced because many companies have public commitments to ES – over 90 percent of large companies in developed countries have published codes of conduct related to ES (Wheldon and Webley, 2013) and 92 percent of the world's 250 largest companies have a formally published public ES report (KPMG, 2015). In such companies, employees will see ES as being symbolic and greenwashing. Then imagine that Company B has the same values, but in applying a three-level model (i.e., ES is included), these values take on a completely different meaning for employees. Employees for whom the aforementioned values are important will find much greater alignment if employees perceive that the company cares for the well-being of stakeholders and of the planet, shows empathy towards stakeholders outside the organization and towards the planet by understanding their needs, and respects all individuals and not just those that can help with profit. In that case, the increased values alignment benefits the organization through increased motivation and performance, and lower turnover.

While I used meaningfulness and values as examples, the same effect could be found with other aspects of one's self such as purpose and self-concept (e.g., having an identity as being a good person). Such an approach answers the first two questions posed in the introduction (i.e., what would HRM look like with a focus on the needs of individuals and if ES was an antecedent). As will be put forward in the following sections, a holistic model enables HRM to focus initially on the individual (e.g., their values, purpose, meaningfulness, self-concept, and other aspects of self). ES is then used as an antecedent, to enable an individual to fulfil their needs and grow.

The third question (i.e., how HRM can enable all to thrive: individual, organization, society, planet) is perhaps not as explicit. Although I wrote about a three-level model in this prior section, ideally this model should be holistic. Because the nature of writing is reductionist, I focused on the interaction of levels. In a holistic model, all thrive. As ES helps individuals fulfil their needs and grow, the individual also contributes to ES. It is a simultaneous process. For example, imagine an employee is attracted to a company because helping the world and the planet is important to her/himself. ES is an antecedent because it enables the employee to thrive (e.g., sense of purpose, values fit, etc.). However, fulfilment of one's purpose and values alignment is stronger if ES is genuine and the employee feels they are contributing to ES.

Theoretical implications of embedding ES into HRM

What are the implications for theories that influence HRM when ES is embedded? In the following subsection, I build on three theories that are influential to HRM as illustrative examples: job design, organizational justice, and engagement. Please note that a full review of each of these theories is beyond the scope of the chapter, so I will focus on elements that pertain to ES. Also, with each aspect of theory below, there is some foreshadowing of the subsequent section on implications for practice.

Job design

Job design is one of the most established areas of management, yet theories have stagnated in the last few decades (Grant, 2007). As put forward by Glavas (2016a) who built on the work of Grant (2008), perhaps a new direction is for job design to focus first on the individual (e.g., their motivation) and then use ES as a driver. Specifically, Grant (2007) posits that job design theory has been focused too much on the job and tasks themselves without taking the individual or external environment into consideration. He proposes a relational job design model in which "enriched relational architectures can motivate employees to care about making a positive difference in other people's lives and can affect what they do and who they become" (Grant, 2007, p. 405). Such a model is enhanced when the relationships are not only internal to the organization (i.e., two-model approach of HRM) but also external. For example, Grant (2012) found that, through contacts with beneficiaries, employees are more motivated. The underlying premise is that individuals have pro-social motivation to varying degrees. If the focus is on the individual's motivation, then ES is an ideal conduit for reframing job design. As in the above hypothetical example of Company A and B, imagine how much more employees who are pro-socially motivated can be positively influenced if they work for Company B – when their work is actually making an impact on external stakeholders and the environment. As an example, I consulted with a company that was in the sanitization industry (note that this is a broad categorization to protect identity). Their employees approached their work from a two-level approach in which organizational performance was improved by creating a superior product to the competition and then executing through high quality management strategies and action. Together with the company, we introduced ES as their mission and truly embedded ES in all aspects of the company. As a result, employees were more motivated. Instead of coming to work focused on their specific tasks, they realized that their jobs were helping to improve the health and well-being of hundreds of millions of people around the world. In turn, their ES performance doubled in the subsequent year. So, in the end, all thrived: the individual, organization, and society/the planet.

Organizational justice

Organizational justice is simply an employee's perception of fairness in the organization (for a more detailed review and definition, see Colquitt, 2012), and it influences HRM and many aspects of management (Folger and Cropanzano, 1998). When ES is embedded into organizational justice, related theories that impact HRM are influenced, such as social exchange, perceived organizational support, and fairness heuristics (Cropanzano and Rupp, 2008). Traditionally, organizational justice has been a two-level model (i.e., individual and organization). For example, when employees feel that their organization is being fair (e.g., through direct treatment of her/himself, processes, distribution of resources, and decisions), employees will be more committed, satisfied, perform better, and will go above and beyond the minimum requirements of their job to contribute to the organization (Colquitt *et al.*, 2001). However, scholars (Rupp, 2011; Rupp *et al.*, 2006) have put forward and tested (Rupp *et al.*, 2013) that, when ES is introduced to organizational justice (often referred to as third-party justice or even simply ES), the relationship goes beyond a two-level model of individual–organization (i.e., in which only the relationship between the individual and organization is important). Positive effects can also be found when employees perceive that the organization is treating those *outside* the organization too (Rupp *et al.*, 2013). Specifically, imagine the influence on GHRM through the following illustrative examples. For recruitment, Jones and colleagues (2014) found that, when prospective employees perceive that the organization is high on ES, many are positively influenced to work there, especially if they believe ES is genuine. In such a case, prospective employees are not only assessing whether the organization will treat *them* fairly (e.g., compensation, procedures, and in general with respect), but also whether the organization will treat *others* fairly. In a study of both prospective and incumbent employees, Rupp and colleagues (2013) found that, despite the effect of how an employee is treated directly, how others outside the organization (i.e., in their study it was local community and environment) are treated is still important, such that perceptions of fairness towards others will positively affect employees. To go back to one of original questions of this chapter (i.e., focus on the individual), such an approach might not seem to be focused on the individual directly. Actually, it is and it expands on our views that individuals only care about what happens to them directly. ES expands the individual focus to also fulfil needs, self-concept, and other aspects of one's self in which a person is positively affected when they see *others* being treated fairly. Moreover, when individuals know they are contributing to an organization that is giving and has a culture of caring, they can be positively affected (Grant *et al.*, 2008).

Engagement theory

Engagement theory is rooted in the concept that, the more an employee can bring of their whole self to work, the more they will be engaged (Kahn, 1990). As Glavas put forward (2016a) and tested (2016b), ES enables employees to show up more whole at work. The author built on prior work of engagement (e.g., Kahn, 1990; May *et al.*, 2004; Rich *et al.*, 2010) to explore the impact that ES can have on employee engagement through four factors that enable employees to show up whole: (1) psychological safety, (2) psychological availability, (3) values, and (4) purpose. First, ES has been found to enable employees to feel safe enough to show more of their true selves at work (Glavas and Kelley, 2014) – ES is related to employee perceptions of fair support from the organization, which in turn provides a "safe" environment in which employees have trust that they have cognitive and emotional safety to be themselves. For GHRM, psychological safety can be enabled through perceptions of fair processes (e.g., promotion), direct treatment (e.g., compensation, rewards, respect), and fair treatment of others outside of the organization (i.e., third-party justice). Second, ES can positively influence the psychological availability to show up whole at work through positively influencing self-esteem (Bartel, 2001) and also enabling an alignment of one's self-concept with the organization (e.g., a self-concept of being a good person) (Dutton *et al.*, 2010). For GHRM, this can be achieved, for example, by making a person's self-concept and the alignment with the organization explicit (e.g., through on-boarding, career development, training and development). The third and fourth factors (i.e., values, purpose) are more straightforward. Employees often feel that they have to leave part of their values and also their sense of purpose in life at the door when they come to work. When employees bring more of their core inner values and purpose, they feel like they are showing more of their whole selves at work and thus are more engaged. Thus, ES enables employees to feel greater values alignment (Vlachos *et al.*, 2013) as well as sense of purpose at work (Glavas and Kelley, 2014). For GHRM, values alignment and feeling a sense of purpose can be fostered, for example, through strategic management and communication (e.g., mission, values), staffing (e.g., targeting a profile of candidates with values and purpose aligned to ES and the organization), including in performance management systems, and embedding values and purpose into career development as well as training and development.

Practical implications of embedding ES into HRM

As foreshadowed in the prior section on theory, there are potentially numerous pathways for expanding HRM when ES is an antecedent and the focus is on the individual. In the following section, I give a few illustrative examples. I would also like to bring to the reader's attention again that, although I use language such as ES being an antecedent, it is a cyclical effect (i.e., ES influences individuals and organizations who then also impact ES). In this way, the individual, organization, society, and planet all thrive.

Prior literature

Although most of the work in this area has been on how HRM can influence ES, there has been emerging work regarding how ES can also influence HRM. For example, in the concluding chapter of a volume related to GHRM, Jackson (2012) puts forward that there are many benefits that organizations find from ES. For example, engaging multiple stakeholders is something many organizations desire to do but have a difficult time doing. ES offers an opportunity to do so. Moreover, ES is cross-sectoral so it offers an opportunity for the organization to align – something that is quite difficult for many organizations that are stuck in silos (e.g., sectors, departments, divisions).

In addition, Aguinis (2011, pp. 865–866) defined six steps through which ES can influence HRM processes. I list them below with comments in parentheses on the first three steps regarding how they link to GHRM as discussed in this chapter. The last three are straightforward connections.

1 vision and values related to ES (related to purpose and values which enable employees to bring their whole selves to work);

2   identification and prioritization of stakeholders' expectations (a design thinking approach in that it is human-centered and starts with the needs of humans first);

3   development of ES initiatives that are integrated with corporate strategy (ensures that ES is substantive and therefore should positively influence employee perceptions of how genuine ES is);

4   employee training related to ES;

5   institutionalization of ES by measuring and rewarding processes and results; and

6   reporting on ES initiatives internally and externally.

In another handbook related to GHRM, in the concluding chapter, Aguinis and Glavas (2013) explicitly state that, although the chapters in the handbook have been on what HRM and related disciplines (e.g., I-O Psychology, Organizational Behavior) can do for ES, there is an important complementary question of what ES can do for HR. The authors give a few examples such as that ES opens up the opportunity for organizations to discuss values more openly and make them explicit. It shifts the conversations in the boardroom and throughout the organization from being focused on financial decision-making to one in which values are legitimately discussed. As a result, values can also be embedded in the culture more explicitly, thus leading to a values-based culture. In addition, ES influences the organization and its members to move beyond treating people as a resource to be managed. Finally, the authors also discuss that, if ES is embedded into performance management systems, it can help shift the culture of the organization.

Future directions

To go back to the original questions mentioned in the introduction, the question is what GHRM would look like if we started with the needs of the individual first – and then used ES to align with organizational objectives. This might seem like a subtle difference from starting with organizational needs first and then aligning with individual needs, but it actually makes a huge difference. In this section I offer a few illustrative examples.

To answer the specific question put forward at the beginning of this chapter of "how can HRM inspire individuals, organizations, and society/the planet to thrive," I build on the theories mentioned in the prior section. Organizational justice underlies all of the implementation of ES in practice in this section because third-party justice is part of ES.

On a related note, it is important to distinguish between organizational justice and just standard good HRM practices. Thus, fair rewards, compensation, and treatment of employees would fall under good HRM. Instead, I focus on a few areas in which ES can help HRM go beyond traditional good practices.

First, ES can be used to create conditions in which individuals can bring more of their whole selves to work, resulting in greater employee engagement. As shown in Table 9.1, the HRM strategies and actions revolve around shifting the culture and practices of an organization from one focused strictly on organizational performance to one that values working for the greater good (i.e., ES). Due to space limitations, I will not expand on each point in Table 9.1, but the message is similar for each one. To give an example, purpose and values are often discussed in organizations but refer to ones that are in the service of organizational performance. When purpose and values are expanded to focus on those outside the organization, it can be perceived as being more genuine and substantive, which in turn can increase alignment of employees with the organization's purpose and values (Glavas and Godwin, 2013). This is quite different from organizations where the discourse revolves mostly around factors that lead to organizational performance. This limits how much a person can bring of their whole selves to work. As mentioned previously, employees will then leave aspects of their selves such as purpose and values at the door when they enter the workplace. On the other hand, ES can be used as a sort of excuse or enabler for individuals to bring more aspects of their whole selves to work. For example, instead of asking an employee directly (e.g., through on boarding, training sessions, feedback) what their purpose is and/or values are in life, sessions could be designed around ES on the surface. Employees could discuss what they feel are important non-financial issues that can increase the well-being of stakeholders, society, the planet. Then, based on those discussions, each individual can find a few issues that resonate for them. In turn, individuals can then contemplate why these issues resonate and how they are connected to their own purpose and values. Once this becomes clearer, the connection back to the organization can be made more salient – specifically, how is what the company doing aligned to their own purpose and values. This can be a method to engage or even rejuvenate employees. This can be done simply through a session (e.g., on boarding, training) or even more structured ways, through development programs that include coaching.

Table 9.1 Engagement: ES conditions that enable employees to show more of their whole selves at/in work

Engagement Factors	How ES can help HRM influence engagement factors
Purpose and values[1]	• Through ES, purpose and values are built around serving the greater good and are not narrowly focused on organizational performance – which in turn, may increase employee perceptions that purpose and values are genuine and substantive, thus increasing individual alignment with the organization. • Specifically, ES can be embedded into HRM (e.g., recruiting, hiring, on-boarding, training, and development) such that individuals are encouraged to get in touch with their own purpose and values, and then connect back to the organization's purpose and values.
Psychological safety	• ES can be used to leverage fair treatment of external stakeholders (e.g., respecting each stakeholder as a human being and not just capital) to foster an internal culture where employees feel they will be fairly treated if they show their true selves. • ES can be embedded in performance management systems as a means to show that non-financial behaviours of individuals are also valued.
Psychological availability	• Through career development, training, and feedback, ES can inspire individuals to become aware of what is important to their self-concept and how it might be aligned to ES and the organization (e.g., identity of being a good person). • Self-esteem can be built by using ES to reward non-financial aspects/contributions of the individual (e.g., acts of caring). • ES can be used as a reason to provide work–life balance.

Note
1 Purpose and values are collapsed into one category because the HRM strategies and actions are similar.

As shown in Table 9.2, ES can also positively influence job and work design, especially the psychological states traditionally associated with job design (Hackman and Oldham, 1976). As shown in the first row of Table 9.2, meaningfulness is expanded when ES is embedded into job design. As Pratt and Ashforth (2003) put forward, individuals can find meaningfulness in work (i.e., in their job and tasks), but also at work (i.e., when their organization contributes to a greater purpose). ES can be a conduit to the latter. ES expands the boundaries of what employees consider to be work. Their work not only contributes to organizational performance but also to improving the world. As seen in the second row of Table 9.2, ES also helps expand the concept of knowledge about results to one that is much more impactful. Rather than a traditional feedback session, actually seeing the impact of ES on beneficiaries will have a greater impact on employees. As mentioned earlier, Grant (2007) proposed that, when work is relational in nature – as is the case with ES due to its stakeholder-oriented focus – then individuals who are prosocially motivated are more positively affected; this effect is strengthened when employees have contact with the beneficiaries (Grant, 2012). As seen in the third row of Table 9.2, ES can help expand models of how organizations try to motivate employees. Many of those models have been based on self-determination theory (Ryan and Deci, 2000) of which autonomy is considered to be crucial. I do not challenge that, but there is a complementary perspective in

Table 9.2 How ES can contribute to job design

Psychological states	Traditional job design	ES contribution to job design
Experienced meaningfulness	Based mostly on task significance but also identification with task and skills employees use	Meaningfulness is not only from the task but goes beyond to what the organization does externally (e.g., fair treatment of stakeholders, society, the planet)
Knowledge of actual results of work activity	Through feedback	ES is used to give feedback internally through traditional mechanisms (e.g., performance reviews) but also feedback comes from contact with beneficiaries of ES
Experienced responsibility for outcomes of work	Fostered through having autonomy and ownership of work	ES is used to build a culture where shared responsibility is important (e.g., for what the organization does in terms of ES)

which having collective responsibility also can be motivating when an employee feels they are part of something larger than themselves. All of this benefits the organization as well. When the focus moves beyond a myopic focus on the job to one in which the broader system (i.e., society, the planet) is taken into consideration, employees are then more willing also to go above and beyond their own job description (i.e., organizational citizenship behaviors). Moreover, this is especially pronounced when employees see the organization going above and beyond its own job description (i.e., organizational performance), as is the case with ES. Therefore, ES has been found to be positively related to organizational citizenship behaviors (Frank *et al.*, 2011; Jones, 2010; Rupp *et al.* 2013).

The above examples are just illustrations of how starting with the individual as the focus and then connecting to ES can help employees thrive, which in turn helps the organization, and of course society and the planet. A few more, briefer illustrative examples are as follows:

- If a human-centered focus of Green HRM is used, then it would follow that cookie-cutter approaches to ES will not work for every-body. Individual differences are important to take into account. For example, those employees low in other orientation might not want to do extra work in ES, but still might enjoy benefits of ES (e.g., reputational ones).
- Career development is different when it focuses on the individual. It can be about life development and living out one's whole self – and using ES for that. For example, if developmental psychology is applied, employees might be influenced by ES differently, as a result of stages of psychological development. As put forward in Glavas (2016a), it has been widely believed that younger generations are more interested in ES (Meister, 2012; Seager, 2014), yet a meta-analysis found that there is actually a slight positive relationship between ES and age (Wiernik *et al.*, 2013). Employees in later stages of psychological development (e.g., perhaps less than a decade from retirement) might be more concerned about the legacy they will leave. For them, ES becomes about leaving the world a better place for their children, grandchildren, and future generations. Instead of using a one-size-fits-all strategy for GHRM, it is important to know how to communicate and engage different groups so as to be able to adapt GHRM (e.g., training, career development).
- As put forward by Glavas (2016a), ES can be used to address diversity issues such as breaking through the glass ceiling and engaging a

larger portion of the workforce. Many individuals do not thrive in corporate cultures that are rooted in competitiveness based around short-term performance. However, ES can be used to create a culture that is more caring and nurturing, which might enable a larger portion of the workforce, which previously was not able to thrive, to be more engaged.

Conclusions

There is a danger that the actual human at work will be overlooked – which then is counter to the very definition of ES in which the well-being of *all* stakeholders is important. Building on the work of Kerr (1975), there is potential folly in creating HRM systems that focus on environmental performance, while also hoping that in the process the actual human being will matter. Instead, this chapter has put forward a few illustrations of how individuals can thrive at work through ES. They can be more engaged, and find greater values alignment and a sense of purpose and meaningfulness. As a result, the organization also thrives from having employees who are thriving. This process is cyclical in that ES can influence HRM and the organization, which then influences ES (i.e, stakeholders, society, and the planet benefit). With a focus on the actual human through the approach put forward in this chapter, the planet and society might end up better off when we put people first – assuming that people's values are aligned with ES. Moreover, there is an argument to be made that many of the ES challenges we have were created by people. So, it is ironic that we sometimes forget the actual person in this whole process. I hope that the acronym HRM will also stand for humans really matter.

References

Aguinis, H. (2011) "Organizational responsibility: Doing good and doing well." In S. Zedeck (Ed.), *APA handbook of industrial and organizational psychology*, vol. 3, pp. 855–879. Washington, DC: American Psychological Association.

Aguinis, H., and Glavas, A. (2013) "What corporate environmental sustainability can do for industrial-organizational psychology." In A. H. Huffman and S. R. Klein (Eds.), *Green organizations: Driving change with I-O psychology*, pp. 379–392. New York: Routledge.

Aguinis, H., and Glavas, A. (2017) "On corporate social responsibility, sensemaking, and the search for meaningfulness through work," *Journal of Management*, advance online publication. DOI: 10.1177/0149206317691575, first published February 1, 2017.

Bartel, C. A. (2001) "Social comparisons in boundary-spanning work: Effects of community outreach on members' organizational identity and identification," *Administrative Science Quarterly*, vol. 46, pp. 379–413.

Brown, T. (2008) "Design thinking," *Harvard Business Review*, June, pp. 85–92.

Colquitt, J. A. (2012) "Organizational justice." In S. W. J. Kozlowski (Ed.), *The Oxford handbook of organizational psychology*, vol. 1, pp. 526–547. New York: Oxford University Press.

Colquitt, J. A., Conlon, D. E., Wesson, M. J., Porter, C. O. L. H., and Ng, K. Y. (2001) "Justice at the millennium: A meta-analytic review of 25 years of organizational justice research," *Journal of Applied Psychology*, vol. 86, no. 3, pp. 425–445.

Cooperrider D., and Fry, R. (2010) "Design-inspired corporate citizenship," *Journal of Corporate Citizenship*, vol. 37, pp. 3–6.

Cropanzano, R., and Rupp, D. E. (2008) "Social exchange theory and organizational justice: Job performance, citizenship behaviors, multiple foci, and a historical integration of two literatures." In S. W. Gilliland, D. D. Steiner, and D. P. Skarlicki (Eds.), *Justice, morality, and social responsibility*, pp. 63–99. Greenwich, CT: Information Age Publishing.

Dutton, J. E., Roberts, L. M., and Bednar, J. (2010) "Pathways for positive identity construction at work: Four types of positive identity and the building of social resources," *Academy of Management Review*, vol. 35, pp. 265–293.

Frank, W. R., Davis, W. D., and Frink, D. D. (2011) "An examination of employee reactions to perceived corporate citizenship," *Journal of Applied Social Psychology*, vol. 41, pp. 938–964.

Folger, R. G., and Cropanzano, R. (1998) *Organizational justice and human resource management*. Thousand Oaks, CA: Sage Publications.

Glavas, A. (2016a) "Corporate social responsibility and organizational psychology: An integrative review," *Frontiers in Psychology*, vol. 7, no. 144, pp. 1–13.

Glavas, A. (2016b) "Corporate social responsibility and employee engagement: Enabling employees to employ more of their whole selves at work," *Frontiers in Psychology*, vol. 7, no. 796, pp. 1–10.

Glavas, A., and Godwin, L. N. (2013) "Is the perception of 'goodness' good enough? Exploring the relationship between perceived corporate social responsibility and employee organizational identification," *Journal of Business Ethics*, vol. 114, pp. 15–27.

Glavas, A., and Kelley, K. (2014) "The effects of perceived corporate social responsibility on employees," *Business Ethics Quarterly*, vol. 24, pp. 65–202.

Grant, A. M. (2007) "Relational job design and the motivation to make a prosocial difference," *Academy of Management Review*, vol. 32, pp. 393–417.

Grant, A. M. (2008) "The significance of task significance: Job performance, effects, relational mechanisms, and boundary conditions," *Journal of Applied Psychology*, vol. 93, pp. 108–124.

Grant, A. M. (2012) "Giving time, time after time: Work design and sustained employee participation in corporate volunteering," *Academy of Management Journal*, vol. 37, pp. 589–615.

Grant, A. M., Dutton, J. E., and Rosso, B. D. (2008) "Giving commitment: Employee support programs and the prosocial sense making process," *Academy of Management Journal*, vol. 51, pp. 898–918.

Hackman, J. R., and Oldham, G. R. (1975) "Development of the job diagnostic survey," *Journal of Applied Psychology*, vol. 60, pp. 159–170.

Hackman, J. R., and Oldham, G. R. (1976) "Motivation through the design of work: Test of a theory," *Organizational Behavior and Human Performance*, vol. 16, pp. 250–279.

Huffman, A. H., and Klein, S. R. (Eds.) (2013) *Green organizations: Driving change with I-O psychology*. New York: Routledge.

Jackson, S. E. (2012) "Building empirical foundations to inform the future practice of environmental sustainability." In S. E. Jackson, D. S. Ones, and S. Dilchert (Eds.), *Managing human resources for environmental sustainability*. San Francisco, CA: Wiley.

Jackson, S. E., Ones, D. S., and Dilchert, S. (Eds.) (2012) *Managing human resources for environmental sustainability*. San Francisco, CA: Wiley.

Jones, D. A. (2010) "Does serving the community also serve the company? Using organizational identification and social exchange theories to understand employee responses to a volunteerism programme," *Journal of Occupational and Organizational Psychology*, vol. 83, pp. 857–878.

Jones, D. A., Willness, C. R., and Madey, A. (2014) "Why are job seekers attracted by corporate social performance? Experimental and field tests of three signal-based mechanisms," *Academy of Management Journal*, vol. 57, pp. 383–404.

Kahn, W. A. (1990) "Psychological conditions of personal engagement and disengagement at work," *Academy of Management Journal*, vol. 33, pp. 692–724.

Kerr, S. (1975) "On the folly of rewarding A, while hoping for B," *Academy of Management Journal*, vol. 18, pp. 769–783.

KPMG (2015) *Currents of change: The KPMG survey of corporate responsibility reporting 2015*. Available at: https://assets.kpmg.com/content/dam/kpmg/pdf/2016/02/kpmg-international-survey-of-corporate-responsibility-reporting-2015.pdf [accessed January 5, 2017].

Kristof, A. L. (1996) "Person-organization fit: An integrative review of its conceptualizations, measurement, and implications," *Personnel Psychology*, vol. 49, pp. 1–49.

Kristof-Brown, A. L., Zimmerman, R. D., and Johnson, E. C. (2005) "Consequences of individuals' fit at work: A meta-analysis of person–job, person–organization, person–group, and person–supervisor fit," *Personnel Psychology*, vol. 58, pp. 281–342.

May, D. R., Gilson, L., and Harter, L. M. (2004) "The psychological conditions of meaningfulness, safety and availability and the engagement of the human spirit at work," *Journal of Occupational and Organizational Psychology*, vol. 77, pp. 11–37.

Meister, J. (2012) "Corporate social responsibility: A lever for employee attraction and engagement," *Forbes*. Available at: www.forbes.com/sites/jeannemeister/2012/06/07/corporate-social-responsibility-a-lever-for-employee-attraction-engagement [accessed October 14, 2015].

Pratt, M. G., and Ashforth, B. E. (2003) "Fostering meaningfulness in working and meaningfulness at work: An identity perspective." In K. S. Cameron, J. E. Dutton, and R. E. Quinn (Eds.), *Positive organizational scholarship: Foundations of a new discipline*, pp. 309–327. San Francisco, CA: Berrett-Koehler.

Renwick, D., Redman, T., and Maguire, S. (2013) "Green human resource management: A review and research agenda," *International Journal of Management Reviews*, vol. 15, no. 1, pp. 1–14.

Rich, B. L., LePine, J. A., and Crawford, E. R. (2010) "Job engagement: Antecedents and effects on job performance," *Academy of Management Journal*, vol. 53, pp. 617–635.

Rupp, D. E. (2011) "An employee-centered model of organizational justice and social responsibility," *Organizational Psychology Review*, vol. 1, pp. 72–94.

Rupp, D. E., Ganapathi, J., Aguilera, R. V., and Williams, C. A. (2006) "Employee reactions to corporate social responsibility: An organizational justice framework," *Journal of Organizational Behavior*, vol. 27, pp. 537–543.

Rupp, D. E., Shao, R., Thornton, M. A., and Skarlicki, D. P. (2013) "Applicants' and employees' reactions to corporate social responsibility: The moderating effects of first-party justice perceptions and moral identity," *Personnel Psychology*, vol. 66, pp. 895–933.

Ryan, R. M., and Deci, E. L. (2000) "Self-determination theory and the facilitation of intrinsic motivation, social development, and well-being," *American Psychologist*, vol. 55, pp. 68–78.

Seager, C. (2014) "Generation Y: Why young job seekers want more than money." Available at: www.theguardian.com/social-enterprisenetwork/2014/feb/19/generationy-millennials-job-seekers-money-financial-security-fulfilment [accessed October 14, 2015].

Vlachos, P. A., Panagopoulos, N. G., and Rapp, A. A. (2013) "Feeling good by doing good: Employee CSR-induced attributions, job satisfaction, and the role of charismatic leadership," *Journal of Business Ethics*, vol. 118, pp. 577–588.

Weiss, H., and Rupp, D. E. (2011) "Experiencing work: An essay on a person-centric work psychology," *Industrial and Organizational Psychology*, vol. 4, pp. 83–97.

Wheldon, P., and Webley, S. (2013) *Corporate ethics policies and programmes: 2013 UK & continental Europe survey*. London: Institute of Business Ethics.

Wiernik, B. M., Ones, D. S., and Dilchert, S. (2013) "Age and environmental sustainability: A meta-analysis," *Journal of Managerial Psychology*, vol. 28, pp. 826–856.

10 From Green HRM towards workforce sustainability?

Douglas W.S. Renwick

Towards a future research agenda in Green HRM

I hope that all the chapters herein act as a research resource to help interested scholars to further identify their own Green Human Resource Management (GHRM) research questions and aid global efforts to mitigate ecological degradation (as per George *et al.*, 2016, pp. 1890, 1892). So, what now for the future in GHRM? In this chapter, I look ahead and discuss some less-examined prospects regarding future research ideas in GHRM, and possible links between GHRM and building more sustainable workforces.

Using theory in GHRM research

Future research could extensively utilize one or more of the many multiple existing theoretical frameworks to examine pro-environmental workplace behaviour detailed earlier (in the Introduction chapter). Here, further research questions, as per Inoue and Alfaro-Barrantes (2015, pp. 155–156), may include:

1   Are the already used frameworks of the theory of reasoned action, the theory of planned behaviour and value-belief-norm theory useful to best explain stakeholder GHRM behaviour worldwide?

Indeed, drawing on Alt and Spitzeck (2016, p. 50), researchers could centre research questions around issues such as:

2   Does social exchange theory fully explain why employees are more likely to display organizational citizenship behaviours to the environment if such staff feel more supported by work organizations globally?

3   Is social identity theory positively related to employee organizational identification and employee workplace outcomes internationally in GHRM?

4   Do the moderator variables of commitment to ethics, equity sensitivity, and staff discretion resonate and apply to GHRM–staff workplace outcome relationships comparatively?

5   Can evolutionary theory explain staff job migration patterns relating to climate change?

6   What other theoretical frameworks usefully explain stakeholder
behaviour(s) in GHRM worldwide? Which ones, and why?

Further, (see Shen *et al.*, 2016, pp. 6, 23), longitudinal data and experimental studies might also help us explore the impact of GHRM interventions, and cross-cultural data could increase the generalizability of
such research findings too.

Concepts and practices in GHRM research

Green leadership

Future research on Green leadership could compare the relative
impacts of environmentally focussed and more general transformational leadership over different cultural and organizational conditions,
and include environmental focus as a control to exclude potential
threats linked to demand characteristics. Scholars might examine
whether various types of target-focussed transformational leadership
(e.g. safety and environmental ones) are empirically separate, which
ones have distinct effects, and the impacts(s) of varying foci of transformational leadership on outcomes. Indeed, researchers may extend
existing findings in longitudinal field experiments among different
organizational contexts to increase existing confidence that leaders'
environmentally specific transformational leadership behaviour causes
changes to employee occupational environmental initiatives, and the
mediating effects of pro-environmental climate overall (Robertson
and Barling, 2017, pp. 2, 27, 28).

Individual variables

Research might benefit from scholars assessing key individual variables,
such as whether supervisors who exhibit environmental transformational
leadership directly impact on staff workplace environmentally friendly
behaviour (WEFB), if employees internalize supervisor-led GHRM

values, and whether positive emotions influence pro-environmental behaviours such as WEFB and harmonious environmental passion motivates staff to engage in pro-environmental activity (Saifulina and Carballo-Penela, 2016, p. 5). Here, researchers could investigate whether traits associated with women such as 'empathy, concern for others, perspective taking, altruism and helping' help explain why females tend to perform more WEFB than men. Indeed, they may also examine whether employees with higher incomes pay less attention to environmental issues at work, and personal and organizational factors such as organizational environmental support promote WEFB too (Saifulina and Carballo-Penela, 2016, pp. 10–12).

Organizational barriers

Scholars could research organizational barriers to EM progress, including whether: internal systems allow corporations to assess, chart and optimize their environmental impact; various stakeholder groups are constrained by limited resources in times of financial turbulence, and conflicts of interest arise among them; complexity in managing and organizing environmental management is heightened for multinational corporations; regions and countries mandate particular aspects of EM for firms operating in their locales; and government and social policies denote their wishes that businesses reallocate some profits towards social development causes as a norm (Wang *et al.*, 2016, p. 535). Moreover, researchers might investigate social variables in new and less-industrialized countries, and contexts which impact on employee green behaviour (e.g. personality traits, environmental attitudes, work values, and organizational power) to facilitate stronger tests of cross-cultural generalizability of current results showing 'negligible age-environmental performance relationships'. Scholars may also undertake longitudinal research on relationships between age and environmental performance to best comprehend age and developmental effects (Wiernik *et al.*, 2016, pp. 12–13).

Levels of analysis

At the institutional, country and company levels, future GHRM research may utilize institutional theory to study varied institutional contexts, and how different staff stakeholders balance and prioritize varying aspects of GHRM at the employee level to deal with complexities in it for multinational enterprises (MNEs). Investigating how organizational motives to engage in GHRM have altered over time might be worthwhile, particularly in emerging economies, as this is less understood there, i.e. whether views of GHRM converge across such countries or not. How MNEs manage stakeholder expectations regarding GHRM across national boundaries could also be an interesting research topic, i.e. if firm social irresponsibility on it occurs via a 'race to the bottom' among countries with the laxest environmental regulations, and in turn, on GHRM globally (Wang *et al.*, 2016, pp. 534, 538–539, 541).

At the organizational level, new scholarship might offer fresh insight into resolving potential and seen staff conflicts arising from enacting organizational GHRM initiatives between interdependent, yet competing, internal stakeholder, and external non-shareholder, groups, such as 'homeowners, environmentalists, individuals and the government'. Here, (see Wang *et al.*, 2016, pp. 534, 540), researchers could examine any trade-offs such stakeholders make under the conflicting firm goals of compliance and commitment as motivations for engaging in GHRM, and whether staff engage in extra-role pro-environmental behaviours in exchange for fair treatment from employers at work (Saifulina and Carballo-Penela, 2016, p. 4). Researching individual roles in GHRM may also be needed to assess emerging responses to workplace accidents and disasters such as tsunamis (e.g. Fukushima, in Japan), which could have implications for staff well-being, happiness, and job satisfaction (Wang *et al.*, 2016, p. 541). Indeed, scholars might research the roles HR managers play in GHRM and developing sustainable organizations by influencing employee activities, and thus changing workplace environments via new behavioural patterns too (Saifulina and Carballo-Penela, 2016, p. 2).

For OCBEs, research may wish to assess whether affective staff commitment to environmental change displays emotional buy-in to GHRM initiatives, the possible mediating factors between GHRM practices and collective OCBEs, and the roles that normative and continuance commitment might play in this process. Moreover, scholars could investigate if OCBEs lead to better environmental performance, whether any relationships exist between top-down Green initiatives and staff environmental behaviours (Pinzone *et al.*, 2016, pp. 202–203, 208), and if organizations with enhanced shared vision are more successful in embedding staff green behaviours into their cultures (Alt and Spitzeck, 2016, pp. 50–51).

Researchers could critically assess whether, as per recent studies on employee green behaviours (EGBs) in China, a lack of persuasive theory-based empirical work on employee workplace outcomes arises from enacted GHRM, and if GHRM both directly and indirectly influences in-role green behaviour, and only indirectly influences extra-role green behaviour through the mediation of psychological climate (Dumont *et al.*, 2016, pp. 1, 10).

New cross-cultural research might help develop more globally useful measures for GHRM, perhaps drawing on the new measurement scales recently developed by Tang and colleagues (2017) to complete longit-udinal studies investigating changes to staff green behaviour arising from adopting GHRM, and usefully explore different predictor variables from human capital (skill enhancement) and motivation (job satisfac-tion). Indeed, GHRM employee green behaviour relationships may be examined at higher unit and organizational levels to display a multilevel approach, accounting for the effects of organizational context, and the impact of GHRM on non-green work attitudes and behaviour too (Dumont *et al.*, 2016, p. 12).

Psychological climate

Future research on green psychological climate could move away from using participant self-reported EGB to more objective 'other' supervisor or peer-ratings, observations, and archival data, to develop theory and test hypotheses on boundary conditions, and examine whether theories of relationships between intentions and work behaviour incorporate the moderator of psychological climate. Indeed, future daily EGB research may further distinguish between active behaviours and those not doing something, develop measures to distinguish between them, and also examine different relationships with antecedent variables, activity levels, and habitualization of EGB (Norton *et al.*, 2017, pp. 14–16).

Workplace Green behaviour

Scholarship on workplace pro-environmental behaviour might benefit from investigating employee decisions to adopt technological innova-tions that may reduce the impact organizations have on the environ-ment, and staff pro-Green behaviours classified as environmental (non) activism to best understand why employees engage in such activities. Here, researchers could examine the role emotions play in shaping staff pro-environmental behaviour, how external factors such as monetary incentives influence employee pro-environmental activities, and whether, and how, employee perceptions of economic constraints such as recessions impact on staff decisions to engage in pro-environmental behaviours too (Inoue and Alfaro-Barrantes, 2015, pp. 153–155). Studies investigating eco-initiatives and workplace social exchange networks may also assess the usefulness of social exchange variables, such as trust, justice, and the psychological contract, to better comprehend underlying reciprocity processes in environmental sustainability (Alt and Spitzeck, 2016, p. 56), and the role of organisational context as a factor contributing to understanding the nature of workplace green behaviour as a specific form of job performance (Norton, 2016, p. 1).

Critical analysis

Using more critical frameworks, researchers could look to uncover, and critique, dominant discourses explaining issues of ownership, control, production, and industrial work relations in environmental labour studies, the role of union stakeholders as climate change actors (Hampton, 2015, p. 7), and any part played in determining union roles by the many organizational and external contextual factors illustrated by Farnhill and detailed in the Introduction chapter (see Farnhill 2016a, pp. 273–274; 2016b, pp. 18–19; 2017, p. 23). On regulation (i.e. conditions and context), scholars might usefully examine whether organizations in other countries make significant inroads into green Health and Safety at work enforcement. They might also examine whether organizations follow or deviate from patterns seen in Australia of organizations responding to new environmental regulations with few substantive efforts aimed at reducing their carbon emissions, or, as per some European studies, investing in green technologies instead (Teeter and Sandberg, 2016, p. 12). Here, researchers might focus on detailed organizational case studies and their 'ongoing internal and external political and environmental dialectics', and also formulate alternative large, statistical, and survey-based studies to explore the antecedents to such responses (Teeter and Sandberg, 2016, p. 14).

Building on the literature-based ideas for future research above, GHRM researchers may (see Bell *et al.*, 2016. p. 11) need to unravel the ethical nature of the GHRM research process, the outcomes it produces, and any imbalances in the production of GHRM knowledge it reveals. Here, scholars might wish to frame new particular GHRM research questions, on the following specific themes and issues. Such questions could include:

7   Is GHRM ethical? Is setting staff green targets in performance appraisals and allocating managers bonuses for achieving such goals the 'right thing' for organizations to do? Are organizations moral in undertaking such Green HRM initiatives?

8 Could staff green targets and bonuses put too much (unwanted?) pressure on non-Green (anti-Green/neutral) staff to 'go Green'?

Here, researchers might make use of Jacques Maritain's concept of 'personal humanism', in which people share a common human nature and strive to the achieve the 'common good' (see Acevedo, 2012), and/or the theoretical lens of human rights theory, to surface and discuss such ethical issues.

Drawing on Bukharin and Preobrazhensky's (1919) notion of state (governmental) assistance for agriculture and their concept of a 'smychka' (or union) between agricultural and other workers, scholars could investigate research questions concerning whether nation states and organizational stakeholders are helping vulnerable agricultural workers in flood-prone countries such as Bangladesh and de-forestation locales such as Brazil[1] (among others) to find new jobs and employment. Researchers may investigate specific research questions including:

9 Do agricultural workers see significant threats to their livelihoods emerging from crops either being flooded due to rising sea levels and/or eradicated through de-forestation? How do these workers show resilience and/or adapt to such changing circumstances?
10 Are agricultural workers suffering job loss due to climate change events?
11 Is farming viable in flood-prone or de-forested locations? Do agricultural workers need re-training/re-skilling to work elsewhere? If so, where?
12 Are clear job migration patterns emerging from agricultural workers moving into non-agricultural, and/or de-forested employment (perhaps in tourism/service-sector jobs)?[2]
13 What shape do climate-led job migration moves take? How are they enacted? And what consequences arise for all organizational stakeholders from such developments?

A related research issue arises regarding the ability and resilience of people (in)directly affected by climate change to cope with it. Examples include agricultural workers in France and Italy and factory workers in India and China (among others). Here, scholars might also investigate related research questions such as:

14 Do vineyard workers suffer from inhaling pesticide spray used to increase vine yield and/or through contaminated land and local water supplies due to pesticide run-off?

15 Are factory workers inhaling polluting fumes from toxic factory leaks and related smog in harmful and non-sustainable quantities?
16 What are the health consequences arising for workers from inhaling polluting workplace-based fumes?
17 Are staff employed in the 'polluter industries' able to work fully in such arguably 'bad' workplaces? What do they think of organizational (in)activity to combat climate change?

Researchers may also wish to focus their research questions to investigate the origins, coverage, and extent of any new Green jobs emerging as a potential new growth area in global employment.[3] This is because current moves towards a Greener economy are estimated to be creating 60 new occupations incorporating environmental aspects (Wiernik *et al.*, 2016, p. 1). For example, scholars could frame research questions on:

18 Do potential alleged 'pro-fossil fuel' jobs being created under the USA Trump administration out-number the so-called 'Green jobs' created under the Obama administration, or vice-versa?
19 What is the breakdown in terms of Green and non-Green job types, work quality, locations, status, sectors, gender, and age globally?
20 What is new in Green jobs comparatively? What noteworthy trends and developments are emerging regarding them worldwide?
21 Are new forms of Green international work and employment truly environmental, or a form of 'Greenwash'? and
22 What impact do any new or existing regulatory environments have on GHRM workplace practices, jobs, work, and employment globally?

Here, scholars might replicate and extend current investigations of where existing external regulatory change seems to impact on Green jobs in Australia (see Teeter and Sandberg, 2016) into other countries where such regulation may now play an increasingly important role in shaping patterns of Green jobs, work, and employment, i.e. in the USA, UK and China among others. Moreover, researchers may wish to critically examine the case that there may be a decrease in jobs globally (see George *et al.*, 2016, p. 1880), and, if observed, what this development may mean for global Green jobs, work, and employment more widely.

Scholars could also extend investigations on the construct of 'ecological embeddedness', to assess take-up among managers on the extent to which they are rooted in the land,[4] and their love for it. Doing so could help us assess whether existing management theory and practice may benefit further from studying indigenous communities such as the Naskapi in the sub-Artic, which have 'successfully avoided ecological collapse' and 'survived for millennia', i.e. would this provide ideas for non-native managers facing difficulties finding 'their own sustainable pathways'? If so, the over 5,000 different indigenous groups existing worldwide (see www.iwgia.org/) may represent a large, untapped resource for researchers when investigating contemporary environmental issues[5] (Whiteman and Cooper, 2000, pp. 1265–1267).

If resources allow, gaining new data from long ethnographic studies among indigenous people at risk from climate change in vulnerable locations such as our deserts, forests, flood plains, and poles, as per Gail Whiteman's work in the sub-Artic (see Whiteman and Cooper, 2000, p. 1268), might add new insights to complement and extend current GHRM research. Doing so could require scholars to use 'an experience-near approach (Geertz, 1974) that focuses on the everyday life-worlds that actors inhabit and render meaningful', and innovative methods of analysis (such as participatory organizational research or digital storytelling) to 'explore diverse forms of knowing', including those drawing on spirituality and/or 'linked to ecological belief systems'[6] (Bell *et al.*, 2016. pp. 4, 13). In doing so, (and see George *et al.*, 2016, p. 1890), GHRM researchers may be obliged to engage in 'reinforcing mechanisms', including 'continued societal vocalism', to shed light on natural and exogenous events seemingly driven by global warming, as this may help illustrate the important need to focus on GHRM as one important indirect way to help tackle climate change.

While grand challenge environments appear to vary regarding their inclusion of advocacy groups, such groups could provide a 'legitimizing influence' (see George *et al.*, 2016, pp. 1885, 1886, 1889), i.e. pro-Green consortiums in Brazil who may lack prior experience, yet provide an inspiration to other related groups globally. Such variation and advocacy is seen in agents such as the Guarani-Kaiowa indigenous people of Midwest Brazil protesting at forced relocation from their natural habitats and cancellation of their land rights (IWGIA, 2010), and local communities opposing the construction of a hydro-electric dam at Belo Monte in Brazil which arguably ignores environmental issues, yet which may affect the lives of 50,000 indigenous people on its route along the Xingu river there (BBC, 2010). I now discuss links between GHRM and sustainability in general, and connecting GHRM to more sustainable workforces in particular.

GHRM and Sustainability

To some authors, 'sustainable HRM' suggests a more holistic approach to employment to extend the HRM role beyond firm boundaries, and to manage and measure corporate social and ecological impacts by redesigning performance reviews to include and use specific sustainability criteria (e.g. Ehnert *et al.*, 2016, pp. 101, 103). Such ideas link to the notion of building an 'Economy for the Common Good (ECG)' (which itself partly links to ideas of 'B Corporations' and the 'conscious capitalism' literature), and includes the case study of Sonnentor[7] as an example of how to begin building an ECG[8] in action (Müller-Camen and Camen, 2017). A clear assumption of ECG supporters is that there will only be a decisive change in business attitudes if governments actively support organizations oriented towards 'the common good' (Müller-Camen and Camen, 2017, p. 1). Here, ECG is no pipe dream, as over 1,700 companies globally have endorsed its principles (University of Chicago Press, 2017, p. 1). However, many influential opponents of ECG exist, including those arguing that introducing an ECG would lead to a disruption of economies, and thus political chaos (see Furst, 2016, in Müller-Camen and Camen, 2017, p. 1). Indeed, as moves towards an ECG link to the need for significant pro-Green regulatory change (and for the reasons outlined in this chapter and the Introduction) they currently seem less likely to be enacted in the USA, UK, and Australia.

Nonetheless, an ECG could be a new organizational and workplace model of the future, as it has been recommended by the European Economic and Social Committee to be included as part of the European legal frameworks (see Müller-Camen and Camen, 2017, p. 2). Moreover, (see Hampton, 2015), an ECG may provide a much-needed workplace and societal vision which arguably helps us progress further from implementing GHRM initiatives and building Greener workplaces, towards the wider, more holistic concepts of realizing more socially responsible HRM (Shen and Zhang, 2017) and constructing Sustainable Workforces in Management Studies (SWiM), which I now detail.

Sustainable Workforces in Management Studies (SWiM)

Connecting GHRM to workforce sustainability requires a wide understanding, and an exploratory concept to do so, which I term Sustainable Workforces in Management Studies (SWiM). The SWiM concept derives from me thinking about how and in what ways global work-places currently do not seem sustainable when viewed from the perspective of some of their less-included, marginalized, and disadvantaged workforce members. Such limitations appear through current organizational focus on the delivery of shareholder profits; control of organizational costs; use of labour as a resource or commodity; introduction of flexibility policies; social exclusion of part-time, zero hours, female, and black and minority ethnic staff; and marginalization of trade union members. To me, several contextual (regulatory, social, economic, and political) and organizational initiatives are needed to make workplaces globally more sustainable for their staff in action. Such initiatives include organizations: having greater concern for their societal impact; making enhanced use of employee voice tools; introducing diversity, green, and sustainability strategies, policies, processes, procedures, and practices; making a shift to an ECG; and using more 'social enterprise' forms of organizing work. I aim to develop the SWiM concept further at: www.sustainable-workforces.co.uk/ and detail country and organisational practices as a means of stimulating initial ideas, discussion, and uptake surrounding it.

For now, I note the relatively new standard for HR of 'BS 76000 Human Resource', published by the British Standard Institute (2015) as one potential example of how to begin building SWiM in practice. The main principles of BS76000 are that the:

> Interests of staff and other stakeholders are integral to the best interests of an organisation; organisations are part of wider society and have a responsibility to operate in a fair and socially responsible manner; commitment to valuing people comes from the most senior leaders of an organisation; and people working on behalf of the organisation have intrinsic value in addition to their protections under the law or in regulation, which needs to be respected.
>
> (see BSI, 2015, p. 1 at www.bsigroup.com)

Indeed, the development of BS 76000 has recently been complemented by work undertaken by the UK-based Chartered Institute of Personnel and Development on professional principles for the British HR profession to 'champion better work and working lives for the good of wider society' (CIPD, 2017, see www.cipd.co.uk/news-views/future-profession/principles). Additionally, a new UK government review of work recommends a move away from 'bad work' (e.g. zero hour contracts and the 'gig economy') and to 'good work', which 'thinks about the quality of people's work experiences' (Ahmed, 2017, pp. 1–3) (see www.bbc.co.uk/news/amp/39849571). If implemented, such recent socially and environmentally progressive trends in British HRM research and thinking such as the BS 76000, CIPD and government principles above may help stimulate moves towards organizations enacting SWiM in practice, and may locate GHRM within SWiM too. That is to say, and to answer the question-type title of this chapter, that GHRM may be part of the future in building sustainable workforces, but it is not the be-all and end-all of them. In essence, 'going Green' in HRM does not automatically equate to, nor necessarily always produce, such sustainable workforces. Instead, much more organizational theorizing, research, and implementation (including trial and error) is needed for organizations to fully enact a sustainable HRM approach, as works by Ehnert (2009), Ehnert, Harry and Zink (2014), and the chapter by Xu and colleagues in this volume clearly illustrate.

Closing remarks

Overall (see George *et al.*, 2016, p. 1893), helping to tackle climate change through GHRM workplace-based interventions is not just about GHRM theory and research, as all relevant stakeholders also have obligations to serve 'the globally and locally unemployed, displaced, and disenfranchised' too. If accepted, this viewpoint means that GHRM educational initiatives could benefit from embracing different business models and pedagogical initiatives to retrain staff to develop the new skills required to work in the non-polluting industries. Indeed, such obligations may also require us to critically ask whether organizations have enough of the right talent to enact Green initiatives, and to assess whether important organizational actors, such as non-specialist line managers, have the personal capability, commitment, and consistency needed in practice to 'own' environmental management initiatives and 'go Green' (see Rayner and Morgan, 2017), and to persuade their direct employee reports to do likewise. For example, can we, and will we, ever talk of 'Green line managers' and eco-friendly willing employee recipients of 'Green schemes' in years to come?

In closing this chapter and this book, I re-iterate the much-used (even clichéd) quote from the UN's Secretary General H.E. Ban Ki-Moon that: 'there is no Plan B for action, as there is no Planet B' (in George *et al.*, 2016, p. 1893). I say this as, to return to a point in my earlier chapter, the physical changes happening to our planet seem to be moving at a quick pace. For example, if we look at pictures of the Earth taken over recent years from the International Space Station (see www.nasa.gov/subject/3127/climate/), a very real and humbling sense of the level and scale of deforestation, desertification, water shortages, and resulting human and animal migration patterns emerges, which partly seems to arise from climate change events. As others recognize (see George *et al.*, 2016, p. 1893), a moral case therefore exists for us as management educators and business stakeholders to generate abundant research studies in GHRM to help tackle the global problem of climate change indirectly, however big or small such research contributions are judged to be by the next generations.

Of course, some arguably significant and positive human-led initiatives are occurring to tackle global warming today. These efforts range from the relatively recent macro-level Paris climate change agreement, to meso-level regional initiatives in Spain, Morocco, and South America which increase the use of solar power and irrigation projects in Australia (to enhance cotton blooms in the desert) and in Jordan (to store water underground to help grow food crops and produce 'living deserts' which reduce non-Green food imports) (BBC 2017a), to micro-level City schemes in Rotterdam to capture heavy rainfall and release it into waste systems and the construction of 'floating houses' as a new and different way to live (Channel 4, 2017).

Nonetheless, I conclude by noting that 'every single thing around us came from the Earth in some shape or form' (Whiteman and Cooper, 2000, p. 1271), as such 'things' originate from *matter*. This circumstance makes our civilization vulnerable,[9] as, while the last 7,000–8,000 years in which humans have evolved have been very stable,[10] new climate and weather changes – to the matter which surrounds us – are a problem for us as people, as what will happen to human community life because of climate change? As such, it may be time to re-think our place as humans in the world and how we relate to Planet Earth *inside* our workplaces too. This is because, as organizational stakeholders, we can surely all help improve our physical, external, and natural environment and ecology through our GHRM-related workplace behaviours, and act as informed, mindful, considerate, and impactful citizens regarding them. Of course, doing so may require us to make a mental leap, to both understand and re-assess our own place on our Planet Earth, and in the wider Universe too. To do so, in the words of the Kiowa poet N. Scott Momaday (1974), we may need to think, and ask, whether we can positively say:

> You see, I am alive, I am alive; I stand in good relation to the earth; I stand in good relation to the gods; I stand in good relation to all that is beautiful.
>
> (in Whiteman and Cooper, 2000, p. 1280)

Notes

1 It seems important for scholars to gather data from managers in newly industrialized countries such as Brazil and China (among others), because of increasing concern about their environmental impacts (Inoue and Alfaro-Barrantes, 2015, pp. 155–156). Investigating 'views from the periphery' in such less-researched countries may require us to assess and question existing developments in GHRM scholarship. Doing so over time may facilitate new 'bicultural and decolonizing' works on how researchers based in the Northern and Western 'centre' of academia could work with, and 'bring in', more Southern and Eastern-based voices in GHRM research (see Bell, *et al.*, 2016, pp. 2–5).

2 '[Denaturalization involves opening] up spaces for indigenous research methodologies that draw on local traditions of knowledge' (Bell *et al.*, 2016, p. 12).

3 For example:

> Renewable energy industries already employ more than three-quarter of a million Americans. In fact, jobs in solar and wind are growing at a rate of 12 times faster than the rest of the US economy, and according to the Department of Energy, solar in the US now employs more than oil, coal and gas combined. Another 2.2 million Americans work in the design, manufacturing or installation of energy efficiency products and services.
>
> (Annan, 2017, p. 2)

4 'People who are physically located in ecosystems are more committed to sustainable management practices than those who do not share these characteristics' (Whiteman and Cooper, 2000, pp. 1265, 1279).

5 Indeed: 'following Usher (1987), utilizing indigenous approaches might move natural resource management away from problems of global access to resources, which currently seem to lead us towards exhausting such resources' (Whiteman and Cooper, 2000, p. 1267)

6 If, as Connell (2007) suggests, management researchers located in South Africa, Brazil and India [can] organize laterally with scholars in other peripheral locations to identify common interests and overlapping problem areas, and form networks of cooperation and knowledge sharing that challenge intellectual dependency on the West [and reveal] spaces for more diverse post-Enlightenment narratives.

> (Bell *et al.*, 2016, pp. 13–14)

7 Sonnentor (Gate of the Sun) is an Austrian company that produces and sells about 800 items of which 85 per cent are organic teas and spices, and was a pioneer in the Economy for the Common Good (ECG) movement. Sonnentor encourages an ecological lifestyle for its workforce by providing free organic food and subsidies for eco-friendly electricity and travelling to work jointly by sharing cars, and tries to limit work-related travel.

> (Müller-Camen and Camen, 2017, pp. 1, 9)

8 Christian Felber coined the term Gemeinwohlokonomie (ECG) and argues it means 'everyone's well-being counts' (Felber, 2015, p. xvi). ECG has three major focuses: to align the values of business and society

... that the values and goals laid down in constitutions should be systematically integrated into business practices, [and] that the main purpose of all business should be to promote the common good and not to maximise profits ... [which] goes beyond the pursuit of a triple bottom line approach.

(Müller-Camen and Camen, 2017, p. 2)

9 Professor Stephen Hawking states that our vulnerability means humans may need to colonize the Moon and leave the Earth (BBC, 2017b, p. 1).
10 For example, 40 per cent of us live only 60 miles from an ocean, but this figure may fall (Channel 4, 2017).

References

Acevedo, A. (2012) 'Personalist Business Ethics and Humanistic Management: Insights from Jacques Maritain', *Journal of Business Ethics*, vol. 105, pp. 197–219.

Ahmed, K. (2017) 'Is work "fair and decent"? That's not how the voters see it', BBC News, 8 May, pp. 1–11, Accessed 9 May 2017 at: www.bbc.co.uk/news/amp/39849571.

Alt, E. and Spitzeck, H. (2016) 'Improving Environmental Performance through Unit-Level Organizational Citizenship Behaviors for the Environment: A Capability Perspective', *Journal of Environmental Management*, vol. 182, pp. 48–58.

Annan, K. (2017) 'Paris Agreement: Donald Trump's decision will hurt Americans', LinkedIn, 6 June 2017, pp. 1–3.

Bell, E., Kothiyal, N., and Willmott, H. (2016) 'Methodology-as-Technique and the Meaning of Rigour in Globalized Management Research', *British Journal of Management*, forthcoming, pp. 1–17 DOI: 10.1111/1467-8551.12205.

British Broadcasting Corporation (BBC) (2010) 'Brazil government gives go-ahead for huge Amazon dam' www.bbc.co.uk/news/world-latin-america-11101842 pp. 1–3. Accessed 6 May 2017.

British Broadcasting Corporation (BBC) (2017a) *Newsnight*, 2 February 2017.

British Broadcasting Corporation (BBC) (2017b) 'Hawking urges Moon landing to "elevate humanity"', *BBC News*, 20 June 2017, pp. 1–3.

British Standards Institute (BSI) (2015) *New HR Standard*, pp. 1–5. At: www.bsigroup.com. Accessed 4 December 2016.

Bukharin, N., and Preobrazhensky, E. (1919) *The ABC of Communism*, London: Merlin Press.

Channel 4 (2017) 'Man made planet: Earth from Space', *Channel 4*, 22 April 2017.

Chartered Institute of Personnel and Development (CIPD) (2017) 'Professional Principles', pp. 1–11 Accessed 9 May 2017 at: www.cipd.co.uk/news-views/future-profession/principles).

Dumont, J., Shen, J., and Deng, X. (2016) 'Effects of Green HRM Practices on Employee Workplace Green Behaviour: The Role of Psychological Green Climate and Employee Green Values', *Human Resource Management*, Early View DOI: 10.1002/hrm.21792, pp. 1–15.

Economy for the common good (ECG) (2016) 'Ecological Behaviour of Employees – ECG – Balance Website', pp. 1–3. http://balance.ecogood. org/matrix-4-1-en/guidelines/c3-ecological-behaviour-of-employees Accessed 19 December 2016.

Ehnert, I. (2009) *Sustainable Human Resource Management: A Conceptual and Exploratory Analysis from a Paradox Perspective*, Berlin: Physica-Verlag.

Ehnert, I., Harry, W., and Zink, K.J. (Eds) (2014) *Sustainability and Human Resource Management: Developing Sustainable Organizations*, Berlin: Physica-Verlag.

Ehnert, I., Parsa, E., Roper, I., Wagner, M., and Müller-Camen, M. (2016) 'Reporting on Sustainability and HRM: A Comparative Study of Sustainability Reporting Practices by the World's Largest Companies', *The International Journal of Human Resource Management*, vol. 27, no. 1, pp. 88–108.

Farnhill, T. (2016a) 'Characteristics of Environmentally Active Trade Unions in the United Kingdom', *Global Labour Journal*, vol. 7, no. 3, pp. 257–278.

Farnhill, T. (2016b) 'A Small-N Cross-Sectional Study of British Unions' Environmental Attitudes and Activism – and the Prospect of a Green-Led Renewal', *Cogent Social Sciences*, vol. 2, pp. 1–21.

Farnhill, T. (2017) 'Understanding British Unions' Workplace Greening Agenda: Three Case Studies', *Aston University Working Paper*, pp. 1–35.

Felber, C. (2015) *Change Everything: Creating an Economy for the Common Good*, Munich: Zedbooks.

Furst, E. (2016) *Katastrophe Gemeinwohlokonomie (Disaster Economy of the Common Good)*. Der Standard 17 April 2016 http://destandard.at/2000034981116/ Katastrophe-Gemeinwohlokonomie. Accessed 15 October 2016.

Geertz, C. (1974) '"From the Native's Point of View": On the Nature of Anthropological Understanding', *Bulletin of the American Academy of Arts and Sciences*, vol. 28, pp. 26–45.

George, G., Howard-Grenville, J.H., Joshi, A., and Tihanyi, L. (2016) 'Understanding and Tackling Societal Grand Challenges Through Management Research', *Academy of Management Journal*, vol. 59, no. 6, pp. 1880–1895.

Hampton, P. (2015) *Workers and Trade Unions for Climate Solidarity: Tackling Climate Change in a Neoliberal World*, Abingdon, Oxon: Routledge.

Inoue, Y. and Alfaro-Barrantes, P. (2015) 'Pro-Environmental Behavior in the Workplace: A Review of Empirical Studies and Directions for Future Research', *Business and Society Review*, vol. 120, no. 1, pp. 137–160.

International Work Group for Indigenous Affairs (IWGIA) (2010) 'Guarani-Kaiowa Indigenous People Are at Risk of Eviction from Ancestral Lands they Recently Occupied in the Brazilian Midwest', www.iwgia.org/news/search news?search=result&search_text=&country_id=5&process_id=0&theme_ id=0&region_id=0&people_id=0&case_id=0&news_language=ENG&advance dsearch=1&pagenr=1. Accessed 6 May 2017, pp. 1–2.

Momaday, S. (1974) 'The Delight Song of Tsoai-talee'. In N.S. Momaday, *The Gourd Dancer*, New York: Harper & Row.

Müller-Camen, M. and Camen, J. (2017) 'Sonnentor and the Economy of the Common Good'. In E. O'Higgins and L.Z. Corvinus (Eds) *For Progressive Business Casebook*, Cambridge University Press, pp. 1–14.

North American Space Agency (NASA) (2017) *Image Galleries, Earth Images,* www.nasa.gov/subject/3127/climate/. Accessed 6 May 2017.

Norton, T. (2016) 'A Multilevel Perspective on Employee Green Behaviour', PhD Thesis, School of Psychology, The University of Queensland, pp. 1–153. DOI: 14264/uql.2016.285.

Norton, T.A., Zacher, H., Parker, S.L., and Ashkanasy, N.M. (2017) 'Bridging the Gap Between Green Behavioural Intentions and Employee Green Behaviour: The Role of Green Psychological Climate', *Journal of Organizational Behavior,* pp. 1–20. DOI: 10.1002/job.2178.

Pinzone, M., Guerci, M., Lettieri, E., and Redman, T. (2016) 'Progressing in the Change Journey towards Sustainability in Healthcare: The Role of "Green" HRM', *Journal of Cleaner Production,* vol. 122, pp. 201–211.

Rayner, J. and Morgan, D. (2017) 'An Empirical Study of "Green" Workplace Behaviours: Ability, Motivation and Opportunity', *Asia Pacific Journal of Human Resources,* Early View, pp. 1–23. DOI: 10.1111/1744-7941.12151. Accessed 4 May 2017.

Robertson, J.L. and Barling, J. (2017) 'Contrasting the Nature and Effects of Environmentally Specific and General Transformational Leadership', *Leadership & Organization Development Journal,* vol. 38, no. 1, pp. 1–46.

Saifulina, N. and Carballo-Penela, A. (2016) 'Promoting Sustainable Development at an Organizational Level: An Analysis of the Drivers of Workplace Environmentally Friendly Behaviour of Employees', *Sustainable Development.* DOI: 10.1002/sd.1654, pp. 1–14.

Shen, J. and Zhang, H. (2017) 'Socially Responsible Human Resource Management and Employee Support for External CSR: Roles of Organizational Climate and Perceived CSR Directed Toward Employees', *Journal of Business Ethics,* Early view, pp. 1–14. DOI: 10.1007/S10551-017-3544-0.

Shen, J., Dumont, J., and Deng, X. (2016) 'Employees' Perceptions of Green HRM and Non-Green Employee Work Outcomes: The Social Identity and Stakeholder Perspectives', *Group & Organization Management.* DOI: 10.1177/1059601116664610, pp. 1–29.

Tang, G., Chen, Y., Jiang, Y., Paillé, P., and Jia, J. (2017) 'Green Human Resource Management Practices: Scale Development and Validity', *Asia Pacific Journal of Human Resources,* Early View, pp. 1–25. DOI: 10.1111/1744-7941.12147. Accessed 4 May 2017.

Teeter, P. and Sandberg, J. (2016) 'Constraining or Enabling Green Capability Development? How Policy Uncertainty Affects Organizational Responses to Flexible Environmental Regulations', *British Journal of Management,* forthcoming, pp. 1–17. DOI: 10.1111/1467-8551.12188.

University of Chicago Press (2017) 'The University of Chicago Press Books', University of Chicago Press, p. 1. Accessed at: http://press.uchicago.edu/ucp/books/book/distributed/C/bo23073339.html.

Wang, H., Tong, L., Takeuchi, R., and George, G. (2016) 'From the Editors. Thematic Issue on Corporate Social Responsibility. Corporate Social Responsibility: An Overview and New Research Directions', *Academy of Management Journal,* vol. 59, no. 2, pp. 534–544.

Whiteman, G. and Cooper, W.H. (2000) 'Ecological Embeddedness', *Academy of Management Journal*, vol. 43, no. 6, pp. 1265–1282.

Wiernik, B.M., Dilchert, S., and Ones, D.S. (2016) 'Age and Employee Green Behaviors: A Meta-Analysis', *Frontiers In Psychology*. (April). DOI: 10.3389/fpsyg.2016.00194, pp. 1–15.

Index

Page numbers in *italics* denote tables, those in **bold** denote figures.

 Taylor & Francis eBooks

Helping you to choose the right eBooks for your Library

Add Routledge titles to your library's digital collection today. Taylor and Francis ebooks contains over 50,000 titles in the Humanities, Social Sciences, Behavioural Sciences, Built Environment and Law.

Choose from a range of subject packages or create your own!

Benefits for you
» Free MARC records
» COUNTER-compliant usage statistics
» Flexible purchase and pricing options
» All titles DRM-free.

Benefits for your user
» Off-site, anytime access via Athens or referring URL
» Print or copy pages or chapters
» Full content search
» Bookmark, highlight and annotate text
» Access to thousands of pages of quality research at the click of a button.

| REQUEST YOUR **FREE** INSTITUTIONAL TRIAL TODAY | **Free Trials Available** We offer free trials to qualifying academic, corporate and government customers. |

eCollections – Choose from over 30 subject eCollections, including:

Archaeology	Language Learning
Architecture	Law
Asian Studies	Literature
Business & Management	Media & Communication
Classical Studies	Middle East Studies
Construction	Music
Creative & Media Arts	Philosophy
Criminology & Criminal Justice	Planning
Economics	Politics
Education	Psychology & Mental Health
Energy	Religion
Engineering	Security
English Language & Linguistics	Social Work
Environment & Sustainability	Sociology
Geography	Sport
Health Studies	Theatre & Performance
History	Tourism, Hospitality & Events

For more information, pricing enquiries or to order a free trial, please contact your local sales team:
www.tandfebooks.com/page/sales

 Routledge
Taylor & Francis Group

The home of
Routledge books

www.tandfebooks.com

For Product Safety Concerns and Information please contact our EU
representative GPSR@taylorandfrancis.com
Taylor & Francis Verlag GmbH, Kaufingerstraße 24, 80331 München, Germany

www.ingramcontent.com/pod-product-compliance
Ingram Content Group UK Ltd.
Pitfield, Milton Keynes, MK11 3LW, UK
UKHW020934180425
457613UK00019B/398